WEEKEND WALKS
IN THE PEAK DISTRICT

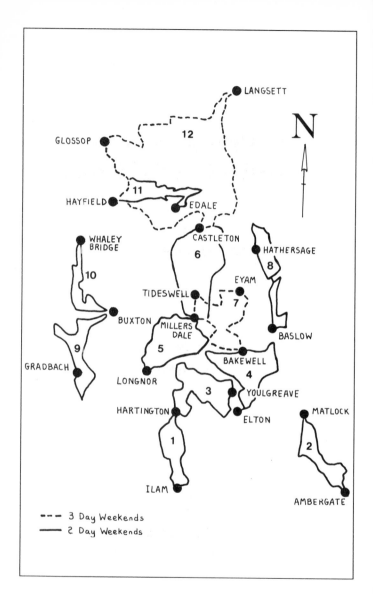

LANGSETT

GLOSSOP

12

HAYFIELD

11

EDALE

WHALEY
BRIDGE

CASTLETON

HATHERSAGE

6

8

10

EYAM

TIDESWELL

7

BUXTON

MILLERS
DALE

BASLOW

9

5

BAKEWELL

GRADBACH

LONGNOR

4

3

YOULGREAVE

HARTINGTON

ELTON

MATLOCK

1

2

ILAM

AMBERGATE

N

- - - 3 Day Weekends
——— 2 Day Weekends

WEEKEND WALKS IN THE PEAK DISTRICT

by

John and Anne Nuttall

Maps and drawings by

John Nuttall

CICERONE PRESS

MILNTHORPE, CUMBRIA

ISBN 1 85284 137 0

A catalogue record for this book is available from the British Library

ACKNOWLEDGMENTS

*Our thanks go to Roland Smith of the Peak Park Planning Board
for checking the manuscript*

Also by John and Anne Nuttall

CONTENTS

KEY

road	
track	= = = = =
path	- - - - - - -
river	
stream	
footbridge	FB
Church	■ Ch
Youth Hostel	● YH
houses	
lake	
railway	+++++++++++

fence	
wall	•-•-•-•-•-•

fences and walls beside tracks omitted for clarity

wood	
contours at 50m	300 350 400
cliffs and steep rocks	
scree	
2000ft summit	▲ 610 height in metres
other cairns	Δ
Start each day	(S)

Route

on path	on track	on road
- - -	= = =	▬▬▬▬

Route at edge of map marked in margin thus

From previous page ◯

To Map number ➤ 9·2

SCALE 2½" = 1 mile

INTRODUCTION

Living as we do on its western fringe, the Peak District is not only one of our favourite areas, it is also close enough for an evening walk. Within an hour of leaving home we can be standing on the summit of Shutlingsloe and a particular treat of a summer evening is to take a picnic and have dinner beside the trig point. While the moors are still lit by the low slanting rays of the sun, far below long shadows reach out across the valley and afterwards we descend at dusk with the lights of the distant towns forming jewelled patterns in the darkness.

On other evenings we stroll down the Goyt Valley through the rhododendrons and azaleas that surround the ruins of Errwood Hall, or wander over the heather moors, while sometimes the Roaches beckon, their gaunt rocks black against the reddening sky. Stolen moments like these, a quick visit to paradise before a return to weekday tasks, bring contentment out of all proportion to the time spent. Weekends of course bring more time, but even a full day is soon over and all too short.

Weekend Walks in the Peak District turns a weekend into a holiday, two or three days away with an overnight stay at a friendly guest house, pub, hotel or youth hostel. This is an opportunity to see more of the Peak than can be done in a day and unlike most holidays there is, after such a break, always another weekend to look forward to.

There are hundreds, if not thousands of enjoyable day walks in the Peak District, but to find two that link together to provide a satisfying weekend is more of a challenge. We have certainly enjoyed our explorations and having walked all the routes twice, and lots of them many more times, we spent a delightful week last autumn stringing several weekends together into one long tour of The Peak. Each evening we came down to the welcoming glow of a farmhouse or cottage or pub and felt at the end of the holiday that we had got to know an old friend even better.

Not only do we live close to the Peak District, but it is also within an hour's drive for half the population of Great Britain. Yet despite this and the fact that more and more people are discovering the delights of walking, it is still perfectly possible to walk for hours without meeting anyone else. Perhaps on a Bank Holiday the stepping stones in Dove Dale are a little crowded and Bakewell too can look rather over full, but on one such glorious sunny weekend we walked the moors above the source of the River Derwent with no other person in view.

There is such great variety in the Peak District. It is both a flower garden and a wilderness. From its flower filled dales to the wild gritstone moorland and from the height of hazy summer to the depths of ice hard winter, the range of scenery and seasons is immense.

Spring memories are of the dales bright with violets, cowslips and the early purple orchids contrasting with the delicate white petalled wood sorrel, and of Deep Dale appearing white as new fallen snow with the hawthorn trees in blossom and the ground beneath them covered in meadow saxifrage. But soon summer arrives with the gold of rock roses, the brilliant red of the bloody cranesbill and mats of purple thyme. To list even a tiny fraction of all the beautiful flowers of the Peak District would fill many pages, for in spring and early summer even a short walk can yield over 100 different species.

Summertime too is of long days on the moors and in the dales, while following the course of the Peakland rivers again provides variety. On the gritstone there is the splashing exuberance of the infant River Dane which contrasts with the mature, wide, slow flowing course of the Derwent and on the limestone there are the clean clear waters of the Lathkill, the disappearing Manifold and the lovely Dove while down beside the River Wye as it flows gently beneath the trees the white throated dipper flits from stone to stone and a streak of blue is the kingfisher.

The high moorland, the Dark Peak, provides some of the toughest challenge walks with mile after mile of wild open country, cotton grass, mat grass, heather, crowberry, bilberry and peat. And here too are treasures to be found with the tiny delicate flowers of the cranberry, its curled back petals massed in a pink carpet covering the boggy moor.

Autumn brings the honey scented heather and black, finger-staining bilberries and as the bracken slopes glow orange in the light of the afternoon sun, walks finish late by torchlight knowing that soon the short days of winter will be here.

Winter memories are of cross country skiing when the snow lies feet deep and everything is still, save for the wind driving the snow, and the moors are an ice hard wilderness of black rocks and blue shadows against the white brilliance. Winter too is when ice axes and crampons appear as eager figures climb towards the arctic conditions on the plateau of Kinder and Bleaklow. But winter too is the beauty of ice rhimed reeds and grasses, of icicles that overhang the frozen streams, of arctic hares in their white coated camouflage and grouse that start up from beneath your feet.

An owl called softly in the fading twilight as we picked our way slowly up the dale. Soon it would be night and the end of another holiday, but next weekend we would be back, for whatever the scene or season the Peak District is a place of which we never grow tired.

NOTES

Although Britain's first National Park, the Peak District, which covers an area of 555 square miles, celebrated its fortieth birthday in 1991, the area has been known as The Peak for much longer. The name comes from the Old English peac, a knoll or hill and over 1000 years ago this was known as Peacland.

With 4000 miles of footpaths and with free access to many of the high moors there is a great tradition of walking and an immense variety of walking terrain, but while the National Park attracts around 22 million day visitors a year, there is only one better way of spending a day in the Peak and that is to spend two! So after a walk in such glorious countryside why not stay the night at some pleasant cottage, pub or hostel and then return by a different route the next day?

Weekend Walks in the Peak District describes twelve walks, comprising ten 2-day Weekends and two 3-day Long Weekends. The walks, most of which are within the National Park, have been chosen so that there is somewhere to stay at both ends and as all the walks are circular you can also begin at the other end and do Day 2 first. In general the weekend starts from a place well served by public transport with plenty of room to leave a car, and finishes for the night where there is ample accommodation.

Accommodation

At the start and finish of each day there is a choice of accommodation varying from hotel or pub, to bed and breakfast or youth hostel. There are also campsites and camping barns. While the Peak District is well supplied with places to stay it is also popular and youth hostels do have closing days, so it is advisable to book ahead especially where accommodation is limited. A table on page 289 shows the range of facilities available.

The Peak Park Information Centre at the Old Market Hall, Bakewell (Tel 0629 813227) is open all year and will help with accommodation enquiries.

Maps

The detailed route maps are at a scale of 1:25,000 and have all been drawn with north at the top which is how most people like them. A key to the maps is given on page 6. The state of paths varies and not all will be equally clear on the ground, but with the detailed annotations of walls, stiles and gates, the routes should be easy to follow. We debated at length what to call a stile next to a gate. Is it a stile, or is it a gate? The rule is that "gate" means either a gate, or a stile close to a gate.

Ordnance Survey maps are generally reckoned to be the best in the

world and no-one will be disappointed with an investment in them. To complement the walks the
OS Peak District Tourist Map
is useful for giving a general picture of the countryside.

The weekends are also covered by
1:50 000 Landranger Series 110, 118 & 119.

The best maps if you intend to explore off the route are:
1:25 000 Outdoor Leisure The Peak District - Dark Peak area
1:25 000 Outdoor Leisure The Peak District - White Peak area
These cover all the weekends apart from a small area around Hathersage for which you need
Pathfinder SK 28/38

Car Parking

Each walk starts where there is ample car parking space. The Peak Park car parks display a notice which states "No overnight parking". The Peak Park authority has confirmed that this can be taken to mean no overnight occupation of vehicles. However you are strongly recommended to inform either a local ranger or the police if you are leaving your vehicle in an isolated spot so as not to cause concern. Parking is at your own risk and they will of course take no responsibility for any damage done or any theft that may occur. It is advisable to leave the car as empty as possible.

Access

The walks use public footpaths or concession paths or routes which have been in use for a long time. On much of the high moorland Access Agreements have been made with the owners giving the public the right to wander at will over open uncultivated land (but see Grouse Shooting below). This Access Land covers over 80 square miles of open country, but it is still privately owned and provides sheep grazing and grouse moorland.

Grouse Shooting

During the grouse shooting season, 12 August to 10 December, the Access Agreements allow each moor to be closed to the public for up to 12 days a year. Weekends 11 & 12 cross grouse moors and dates when the moors will be closed are available from the Peak District Information Centres and also from the police. Rights of way are not closed and there is no shooting on Sundays.

Equipment

The weekends vary from easy strolls over the White Peak when a pair of trainers and a cagoule will be sufficient, to long walks crossing the high exposed moors of the Dark Peak. For these boots, waterproof and windproof clothing, a compass and an ability to use it are essential.

WEEKEND 1: THE DOVE AND MANIFOLD VALLEYS

DAY 1: *STARTING POINT:*	Ilam to Hartington 8½ miles (132506) Ilam Hall 3 miles north- west of Ashbourne
DAY 2: *STARTING POINT:*	Hartington to Ilam 11½ miles (128604) The centre of Hartington
ROUTE SUMMARY:	Up the Dove and down the Manifold. Gentle walking on good paths follows the course of these two famous Peakland rivers.

DAY 1: ILAM TO HARTINGTON

Rising within half a mile of each other on the high moorland south of Buxton, the rivers Dove and Manifold spend much of their early lives separated by at most a few miles of field and moorland. The little village of Longnor is passed by the Dove to the north and by the Manifold to the south and this separation is maintained as the rivers, each in its rocky bed, meander south past Hartington.

Although born on the gritstone moorlands of the Dark Peak, the Dove and Manifold run for much of their course on limestone and it comes as a surprise to find the rivers there at all. Limestone is of course soluble in slightly acid water, atmospheric pollution alone is sufficient to impart to rainwater the acidity which dissolves away the hard white rock, and rivers on limestone have the habit of disappearing down cracks and fissures

11

Dovedale

into a subterranean world. The Manifold runs true to form and just below Wetton Mill the river drains away through fissures in its bed leaving the downstream course an arid desert. Sheltering one autumn from the first of that season's downpours, we ate our lunch in the dry bed of the Manifold beneath the protection of Weag's Bridge.

The Dove is different. Despite all the rules it stays obstinately above ground, down past the meanderings of Beresford Dale where the ruins of Charles Cotton's fishing temple may still be seen through the trees, down through Wolfscote Dale where caves high on the hillside speak of the river's former power, and down into Dove Dale itself where Victorian tourists who thought this the most delectable of dales named every pinnacle and rock in romantic allusion.

With over 750,000 visitors every year and with many more words written in praise of it, what is there new that can be written about Dove Dale? The dale is certainly different from when Victorian ladies in flowing ankle length dresses were assisted across the stepping stones by earnest young men in fashionable waistcoats and tweeds. For one thing in those days you could see the rocks, and old photographs show a valley which would be almost unrecognised by today's visitors. No trees masked the limestone cliffs and pinnacles which so impressed the visitors of a century or more ago. Then grazing habits changed, the trees grew and there was little of the rugged Dove Dale on view.

It was with consternation that we saw JCBs in the valley. Chain saws were at work and for one horrible moment it appeared that a new select housing development was to appear beneath Ilam Rock. When it transpired that the National Park and the National Trust were the culprits alarm turned to disbelief. Trees crashed to the ground, tracks were churned in the mud and bonfires of brushwood blazed beneath the cliffs. What could they be up to? Now the scars have healed, the result of their efforts has begun to blend into the scenery and it must be agreed that it was all worth while. Crags long lost behind a screen of ash have appeared once more and the limestone faces are clear of their veil. Perhaps the quarter of a million pound path, a gleaming white ribbon that replaces the muddy trail into which we used to sink to mid calf is less successful, rather too park-like. Perhaps it was elitist, but the mud we felt, kept Dove Dale for the "proper" walkers. Now it is perfectly possible to negotiate the length of the dale in a pair of high heeled shoes.

The winding pattern of the Dove is that of a river of the plains, yet here it is in a steep sided gorge. Once indeed it wound its way across a plain marked today by the tops of the surrounding hills. These hills whose summits are all at the same level, are the remnants of an ancient plain into which the rivers and streams have incised their valleys. When the land was lifted up in the massive earth movements of mid Pliocene times, the river once again started to cut its way down, its course already set in the form of its early years.

Although over a third of a millennium has passed since Izaac Walton published his *Compleat Angler* the little packhorse bridge over which you enter the hamlet of Milldale is still known as Viator's Bridge. A linen-draper born in Stafford in 1593, Izaac Walton was nineteen when Shakespeare died. Although he didn't produce his major work until he was sixty, he lived to the age of ninety surviving his close friend Charles Cotton who was some forty years his junior.

The ash woodland on the west bank of Dove Dale is treasured by botanists as relict woodland, for trees have grown here in natural succession since the last Ice Age without the interference of man. It is registered as a Grade 1 Site of Special Scientific Interest, but whether you come to Dove Dale for its ecological, geological and botanical importance, or just for the scenery, it is still one of the loveliest dales in England.

ROUTE DESCRIPTION
Dove Dale

From Ilam Hall take the path past the church then follow the tarmac down to the model village of Ilam which, despite its row of modern houses, is still very attractive. Turning left by the Victorian Gothic cross take the footpath through the small gate after the last house to cross the fields beneath Bunster Hill. Heading straight for the truncated pyramid of Thorpe Cloud and passing to the rear of the Izaak Walton Hotel, the road is met by an enormous car park where the crowds are joined to walk beside the river.

The quickest and easiest way up Dove Dale is to stay on the road beside the river and follow it to the stepping stones. If the river is in spate the footbridge may be preferred, though its exact position is at present in doubt with plans to move it upstream under discussion.

The more energetic will be tempted to climb Thorpe Cloud itself. The eroded steep edge is being protected from further damage by the National Trust which has erected fencing to allow the slopes to re-vegetate, but the path to the right soon leads to the open hillside where you can climb 500ft straight up to the top. The summit of this ancient coral reef knoll has been polished smooth by the thousands of visitors that stand here to admire the view of Dove Dale far below.

The ways join again at the famous stepping stones, the limit for many who wander into Dove Dale, but the whole valley is now so popular that the once muddy track has been sanitised to a clean white path. After climbing the steps to Lover's Leap where you can see corals, shells and crinoids which make up the hard limestone, the strollers are left behind and only bona fide walkers continue up the dale. In March 1985 the woodland opposite, around the limestone pinnacles of the Twelve Apostles, was cleared by the National Trust and now this viewpoint must be much as it was when the Victorians

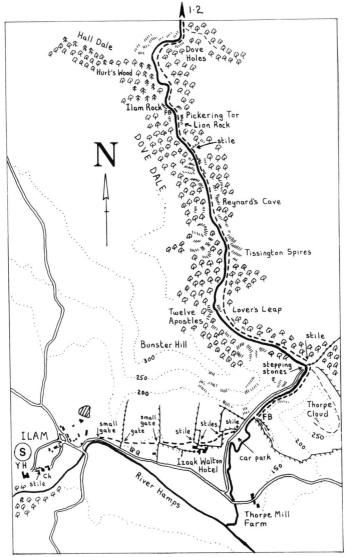

named the rocks.

Tissington Spires with a little cave at the base comes next and then a half sunken dungeon, the first of a series of ram pump houses which used the power of the river to pump spring water to the fields above. The massive natural arch of Reynard's Cave soon follows which before the National Trust set to work was completely hidden by the trees. Next the valley narrows with the sides dropping straight to the river, but a wooden walkway enables this section to be negotiated even when the river is high.

Below Lion Rock which frowns over the path there is a memorial plaque to FA Holmes and his son, through whose efforts Dovedale came into the care of the National Trust, then rounding the bend Ilam Rock comes into view, the most impressive rock in the whole of the dale. The south side overhangs for its full height and is a noted rock climb. Although the edge has been scaled free, the face requires pegs and as the leader nears the top the rope hangs several feet clear of the rock. Underneath is a hidden cave and though the entrance is only 4ft high the roof inside rises to 30ft. There is another small cave on this side of the river below Pickering Tor.

Beyond is Hall Dale, the first of the side dales, then the valley becomes more open and less enclosed. Dove Holes, once hollowed out by the river is all entrance and no cave, then leaving the woodland Ravens Tor rises from grassy slopes and you swim against a tide of visitors streaming down from Milldale, the next access point for a car.

Milldale

Viator's Bridge leads to an Information Barn which tells how the little packhorse bridge acquired its name. Milldale's mill stood just upstream and though the National Trust describe it as a corn mill other sources claim it was an Ochre Mill producing the coloured powder from iron ore mined at the nearby village of Wetton. Milldale is an attractive cluster of houses and has a shop selling refreshments.

For half a mile the route now follows the quiet road beside the river to Lode Mill. This old lead smelting mill was later used as a corn mill and the waterwheel and machinery are still in place. After the war it became a saw mill and coffins were made here by the undertaker who lived in the house above.

Though less dramatic than the lower reaches and with fewer rocky outcrops the next section of Milldale is still a delight. The woodland alternates with open grassy slopes and beneath the alder trees which line its banks the river flows peacefully over little weirs.

Wolfscote Dale

After 1½ miles a small cave at the end of Biggin Dale tempts exploration, then as you pass the pinnacles of Peaseland Rocks the character of the dale

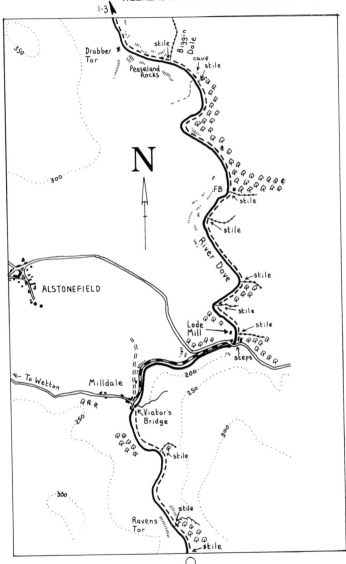

1·3

350

Drabber
Tor

stile

Biggin Dale

cave
stile

Peaseland
Rocks

300

N

130

FB
stile

stile

River Dove

stile

ALSTONEFIELD

stile

stile

Lode
Mill

stile

steps

← To Wetton   Milldale

200

250

250

Viator's
Bridge

300

stile

300

stile

Ravens
Tor

stile

stile

17

again changes. With its open slopes almost bare of trees the screes of Wolfscote Dale sweep down to the trout filled pools of the river. At the end of the dale the sides close in and Frank i'the Rocks cave, the large entrance to the right, is well worth visiting. Just inside is a narrow passage which emerges onto the hillside close to a second rift cave.

Beresford Dale

Passing a footbridge to enter Beresford Dale, go over a wide field to a second footbridge, where you cross to the other side of the Dove and enter a wooded gorge. The murky depths of Pike Pool, just before a third footbridge, was named not after a fish, but for the column of limestone above it. After you emerge into the open field look back to see almost hidden in the trees the little square fishing temple, which was built by Charles Cotton in 1674 in the grounds of Beresford Hall. Only a tower of the hall now remains, as the building was demolished around 1900. Crossing the fields to a green lane, take the rightmost stile and keep straight on into Hartington.

Hartington

Standing aloof from the River Dove, Hartington is an attractive village with houses grouped around a spacious square and a village green with a mere. Hartington's main claim to fame is that 350 years ago Charles Cotton the poet lived here. The squire of Beresford, who was born and lived at Beresford Hall, was a friend of Izaak Walton and wrote the second part of the *Compleat Angler* in ten days. This was first published in 1653. The two friends appear to have led an idyllic life, either fishing or whiling away their time by the Fishing Temple Cotton built in the grounds of the hall.

> *Oh, my beloved nymph, fair Dove,*
> *Princess of rivers, how I love*
> *Upon thy flowery banks to lie,*
> *And view thy silvery stream*
> *When gilded by a summer's beam.*

The Market Hall is now a general store, a couple of former coaching inns offer accommodation, there is a cycle hire centre and a cafe, while among the several tourist shops is the Old Cheese Shoppe. Though this might appear to be just another tourist trap, Hartington is widely known for its cheese and just round the corner is Nuttall's Cheese Factory where our namesakes produce a fine Stilton. The factory was established around 1900 as a co-operative by the Duke of Devonshire and the cheese, which is much prized and the winner of many awards, is exported all over the world.

A former market town, Hartington was granted the first Market Charter in the Peak District by King John in 1203. Once a place of some importance, the town was associated with lead mining and with the copper mines of Ecton

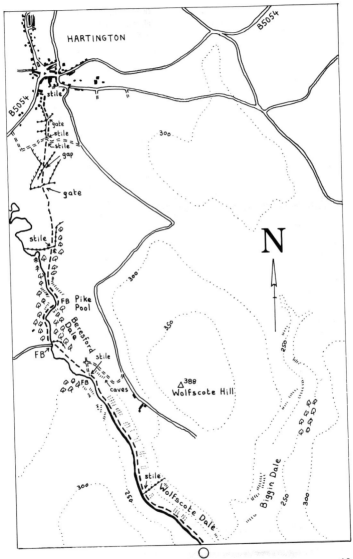

Hill in the Manifold Valley. The mid-thirteenth-century St Giles Church has medieval wall paintings and some interesting gargoyles.

Hartington like several other Peak District villages has recently decided that it too ought to have a well dressing ceremony. The commercialism can be forgiven though as the results are delightful and since 1980 screens have been erected on the green by the village pump on Wakes Saturday, the second Saturday in August.

DAY 2: HARTINGTON TO ILAM

The River Manifold, twin sister of the Dove, passes Hulme End a little to the west of Hartington and then meanders south for another nine miles before the two rivers merge at Ilam. Like its more famous twin, the Manifold has limestone caverns and cliffs, but though less celebrated and a much quieter valley, it has some spectacular scenery.

The Manifold is born on the gritstone upland moors to the north, but shortly after it reaches limestone country at Hulme End the effort of remaining above ground becomes too much and just below Wetton Mill the river sinks through fissures in its bed leaving the downstream course mere whitened stones. Except in very wet weather the Manifold does not appear again until Ilam, where in the grounds of Ilam Hall the water wells up from the Boil Hole and suddenly the river is full.

From Hulme End in the north, right down to Waterhouses on the A523 Leek to Ashbourne road the Manifold is accompanied by a track. In places this has been usurped by the road, but for much of its length there is a footpath and cycle route. This was the course of the Leek and Manifold Light Railway, which had it survived until more affluent days when railways are kept just for tourists, would surely have been a major attraction. It was constructed in 1904 at the end of the railway building era to serve the farms, all of which were situated on the limestone plateau far above the valley floor. Passengers, of whom there were few, had a long climb at the beginning and end of their journeys and while hopes of a revival of the Ecton mines were disappointed, the line survived on weekend tourists and milk traffic for a creamery at Ecton. The Whitsun holiday of 1905 brought 5000 passengers, but when the creamery closed in 1933 the line followed a year later. The track was converted to its present use as a footpath by Staffordshire Council as long ago as 1937.

Looking down on the river from a sheer rock face high on the valley side is Thor's Cave. Apart from the position, its most spectacular feature is the 60ft high entrance. In 1864 the cave was excavated but very little can be said about its history save that it contained Romano-British remains of pottery and bronze and iron knives. Nowadays archaeologists remove earth in layers so that their finds may be dated by the level at which they are found,

Beeston Tor

but the floor of Thor's Cave was thrown out to lie in a heap below the entrance. Elderbush Cave close by wasn't discovered until 1935 and modern methods have shown it was in use in late Palaeolithic times, probably by hunters whose flint implements have been found.

A little downstream from Weag's Bridge is Beeston Tor. This too has a cavern, St Bertram's Cave, named after the Anglo-Saxon hermit who converted the district to Christianity in the thirteenth century. A hoard of Saxon coins and jewellery was discovered here in 1924. The cliff itself is the most striking in the whole of the valley. Rising straight from the water's edge, the smooth white limestone wall rises sheer until 150ft above the river it arches out in a huge overhang. Above, the wall continues to a top nearly 300ft above the river bed.

The rock climbs here are mostly graded at Very Severe and above. There is Central Wall, one of the easiest, but also one of the best where on the main pitch, nearly 100ft of climbing on a rising traverse across a blank wall, there is no ledge bigger than a man's hand on which to rest. West Wall is longer and harder, but the Thorn is, for the average climber, undoubtedly the best. Put up by Joe Brown in 1954, when few climbers were venturing onto limestone which was thought of as loose and dangerous, the Thorn climbs direct to the huge overhang of Ivy Gash before escaping round it up the impending wall to its left. The crucial overhanging section is sometimes done free which makes it at least one grade harder, but most climbers are happy to haul themselves over the crux with the aid of a length of nylon sling on a strategically placed peg. Why "The Thorn"? Well, the finish as the climber thankfully reaches the top of the cliff is through a very scratchy hawthorn bush.

The rounded shape of Ecton Hill is honeycombed with disued shafts and levels. To the east fields separate its grassy slopes from the valley of the Dove, while the western side falls more steeply to the Manifold that meanders slowly past its foot. Sheep graze the steep flanks and the hill top is a pastoral scene with white walled farmhouses and fields of sheep and store cattle, but of its former mineral wealth there is very little sign.

The Ecton copper mines, unlike the rest of the Peak District mines, did not come under the jurisdiction of the Barmote Court but were leased to speculators. When the lease ran out shortly after a rich vein of copper was discovered, the landowner, the Duke of Devonshire, took over the mines and during the eighteenth century reaped a profit of over £1,000,000. The Crescent in Buxton is said to be the result of this mining venture. The mines date from much earlier than this and the first recorded use of gunpowder underground took place here in the seventeenth century. As the mines prospered boats were used in the tunnels and one of the earliest James Watt rotary steam engines was employed as a winding engine.

It is just over 100 years ago that the last mine closed and spoil heaps no longer dominate the hillside above Ecton, the open shafts breath a soft mist into the cold air and the engine house, now a barn, stands forlorn on the hilltop.

ROUTE DESCRIPTION
Hartington Bridge

Hartington is left by the back door; one minute you're in the middle of the village and the next in quiet countryside. 50 yards up the road to Warslow, to the left of the house next to the Charles Cotton Hotel, the footpath squeezes through a stile between the houses, then passing a modern barn the houses are left behind as you cross the fields. The buildings to the right

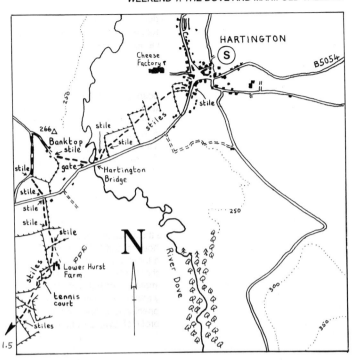

are Nuttall's Cheese Factory and in the distance is the switchback range of hills above the Manifold Valley. Arriving at Hartington Bridge beside a converted water mill which still has the old millwheel in place, the shortest route is up the B5054, but with high speed traffic and negligible verges a more circuitous route is pleasanter. Take the footpath up the field to Banktop whose drive leads to a minor road then go left down the road to a corner where a footpath brings you back to the main road.

Ecton Mill

Go straight across to follow the stiles over the fields and where the path forks, pass to the right of the buildings of Lower Hurst Farm. Crossing another field keep straight on past a tennis court and through more waymarked fields to the lane. The long ridge to the left is Wolfscote Hill.

Turn left to the crossroads then go right for a few yards to a footpath just beyond a little hut with a bell turret which was an Anglican Mission last used

40 years ago. Walking across the fields and round the back of Archford Moor Farm where twin stiles indicate a parting of the ways, keep straight on following a little walked path over a series of sturdy new stiles and an old squeezer stile isolated in the middle of a field. Ahead on the far side of the valley lies Ecton Hill, the traces of old copper workings still visible on its slopes. Crossing the lane the path continues downhill and into the adjacent field at a kink in the fence, then slants across the hillside to pass below a cottage to join the road by the cottage drive.

Turn left to the junction, where an interesting cave by an old quarry a few yards along the road is worth a detour. Just past the cottage towards Back of Ecton there is a stile on the right. Climbing up to the top of the field, join the footpath which contours along the hillside through the woodland above a wall. Through the trees you catch occasional glimpses of the Manifold Way below, the track of the former light railway. After a third of a mile the path descends to a stile by a Gothic castle whose copper spire came from a

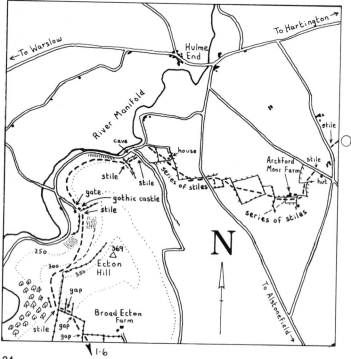

Swainsley Hall from Ecton Hill

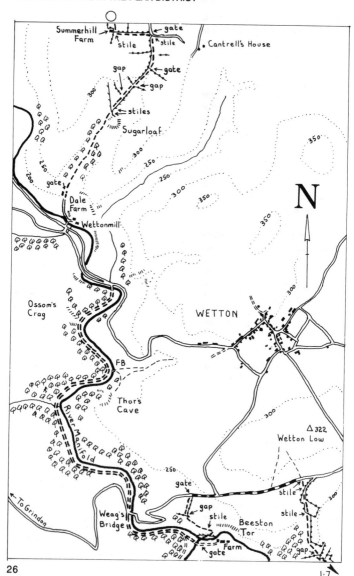

demolished chapel. The castle was built in 1933 by Mr Arthur Ratcliffe, MP for Leek, and is now a Field Centre. Go round the building, under an archway and over a stile onto the open hillside.

A grassy path slants up across the hillside below the Dutchman Mine, now screened with trees. The screes are the spoil from the copper mines and below is the site of the smelting mill, the railway station and the dairy. The path climbs steadily with a superb bird's-eye view of the Manifold Valley. In summer the bare hillside is dotted with buttercups and daisies, the rarer rock roses and mountain pansies. Joining a higher path coming from the building on the skyline which was the engine house of the Deep Ecton Mine, you round the corner to look down upon Swainsley Hall, built in 1867 by a London solicitor. There is a dovecote in the grounds and in order to preserve the view from the hall the Manifold Railway was concealed in a 150 yard long tunnel. With the ground still dropping away steeply to the right the angle relents across the hillside to an old hedge line of battered hawthorn trees, where after a final effort a stile is reached in the stone wall above.

It is now an easy walk over the fields across the top of Ecton Hill. Going through a gateway to the right of a belt of trees, pass an old lime kiln in a quarry to a stile below Summerhill Farm and then go down beside the wall to a gate by a duckpond. Joining the lane leave it again immediately over a stile for a gentle downhill stroll beside the wall. The landmark of Grindon Church steeple appears ahead and passing the Sugarloaf, an imposing isolated limestone reef knoll, the path then descends quite steeply to the grassy valley bottom and down to the road at Dale Farm, where walkers taller than 5ft 8in must mind their heads!

Manifold Valley

Wettonmill is a culture shock, suddenly it's busy again. After the peace and seclusion of the last five miles, the visitors, the ice-creams and the bicycles come as a surprise. The mill which dates from the end of the sixteenth century was a corn mill and a stile by the entrance leads up to Nan Tor Cave which is fun to explore.

Crossing the bridge turn left down the road which divides only to rejoin shortly, then when you cross the river again it is usually dry having gone underground at the swallets just after the mill. The next section, though still tarmac and a bit hard on the feet, is for walkers and cyclists only. After passing under Ossam's Crag, the huge opening of Thor's Cave appears ahead high above the valley. You don't have to visit the cave, but it's worth the climb to see at close quarters one of the biggest cave entrances in England. A footbridge leads over the river bed with a flight of steps up the hillside. Thor's Cave was excavated by Wetton schoolmaster Samuel Carrington who found Romano-British remains which are now in Sheffield and Buxton Museums. Below, by the river bed, are another two small caves known as Radcliffe's Stables where a local farmer hid his horse from the marauding troops of the 1745 rebellion.

The track of the old railway continues along the valley until the narrow road from Grindon to Wetton is met at Weag's Bridge. If the river hasn't disappeared and there is much more than a trickle it is advisable to cross here and follow the road up towards Wetton, but if the bed is dry take the left hand track of the dual carriageway ahead. The old railway now turns away beside the River Hamps where the station tea-room still stands forlornly in the field, then just before Beeston Tor Farm a small double gate leads to stepping stones across the Manifold. The great white wall of Beeston Tor rises straight from the river nearly 300ft in height and is one of the biggest rock faces in the Peak District. It is a popular climbing cliff with some excellent routes.

If the river is dry, walk downstream for a few yards to visit St Bertram's Cave at the base of the cliff. This was used as a refuge from the invading Danes. It has an iron bar across the entrance which is helpful when climbing out again. The saint's cave which at one time had a door, has narrow muddy passages leading to other small chambers with one emerging 50ft up the cliff.

Surprisingly there is no right of way beside the Manifold, so the route now leaves the valley going to the left of the cliff. Climbing steadily to a gateway, turn up beside the wall to join the road at a stile. Following the road uphill, keep straight on at the junction along a narrow little lane for a third of a mile over the crest of the hill to the dip, and then take the footpath to the right which cuts across the corner of a field. The path contours the hillside along the valley edge where rock roses and purple mounds of thyme brighten the slopes. Looking back Beeston Tor is seen in profile with above it the landmark of Grindon Church spire. Below is the dry bed of the River Manifold and you can see very clearly how it has cut its way down through the plateau. After passing the quite extensive spoil heaps of Bincliffe Mines, which had eleven adits, the right of way turns off left into the fields, but a concession path created by the Staffordshire Wildlife Trust stays along the valley rim. The reserve has been an SSSI since 1972. Re-joining the right of way in a large field, curve round the head of a little side valley across to a gate in the corner.

Continue through the fields to the lane that passes behind the sixteenth-century Castern Hall which once again belongs to the Hurt family who named it after their iron works. Across the valley is Throwley Hall, a roofless ruin. The roof itself is in the city of York. A former owner, a Mr Cathcart, took a fancy to it and removed the lot, destroying this fine fourteenth-century house.

Ilam Estate

The tarmac loops down to the road, but you can short-cut across the grass, then at the junction keep straight on to River Lodge which was built when Ilam village was remodelled and the hall rebuilt. Take the footpath through the

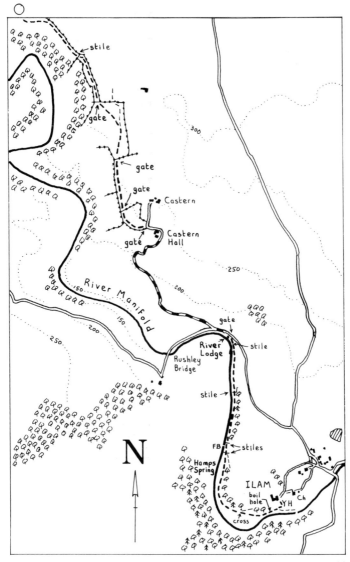

garden where "All persons using this road must pay 1NP at the lodge". Walking beside the river, whose banks in summer are massed with red campion and forget-me-nots, Ilam Country Park is entered on the path known as "Paradise Walk" which was created as an informal promenade for the residents of the hall. There is usually now some water in the river bed as the River Hamps, after performing another disappearing act, emerges at Hamps Spring on the opposite bank.

After passing the Saxon Battle Cross, the path has a tropical air with its edging of bamboo. Next you come to a small cave where tradition says St Bertram lived as a hermit, then the River Manifold bubbles up at the "Boil Holes" or "Raspberry Rising". Emerging after its six mile journey underground from Wetton Mill the river now passes peacefully on its way towards St Bertram's Bridge, looking as if it has never had an adventure in its life. Veer left up into the Italian Formal Gardens of the hall to explore the turret and parapet, which were built about 1830, before finishing with a visit to both the National Trust Information Centre and the tea room.

Ilam

The model village of Ilam, set respectfully apart at the gates of the once great Ilam Hall, was like Edensor on the Chatsworth estate especially created. Jesse Watts-Russell, a London business man removed those houses too close to his pseudo-Gothic towered and turreted mansion and went on to demolish the rest of the village before rebuilding it in a suitably rustic alpine style with steep gables and ornate bargeboards. It is very pretty, but so much resembles the set of a pantomime that you half expect a chorus of milkmaids to skip out of the cottage gardens and dance round a maypole.

The old road to Blore which used to pass uncomfortably close to the hall was realigned and is now at the other end of the village. The half timbered building which resembles a church is the village school, built in 1854, and the adjacent house was for the school master. The large Gothic cross was erected by Mr Watts-Russell in memory of his wife Mary and he also had a go at improving the thirteenth-century church adding an octagonal mausoleum. Gilbert Scott, who designed the village early in his career, became very successful undertaking nearly 1000 other projects including the Albert Memorial, the Midland Grand Hotel at St Pancras Station and the Foreign Office. He would be dismayed to see one of the village buildings being used as a bus depot.

During the remodelling of the old village a Saxon Battle Cross was discovered in the foundations of one of the cottages and this has now been erected at the end of Paradise Walk. Of the original hall only about a quarter remains. It was built in the 1820s on the site of an earlier sixteenth-century dwelling but the hall only stood until the 1930s when after much of it had been demolished, the building was purchased by Sir Robert McDougall, the flour baron. He made the remaining portion safe and gave it together with the grounds to the National Trust in 1934 on the understanding that like Ravenstor in Miller's Dale it was to be used as a youth hostel. It also houses a National Trust shop, an interesting information centre and a tea room.

Ilam

WEEKEND 2: MATLOCK AND THE DERWENT VALLEY

DAY 1:
STARTING POINT:

Ambergate to Matlock 9 miles
(348516) The Hurt Arms in the centre
of Ambergate

DAY 2:
STARTING POINT:

Matlock to Ambergate 9½ miles
(296603) Matlock Railway Station

ROUTE SUMMARY:

Exploring the wooded vale of the
Derwent the route takes in the High
Peak Trail, Black Rocks and
Cromford, with a return past Riber
Castle, Cromford Canal and the
Tramway Museum. A few short steep
climbs, but mainly easy walking.

DAY 1: AMBERGATE TO MATLOCK

From Matlock the River Derwent glides south through a narrow limestone gorge lined on one side by tier upon tier of houses clinging to the steep hillside and on the other by the sheer white wall of High Tor. Until the early

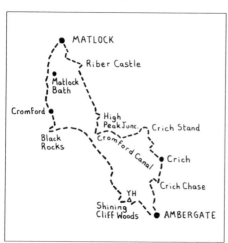

nineteenth century this was secret territory with no road up the valley and the only approach was a steep lane which twisted its way down the wooded sides. But despite the difficulty of access the fame of Matlock Bath was already established with three hotels and numerous other houses, and when in 1815 Scarthin Rock was blasted away and the turnpike built, the valley was opened up to become a most fashionable resort.

Cromford Canal

Yet when the railway arrived in 1849, driven through tunnel after tunnel up the valley beside the Wye, instead of redoubled success for the spa, Matlock Bath was transformed. With every train disgorging tourists on a day trip from Derby and other vulgar Midland towns, it was no longer a congenial place for the former genteel visitors so, leaving the village to the hordes, the clientele moved their allegiance upstream to Matlock Bank. The lowered tone of the spa is captured in James Croston's 1876 *On foot through the Peak* "No visitor can remain many hours in Matlock without becoming aware of the fact that the inhabitants are a money-getting race. Nature has dealt bountifully with them and they eagerly avail themselves of every opportunity of turning these advantages to account."

Though gradually the valley lost its isolation as canal and road links to the south were built, no canal could breach the westward barrier, no flight of locks could climb the 1000ft to the plateau, but hidden within the woods is Sheep Pasture Incline. This steep slope, so long that in both directions the ends disappear from sight into the distance, was the route by which railway trucks were hauled from the wharf on the Cromford Canal to the heartland of the White Peak. This was the first stage of the Cromford and High Peak

33

Railway, one of the earliest railways in Britain. A massive steel cable wound round a drum was driven by a steam engine whose empty shell of an engine house still stands at the top of the incline. At the foot the line has a kink in it, not to avoid an obstacle, for nothing got in the way of the straight track which was quarried through solid rock, but if the cable broke and the trucks rushed downhill out of control, then they would leave the track at the kink and be caught in a tunnel, a kind of subterranean sand trap. The remains of one such runaway are still to be seen nearly buried in the catchpit at the base of the incline. Now the railway is gone, the rails removed and the only hazard on the incline is runaway cyclists who hurtle silently down the slope.

As the incline levels out after its exhausting climb from the valley, it rounds the foot of Black Rocks. These steep gritstone crags now busy with rock climbers, were a popular excursion even in Victorian times when tourists made the trip from the village of Cromford. Cromford is forever associated with Richard Arkwright who in 1771 built the first water powered cotton mill in the world at the foot of Bonsall Brook, just before it joins the Derwent. Although water power had been used long before, this was its first major industrial use and the millpond which served to maintain power during times of drought is still a central feature of Cromford. Six years later Arkwright built a second mill close by, but this time the water came not from the brook, but from the more reliable flow of a sough from an otherwise unsuccessful mine on the Via Gellia. This incongruous Latin name for the more prosaic A4012 was bestowed by the Gell family, the builders of the dale's first road, and there is an even more modern link as the name gave rise in the twentieth century to the trademark Viyella.

Over the next few years Arkwright's mills proliferated in the Peak District and then in 1783 he tackled the powerful River Derwent itself. Masson Mill still dominates the roadside and the dam still holds back the river, while in the village of Cromford his legacy is a whole street of houses built opposite his Greyhound Inn for the work people. Close by Masson Mill on a flat shelf quarried from the hillside, and almost encircled by the great bend in the Derwent as it veers away seeming suddenly to take an aversion to Cromford, is Willersley Castle. Intended as a palatial home it was never occupied by Arkwright who, before it could be completed, died at Rock House on the hillside above his mills. Cromford has not forgotten Arkwright and his first mill is now open to the public every day.

ROUTE DESCRIPTION
Shining Cliff Woods

From the Hurt Arms in the centre of Ambergate follow the main A6 towards Derby then turn right in front of the late Victorian St Anne's church. Holly Lane crosses Ha'penny Bridge by the confluence of the River Amber with the

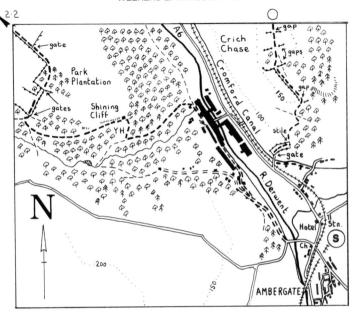

Derwent and also spans the tail race from the mills upstream. Turn right along the bridleway forking right downhill to pass the factory. The Wire Works here was established as long ago as 1876 on the site of an earlier iron-smelting forge and rolling mills.

Turning left after the buildings and up through the woods signed to the youth hostel, the industrial area is soon left behind as you follow a broad track through the trees. Take the first right turn in about a third of a mile by a map board and climb to Shining Cliff Youth Hostel which nestles under the tall cliffs. The original hostel was destroyed by fire but it has now been rebuilt. The track from the hostel contours along the hillside for another third of a mile to a T-junction where you turn uphill and then go right again to leave the wood through a gate and enter the fields.

Alderwasley

Keeping straight on through Park Plantation you emerge from the trees into Alderwasley Park. Across the Derwent Valley is the conspicuous tower of Crich Stand on top of a limestone cliff, to the right the village of Crich is hidden by a fold of the hills and only its church spire can be seen standing isolated. Follow the wall down past the huge mansion of Alderwasley Hall, the former

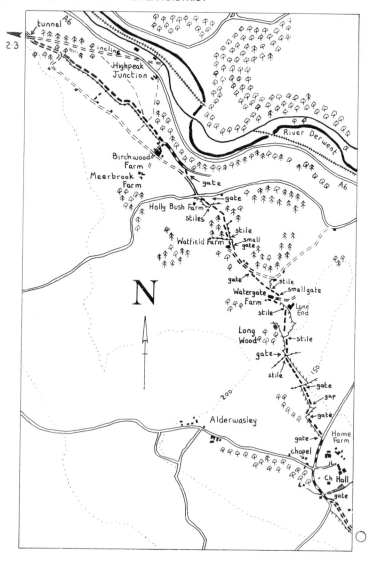

Georgian home of the local industrialist Francis Hurt who in the 1780s built iron furnaces in the valley below, where the modern wire works now stands. The hall houses a special school which takes children from both north and south Derbyshire and in its grounds is All Saints Church which was built in 1850.

Higg Lane leads up the hill then at the junction keep straight on along New Road. To the left on Chapel Hill is the restored sixteenth-century building of St Margaret's Chapel which belonged to the Hurt family. In 200 yards a footpath leads across the fields bending downhill after the first gate into the next field and crossing a ditch before climbing to the ridge ahead. Go through the adjacent stile on the right and downhill by the side of Long Wood to join a track to the left of Lane End. A footpath crosses Mere Brook by Watergate Farm and climbs to another track below a wood. This is followed for a short way past the houses then you turn right up the side of the outbuildings of Watfield Farm. A path follows the edge of Flat Wood then it turns into the trees going down the hill to a narrow walled track and along the field boundary to meet the road to the right of Holly Bush Farm.

High Peak Trail

The road opposite leads to a caravan site, but at the site entrance you turn off into the trees to join the lane along the top of Birch Wood. After passing Birchwood Farm the track continues through the trees. Keep to the higher path by the edge of the wood to meet an old road which passes under the Cromford and High Peak Railway. Just before the tunnel climb left to join the track which is now the High Peak Trail. Sheep Pasture Incline at a gradient of 1 in 8 leads to Sheep Pasture Engine House where there was a single stationary engine to haul the waggons up the ³/₄ mile long incline. It was modernised in 1964 with an electric engine, but in spite of this only worked for three more years. The top of the incline is a fine viewpoint from which to look down upon Willersley Castle which faces Arkwright's 1771 mill across the river. The 40ft Victoria Prospect Tower on the Heights of Abraham is on the skyline above, while round to the left is the huge scar of Middleton Quarry.

It is easy walking now for the next ¹/₂ mile past old gritstone quarries to the 80ft high escarpment of Black Rocks. Just before you reach the car park, where there is an information centre and toilets, leave the trail and take the stepped path down through the trees. At a cleared stony area go through a stile by a gate on the far side and follow the wall along the top of the field to a track which leads downhill.

Cromford

Just after the sharp bend by Holly Cottage, go through a squeezer stile and down a tarmac path into Cromford, one of the first factory villages. Passing some new houses Bedehouse Lane goes down by the cottages and behind

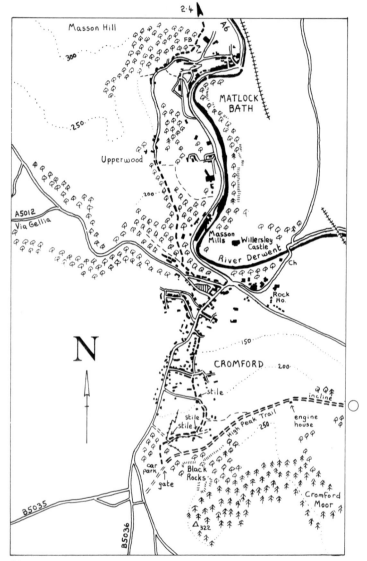

gardens on the edge of the fields. Joining the main road you pass North Street, a cul de sac of three storied terraced houses which together with the school at the end were built by Arkwright. The attics communicated along the whole length of the building and were used for stocking knitting.

Passing in front of the Greyhound Hotel, which in 1788 was also built by Arkwright, turn up Scarthin Road past the Boat Inn and the tempting Scarthin Books. Opposite the Primitive Methodist Chapel a cobbled lane leads to the footpath to Matlock Bath.

Masson Hill

Take the path which runs above the cottage gardens then in 50 yards leave it by a steep scrambly way up. This doesn't look like the proper route but it soon becomes a good path through the trees which contours Masson Hill above the River Derwent and the busy A6. Below is Masson Mills. The northernmost six storeyed red brick building was erected by Arkwright in 1783 and the mill manufactured textiles until the 1990s. The path leads behind the New Tribes Mission by old lead mine entrances and then climbs to a higher level, continuing to the cluster of houses at Upperwood, an old mining settlement where a narrow cobbled lane known as the Wapping joins the path. Before the new road was made along the valley in 1815 this was the only way down into this part of the dale. On the other side of the valley gaunt Riber Castle can be seen silhouetted against the sky. Becoming surfaced Upperwood Road first climbs a little before descending into Matlock Bath above Gulliver's Kingdom and the Pavilion which now houses the Peak District Mining Museum.

50 yards beyond the entrance to the Heights of Abraham the route to Matlock continues up a flight of steps. These pleasure gardens were laid out in 1780 and named after the storming of Quebec by General Wolfe in 1759. The path climbs and crosses the private grounds by an elaborate bridge and then passes under the modern cablecars which have been here since 1984, before descending opposite the massive 350ft limestone cliff of High Tor. Joining the Masson Farm track which leads to a tarmac road, pass beneath the picturesque Chapel of St John, which was built in 1897, and fork left along a path which continues along the hillside beside a wall. Just before the drive to Greenhills Farm turn through a stile and cross the fields with ahead an almost aerial view of Matlock spread out in tiers over the hillside. After descending through the yard of Bridge Farm you arrive suddenly in the town above the main road and the railway station.

Matlock

The busy little town of Matlock is excluded from the Peak National Park because like Buxton it is encircled by limestone quarries. There are actually several small villages all called Matlock. Matlock Bank, Matlock Bath,

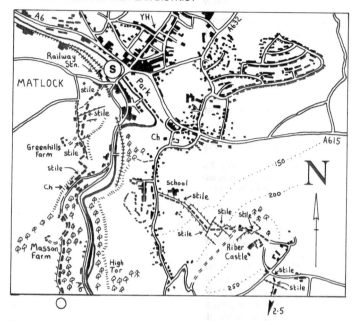

Matlock Bridge, Matlock Dale, Matlock Green and Matlock Town, but nowadays with the exception of Matlock Bath, they all merge, spreading away up the hill from the River Derwent and its fifteenth-century bridge.

Though the hillside is now covered by trees the ancient mines remain, some of their tunnels converted by the Victorians into show caves. Matlock is thought to have been a centre of lead mining in Roman times and it is lead that gives it a mention as Metesford in the Domesday Book. Five turnpike roads converged at this important river crossing and later the magnificent scenery of the gorge encouraged tourists who, from as early as the seventeenth century, came to take the waters.

In 1893 a cable tramway was built at Matlock Bank which claimed to be the steepest and the only single-line cable railway in Europe. On meeting financial difficulties it was bought by Sir George Newnes, the son of a local Congregational Minister and the founder of Tit-Bits. The ride up Bank Hill was twopence, but it was only a penny to come down and these fares were maintained until the tramway closed in 1927. The engine house and chimney still stand at the top of the hill by the grandly impressive Smedly's Hydro which was open until 1955 and is now the County Council Offices. British Rail still functions, but Paxton's station is the terminus of the line from Derby, though the Peak Railway Society have ambitious plans that one day steam trains will again follow the old 1849 Midland line up the Derwent Valley to Buxton.

The numerous hydros are no more, but there are show caves and cable cars, rowing boats and motor boat trips and plenty of gift shops and amusement arcades for as Croston observed there is ample opportunity for getting rid of your money in this "Blackpool of the Peak". In spite of this the valley has a natural beauty that is unspoilt by the trippers.

DAY 2: MATLOCK TO AMBERGATE

By the time John Smedley built his gothic castle on the skyline above Matlock, society had abandoned the spa at Matlock Bath and Smedley's new hydro was the place for fashion conscious seekers of health in graceful surroundings. The railway which brought the influx of tourists also brought in the customers, over 3000 a year at the turn of the century, but now as you climb steeply away from the valley you look down on an urban sprawl where in its turn the hydro has gone while ahead the once splendid Riber Castle stands gaunt and ruined.

Beyond the castle is farmland and then the delightful lane which crosses Bilberry Knoll descends through woodland and across bracken covered slopes to join the river near the once industrial village of Cromford. Industry has not entirely left these parts and here below the bluebell woods is Lea Mills where the raw materials of cotton and wool are spun and woven and made into clothing, one of the few remaining mills to handle the complete process. The mill has associations with Florence Nightingale who was brought up at Lea Hurst, just up the road and to which she returned after the Crimean War in 1856. Lea Bridge was originally the site of a cotton spinning mill built in 1784 by her great uncle Peter Nightingale.

As the Derwent comes to Cromford it leaves behind the limestone with its narrow gorge, and the winding river continues into the country of Millstone Grits and shales. The valley sides lean back and their wooded slopes look down on the road, the river, the railway and also the Cromford Canal. This was built by Arkwright to open up the area and connected his mills at Cromford with the Erewash Canal fifteen miles to the south. The water for the canal came from the mill which was supplied by the sough of the Via Gellia mine while Leawood Pump House, which stands beside the canal at High Peak Junction, was built about 1840 to pump water from the River Derwent into the canal in times of shortage. The canal of course predates the railway, but it is also earlier than the road for when it was built only packhorse tracks connected the valley with the outside world.

Flowing south to its assignation with the River Amber and the industrial midlands beyond, the Derwent is accompanied by the Midland Railway and the Cromford Canal. The canal has long been abandoned, on its banks grow wild daffodils and across the still surface swims a water rat, its nose held high. Below Lea Hurst the canal tunnels through the hill then as you emerge into daylight, ahead is Crich Stand. Crich Cliff is an island, an upthrust of limestone amid gritstone surroundings and on its western side a quarry has dug deep encroaching within yards of the fine tower that stands at the top, a memorial to the 11,400 Sherwood Foresters who died in the wars. Climbing the staircase which spirals up within, you can see for miles across five counties and at night the beacon shines out over the countryside.

In the quarry beneath is another memorial, one to the beloved tram. This is the National Tramway Museum, a delightful working museum with dozens of lovingly restored tramcars. These are not just trams to look at, but trams to ride on looking very much smarter in their Sunday best than they did when working the streets of Manchester, Sheffield or Leeds.

Crich Stand

Beyond Crich village is the heathland and woodland of Crich Chase. Only a matter of yards from the over busy A6, the bluebell woods and bracken slopes have a quiet and unhurried air and it came as no great surprise to find, one afternoon, a frame tent pitched there in a clearing. More unusual though was the tall latticework mast behind the tent, built of wood lashed together boy scout fashion, with on top a windmill powered electricity generator. "Well," the man said, "it drives my radio, record player and other things." He had been living there for over six months and no-one seemed to mind. We left him beside his camp fire and descended to the A6 where motorcyclists lying flat over their machines watched the needle climb towards 100 miles per hour. It was a harsh return to the twentieth century.

Jeremy at Crich Tramway Museum

ROUTE DESCRIPTION (See map 2.4 page 40)
Riber

From Matlock railway station cross the fifteenth-century Matlock Bridge and walk through Hall Leys Park beside the River Derwent. The ornate cast-iron shelter surmounted by a clock near the park entrance originally stood in Crown Square at the foot of Matlock's cable tramway where the roundabout now is. Passing a footbridge which shows the heights of two December floods, Knowlstone Place is reached. Turn right to cross a little stream and climb steeply up Stoney Way by St Giles Church. Turn right along Church Street in Old Matlock where opposite the Duke William is a lovely old house dated 1781. It has an expensive gritstone façade, but the far side is of cheaper limestone which has been infilled with gritstone at the top making a single pitched roof from the original double one.

A handful of new houses is sprinkled amongst the old cottages, then after ¼ mile you turn up beside the drive of Highfield School. The public footpath climbs steeply heading straight for Riber Castle on the skyline which resembles a lace doily. At the top of the field the path bends left to pass an isolated house and looking back Matlock and the Derwent valley lie spread out below.

The castle with its four 90ft towers was built in 1862 and had its own deep well and gas plant. It became a boy's school after Smedley's death then after standing empty for a few years was bought by Matlock UDC in 1936 and used during the war as a food store. Little more than a shell, it was purchased by the British Fauna Reserve 100 years after it was built for less than one hundredth the original cost. Riber Castle now houses a collection of British and European birds and animals.

Reaching the castle entrance just after a quarry from which the stone was obtained, continue down the lane and turn right by the seventeenth-century Riber Manor. Riber Farm shop and tearoom stand next to the mullion windowed Elizabethan Riber Hall, which is now a hotel.

At the green triangle containing a neatly fenced Ordnance Survey benchmark marking a height of 797.28ft, go just a few steps to the left and take the footpath over the fields. There is a fine view of Crich Stand on top of its limestone cliff and the path passes to the right of Hearthstone Farm then turns left along the road.

Lea Bridge

Forking right after the buildings the track swings up the hill past Bilberry Knoll with Crich Stand again ahead in the distance. After passing a beechwood fork left and go down the other side of the hill past a ruined building to a stile. The path slants down the hillside through Coumbs Wood to another stile which leads into semi-open woodland. The little grassy path through the bracken keeps to the right of a boggy patch then another green path is met

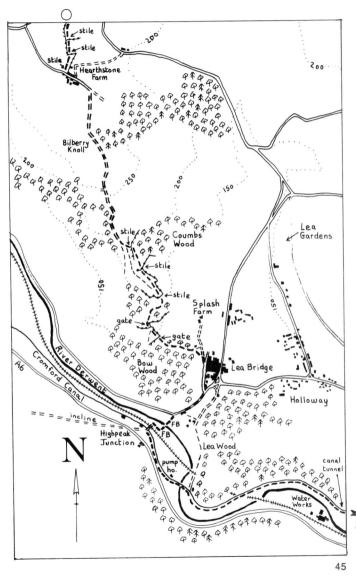

which climbs slightly to a stile by a gate and back into the bluebell wood. The path wanders through the trees keeping straight on through the next patch of open with views across to the village of Holloway. Meaning a hollowed or worn-away route the village was already in existence at the beginning of the thirteenth century and so must have stood on an important ancient route. A grassy track then leads down through Bow Wood and just before the road from Splash Farm is met, the footpath turns right to join it a little further on. The road runs behind the large works at Lea Bridge which has a company shop selling garments to the public.

Cromford Canal

Turn right along the main road to the bend, then take the path over the river and railway to High Peak Junction where by the Information Centre are two restored brake vans. Turning left along the Cromford Canal you pass the Leawood Pump House with its tall chimney. The original Watt type single acting beam engine which operates some summer weekends is still intact and is capable of raising 5 to 6 tons of water per minute. The water level of this section has been raised to accommodate horse-drawn barges which run regular boat trips in the season. The canal is carried over the River Derwent by the 200 yard long Wigwell Aqueduct, which was constructed in 1792.

Continuing past the junction with the overgrown Nightingales Canal, an 1849 cast-iron aqueduct crosses the railway where it emerges from the Leawood Tunnel and the canal then runs below Lea Wood. This section has been repaired by sandbags, for the embankment collapsed and the canal emptied itself into the river. Gregory Tunnel leads to the silted basin at Gregory Dam and as you emerge from the darkness Crich Stand is seen framed by the tunnel mouth. At the bridge go up the steps and cross the canal by the cluster of houses at Leashaw Farm.

Crich

The track leads up to the road where you go straight across past a bungalow and up through Leashaw Wood. Near the top of the wood the path enters a field with Crich Stand again appearing ahead and the road is joined by a gate on the bend at Wakebridge.

Follow the road round the next bend and over Oxhay Brook then turn left up a track in front of the houses. To the left of the track are the ruins of the Wakebridge Mine which was worked from the early nineteenth century until the 1950s. The circular walls in front of the engine house enclose twin 650ft deep shafts. Forking right, pass above Cliff Farm on a path which then bends back to cross the mile long track of the Crich Tramway Museum at its terminus. When they are running it is worth waiting here for a few minutes to watch the trams.

The route now skirts the back of Cliff Quarry. A path joins from the left

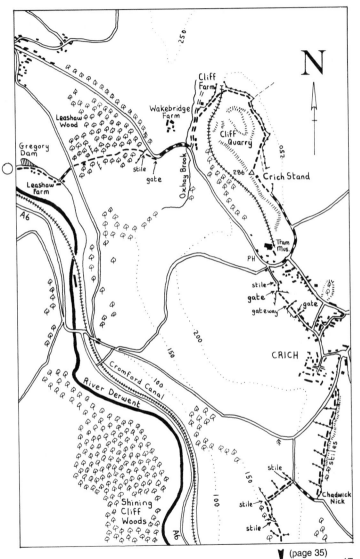

(page 35)

and you can see a long way to the east, out over the landscape of the Derbyshire coal fields. The path continues round the quarry and creeps up on Crich Stand from the rear where a trig point shares the 950ft summit with the war memorial.

The tarmac path leads down from the memorial to join the road. Follow it round the bend and keep straight on past the entrance to the Tramway Museum which is sited on a former mineral railway in the huge Crich Quarry. The imposing façade was taken from the old Derby Assembly Rooms designed by Robert Adams. The museum has a Victorian atmosphere and contains about 40 trams.

Turn off at Carr Lane before the Cliff Inn and then immediately go left down a track. This runs parallel to the old gravity-hauled tramroad which supplied limestone from the quarries to 20 limekilns on the canal at Ambergate and was built by George Stevenson the railway pioneer. The path leads through the fields past a now obsolete bridge by St Mary's Church which was consecrated in 1135. Joining the road end continue down Coasthill and bend left to the square in the centre of the village with its four-fold horse trough and impressive Baptist Chapel. Crich means crag and it was once a stocking making centre as well as being important for lead mining and limestone quarrying.

Turn up Sandy Lane and take the footpath to Chadwick Nick that forks off opposite the Fire Station. This path goes behind a modern house and then follows a gritstone wall along the top of disused quarries. The line of the old tramroad is far below with again panoramic views to the east. To the west across the valley of the River Derwent are the extensive Shining Cliff Woods.

Crich Chase

Joining the lane at Chadwick Nick down a flight of gritstone steps, turn right to the next corner where a metal stile leads into the fields. Reaching Crich Chase go left along the top of the wood where the waymarked path descends gradually along the hillside. Passing a little clearing by a ruin the path swings away downhill crossing a broad path half way down. A field path then leads to a bridge over the Cromford Canal.

(For Shining Cliff Youth Hostel turn right along the canal past Canalside Cottages to the railway bridge. Crossing the busy road go through the factory yard, over the River Derwent and through the works, turning right along the tarmac road at the back of the buildings to join the route from Ambergate.)

For Ambergate turn left along the canal towpath to the next bridge and then follow Chase Road under the railway to the busy A6 where you turn left into Ambergate.

Ambergate

The settlement of Ambergate grew up by the 1820 tollgate at the turnpike junction to Bullbridge near the confluence of the River Amber with the Derwent. With the coming of the railway some twenty years later the cluster of houses grew into a small town dominated by the high railway arches.

Though a good point for starting a walk there is little left to recommend Ambergate as a destination for, since the 1960s, nearly everything of interest has been razed to the ground. In those days Stephenson's battery of twenty lime kilns stood beside the canal, the famous aqueduct at nearby Bullbridge had not been destroyed, the original large stone station and its unusual wooden triangular companion would still have been there, you could have admired Stevenson's Incline and also the tollhouse at the east end of Ha'penny Bridge. Now all are gone save for the bridge, which was built to replace a ferry in 1792 by Francis Hurt of Alderwasley Hall. The toll was $^{1}/_{2}$d.

The 1874 Hurt Arms has pride of place at the busy road junction and is only rivalled by a Little Chef which squats beside the viaduct. The turnpike road from Cromford to Belper has matured into the terrifyingly busy A6 racetrack where you take your life in your hands as you attempt to cross to the other side. One blisteringly hot day while walking in the nearby woods we came across an ambulance parked on a quiet shady track. Leaning against it with the radio murmuring in the background, the two ambulance men told us cheerily that they were just waiting for the inevitable weekend accident to happen.

WEEKEND 3: DALES AND TRAILS, HARTINGTON TO YOULGREAVE

DAY 1:   Hartington to Youlgreave 12½miles
                                      (Short Route 10½ miles)
STARTING POINT: (128604) The centre of Hartington

DAY 2:   Youlgreave to Hartington 13 miles
STARTING POINT: (211643) The centre of Youlgreave

ROUTE SUMMARY: Lathkill Dale and Bradford Dale are
                                      linked by dry limestone valleys to the
                                      Tissington and High Peak Trails.
                                      Easy walking on good paths.

DAY 1: HARTINGTON TO YOULGREAVE

Between the valleys of the Dove and the Wye a broad expanse of high land runs south from Buxton. This is the heart of the White Peak, a limestone plateau around 1000ft above sea level broken into a myriad jigsaw pieces by a network of limestone walls. Here narrow strips of fields date back to the

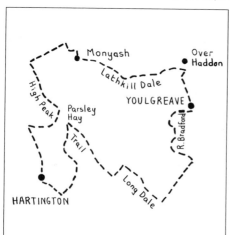

Middle Ages, but other walls that now fit so naturally into the wide landscape arrived in the early 1800s as unwelcome intrusions spoiling the country-side - "Everywhere disfigured with these stone-wall fences", said Rhodes in 1818.

Until the coming of the railways in the nineteenth century this was an isolated wind-swept fastness cut off from the lowlands beyond the Peak. "It is with great difficulty," writes an agent of the London Lead Company in the eighteenth century, "that we got in and out of the county". In winter when the wind sweeps the snow off the fields to cover the road and piles it against the walls burying the sheep huddled in the lee, a simple trip to Buxton can still be a voyage into the unknown. But for most of the year cars speed their way south-east along the busy A515 to Friden, turning left down the Via Gellia to Cromford or continuing south to descend gradually to Ashbourne along the old turnpike routes.

The railways invaded the wilderness, approaching from the south and joining forces at Parsley Hay just north of Hartington for the onward dash to Buxton. The first to be built was the Cromford and High Peak Railway which linked the Cromford Canal near Matlock with the Peak Forest Canal at Whaley Bridge on the western side. This was one of the earliest railways in the country and met the difficulties of crossing the high plateau head on. A series of inclined planes with stationary steam powered winding engines hauled up the trucks and the track then wound its way across the plateau following the contours, keeping gradients to a minimum so that horses could pull the waggons.

The Tissington line was built by the London and North Western Railway in 1899, a link in its objective of joining London and Manchester. Competition with the Midland Railway was always fierce, no physical obstacle was too much and the track was forced through from Ashbourne to join the Cromford and High Peak at Parsley Hay. In the higher reaches near Buxton a huge viaduct was built and the two rivals provided Buxton with two separate railway stations.

The day of these railways is now over and the lines have been converted by the Peak National Park authority to trails for walkers, cyclists and horse riders. Where once smoke and sparks from the engines burnt black the embankments and cuttings, now the grass is patterned with cowslips and orchids.

It was October and the storms that had brought in the beginning of the month had subsided to be replaced by cold clear mornings with fog filled valleys and a sky of perfect blue. In the shadows the frost still held onto the ground, the pools were skimmed with a thin film of ice and only an occasional flower reminded us of the summer so recently ended. Humming to itself Friden Brick Works shimmered in the sun. A group of blue overalled workmen sat, backs to the limestone wall, beside the trail eating their sandwiches and enjoying their break in the open air. The factory makes bricks to line furnaces, not ordinary rectangular bricks, but elegantly curved ones that fit snugly round the furnace walls. The clay used to be mined locally, but now, the men said, it comes from China. There was they added, a vacancy for someone in the office to work the computer if we were interested.

Beyond the brick works and the trails lie the dales, Friden Dale, Long

Dale and Gratton Dale. Friden Dale is the shortest and is fringed with trees, but perhaps due to grazing animals the slopes of Long Dale are bare open grassy slopes where in summer the stemless thistle abounds. Though common in southern England, *Cirsium acaulon* is at its north-western limit in the Peak District.

Gratton Dale is a complete contrast to the barrenness of Long Dale. The change is sudden, a right angle bend in the valley and the limestone bones of the hillside break through, at first small rocks and boulders, but further down the valley rearing up in steeper cliffs and fragmented scree slopes. Mostly scrubland, perhaps too swift growing and hardy for even the sheep to subdue, the valley is a tangle of hawthorn. Then towards its foot Gratton Dale gradually subsides into pastureland with only a tiny stream, mere dried mud on our visits, though others speak of a torrent in wetter years.

It was late afternoon as we came down to the River Bradford, but where was it? Even the head high foliage in the valley bottom had withered in the drought and when we saw the fish pools what a sad sight it was. "Mud unto mud, death eddies near", and here death must we thought have been the fate of many a fat trout for the bed of the pools was but cracked mud. We walked beside the river hoping that the fish had escaped downstream to where the pools still retained a little water. Of the trout only one could be seen, its back nearly breaking the surface. But where were the rest?

"They've gone on their holidays", said our host at Youlgreave. "It's the driest we've seen in twenty years. It's never dried up like this before. There's a fish farm at Raper Lodge in Lathkill Dale, so when the water got a bit low, the fish were sent there for a rest."

ROUTE DESCRIPTION
Heathcote

The road nearly opposite the Market Hall in the centre of Hartington passes the Chapel Bookshop and climbs out of the village past Hartington Hall, the finest youth hostel in the Peak District. Just past the hall a public footpath through a field gate leads through two more gates, cutting across to join Highfield Lane at a stile by a footpath notice. This old packhorse way to Wirksworth, which was probably used to carry copper ore from Ecton in the Manifold Valley to Belper for smelting, crosses a network of fields divided by gleaming white ribbons of drystone walls so characteristic of the White Peak. These were built around the beginning of the eighteenth century with the passing of the Enclosure Acts. The old lane climbs over the top of the hill with to the right the mound of Wolfscote Hill while straight ahead is Biggin village and the square tower of its church.

After about a mile at a staggered crossroads, a left turn dips to the road and the way continues as a footpath following the wall uphill and then through

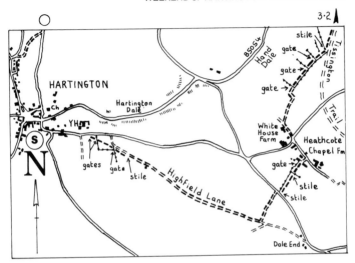

the yard of Chapel Farm. Turning left along the road through the hamlet of Heathcote, keep straight on at the crossroads and at White House Farm turn right along a walled lane. After a fleeting glimpse down into Hand Dale the lane zigzags into a field and vanishes. Continuing in the same direction beside a wall and past old tips of limestone banked with a mass of wild flowers, join the Tissington Trail at Hartington Station which is nice and handy for the village!

Tissington Trail

The station is in fact nearly two miles from Hartington by the most direct route, and the remoteness of the line from many of the surrounding villages was one of the reasons for it's failure and subsequent closure by Dr Beeching. An information centre in the signal box, which has its old lever frames and photos of the line, is well worth a visit and if you are lucky there may be a tea van here.

Short Cut to High Peak Trail

By shortcutting down the station approach to join the B5054 and then following Green Lane over the hill to join the High Peak Trail, Parsley Hay is omitted and nearly 2 miles of trail walking lopped off today's journey. This route has the advantage of passing a pub.

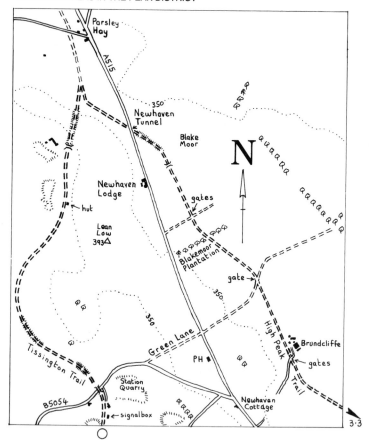

Parsley Hay

Heading northwards along the route once taken by waggons carrying limestone from the quarries to the crushing plants at Buxton, the line passes high over the main road. The trail goes through two rocky cuttings close together then, above Hartingtonmoor Farm, it follows the contours around a big bend on an embankment. A bridge is succeeded by a deep cutting and then the Tissington Trail joins the earlier Cromford and High Peak Railway just before Parsley Hay Wharf. As the line was modelled on a canal the

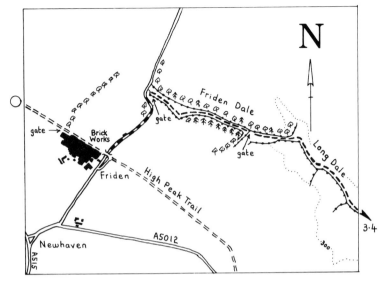

stations were known as wharfs. Parsley Hay now operates a cycle hire centre.

Doubling back along the narrower and much quieter High Peak Trail, the track enters a cutting to pass through the wide Newhaven Tunnel beneath the busy A515. Each end of the tunnel has a different decorative plaque, both showing a railway waggon with the words Cromford & High Peak Railway 1825. The secluded path is sheltered by high banks, then after a crossing the verges widen and you pass through the narrow ribbon of trees of Blakemoor Plantation.

High Peak Trail

Crossing Green Lane, an important medieval road from Hartington to Middleton, the track continues through another cutting, past Brundcliffe Farm and on to Friden Brick Works who were probably the last users of the line before it closed in 1967. Refractory bricks are made from the piles of white and grey sand which, though once mined from pits in the "pocket silicas" occurring here in the limestone, is now mostly imported.

Long Dale

After crossing the bridge, take the slip road down to the front of the works where you can see stacked piles of bricks awaiting delivery. Going under the

55

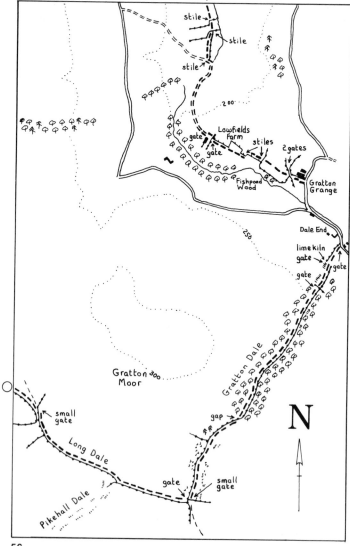

railway walk down the road for a good ¼ mile past a row of cottages. This road was improved in 1830 when an embankment was built across Friden Dale and at the bottom of the hill a gap in the hedge gives onto the line of the original road below, where there is a small gate. A green lane follows the edge of the field in the valley bottom to a stepstile by a gate. The steep grassy sides show the ridges of soil creep for the sides of the dale are gradually moving downhill. At the end of the summer there is a mass of thistledown from the creeping thistles which grow here in abundance, covering the whole valley with a fine silver dust and the treeless grassy slopes of Long Dale are host to numerous stemless thistles. A wall is crossed at a little gate by a lead rake and the path continues down past carpets of purple thyme and golden rock roses, the pretty little eyebright and the large blue field scabious. On hot sunny days there are many butterflies, the peacock and small copper being particularly attracted to the thistles, then after passing the narrow side valley of Pikehall Dale you arrive at a right angle turn down into Gratton Dale.

Gratton Dale

The whole character of the dale now changes with rock-strewn sides which lower down are covered in scrub. Traces of old mine workings remain and spoil heaps, then pylon lines swoop high over the dale by a ruined mine building on the skyline which looks like a gothic folly. Beyond a patch of scree the dale now becomes more thickly wooded, mainly with hawthorn bushes and the rocky sides develop into little cliffs. Below another mine a stream appears coming from a tank beside a small building and you continue down the dale on a track to pass a lime kiln beneath an old quarry, before crossing a field to join the lane. Turning left towards Gratton of which little remains, though it was once an important medieval village, pass the lovely Dale End House and fork right at a large building which was a cheese factory built in 1884. Opposite is an old sheep wash.

Bradford Dale

Reaching Gratton Grange the path passes in front of an open barn, dated 1853, and then goes behind the farmhouse. Crossing a field corner through two gates, the path then makes its way over the fields to Lowfields Farm. Go through the gate and across the yard to follow the farm-drive. After a widely spaced cattlegrid turn the corner to a stile and then walk across the fields. The path crosses Rowter Brook by a large limestone slab then descends a flight of steps into the valley by Fullwood's Rock. This was named after Sir Christopher Fullwood who during the Civil War marshalled a force of over a 1000 local men to fight against Cromwell. When his home in nearby Middleton was destroyed by the Roundheads he fled and hid behind this rock, but he was discovered, shot and captured, later dying from his wounds.

The stream is recrossed at a footbridge and the route passes the source

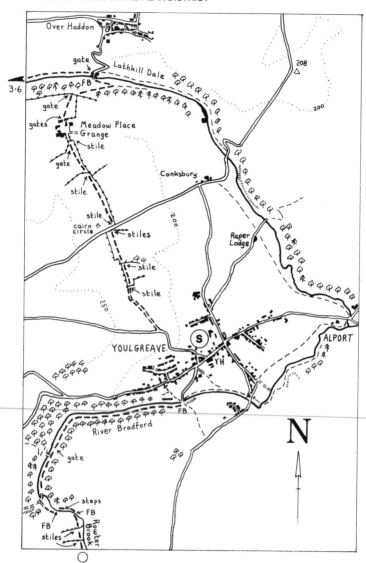

of the River Bradford at a rising under the cliffs where there is an old iron pipe which once supplied the village of Middleton with water. Turning right on the strangely named Stinking Lane continue down the sylvan Bradford Dale. The broad track passes a bridge and Bradford Dams, a series of man-made deep fishponds which after the dry summer of 1991 were nearly empty. The wooded dale continues peacefully to where ducks splash about happily beside a flat stone slab bridge, then Holywell Lane ascends past Meadow Cottage café and the village hall to arrive in Youlgreave opposite the beautiful Old Hall which was built in 1656.

Youlgreave

High above the River Bradford just before it joins with the Lathkill is Youlgreave or Youlgrave, the yellow grove. The village is also known as "Pommy". According to the landlady of the Bull's Head, the village band when first issued with their instruments didn't know how to play them and made do with going pom pom pom!

This attractive little village, which was mentioned in the Domesday Book, was once an important mining centre and many of the old cottages originally belonged to lead miners. The houses are strung along the main street for nearly a mile making it a typical Peak District linear village and it is a thriving community with several shops. Youlgreave was granted a market charter in 1340 and has an 800 year old church with a fine bell tower. The youth hostel is most unusual as it occupies the premises of the three-storied nineteenth-century Co-Op store. It is also unusual in being marked in the wrong place on the Ordnance Survey White Peak map.

Situated on a dry limestone shelf high above the river, a good water supply has always been of importance to Youlgreave. The village was first supplied with drinking water in 1829 when water was pumped from Mawstone Spring on the other side of the river to the unsightly stone enclosed reservoir known as "The Fountain" in the centre of the village. The wells were probably first dressed at this time, then the custom was revived in 1869 when a new water scheme put taps along the village street.

Youlgreave is unique in that it still has a private water supply. The Youlgreave Waterworks Association which belongs to the parishioners has a celebratory well-dressing ceremony which takes place on the Saturday nearest to June 24th.

Youlgreave

DAY 2: YOULGREAVE TO HARTINGTON

The Lathkill is said to be one of the cleanest rivers in the country. Trout spawn in its shallow pools, moorhens scurry about the surface, a white throated dipper bobs curtsies from its perch on a stone in the river, a mallard skims low to land with a flurry and splash, while shy but busy dab chicks dive and swim underwater in search of food.

In its upper reaches the valley is dry. The river that once carved the channel has long vanished and a narrow gorge squeezes between limestone walls. Here is a Nature Reserve, host to thyme and harebells, to meadow saxifrage and rock rose, and especially to one of the Peak District rarities, the purple petalled Jacob's Ladder. There is more of this growing wild here than anywhere else in the country.

The Lathkill rises in winter as a full grown river, a foaming turbulent torrent of water pouring from the black mouth of Lathkill Head Cave. After heavy rain, even this is not enough and every crack and crevice on the hillside is a fountain spouting yet more water to add to the swelling flood. In summer the river is a more subdued affair. The cave is dry and if you stoop through the entrance the chamber quickly closes down to narrow passages where cavers crawl flat into the darkness. The Lathkill now appears gradually, rising through fissures in its bed and in most summers the valley is dry for quite some distance below the cave.

In its early life the stream is shallow, lined with alder trees and rippling over the rocks at the foot of steep grass and scree covered slopes that rise to the vertical white walls of limestone on the valley rim. The river continues past Cales Dale tumbling prettily over a tufa waterfall to reach a weir and the abandoned millstones of Carter's Mill. It now becomes more purposeful and hidden among the trees are tell-tale depressions in the ground that hint at mining and, fast disappearing under the vegetation, are the crumbling ruins of old buildings. This is the industrial past of Lathkill Dale, of mines and levels, of soughs and waterwheels and machinery, of shafts dropping hundreds of feet into blackness, of dirt and noise and money. Money that drove tunnels through solid rock to reach the hoped for rich veins of lead ore; money that built great pumps and waterwheels to drain the tunnels and money that was lost as lead output dwindled, the pumps failed and the water came flooding back.

The lead came millions of year ago. Welling up from the earth's core as immensely hot salt solutions and incandescent gas it filtered into the cracks and joints between the rocks, then as it cooled left crystals of lead and other minerals. Although the Romans mined in the Peak District, the earliest record of mining in Lathkill Dale is the Domesday Book. For five hundred years the miners did little more than scratch the surface, but as they dug deeper following the veins of ore down into the earth, the mines began to flood. A river carries but a tiny fraction of the water in limestone country, for at every opportunity it dissolves away the rock to make underground channels for itself and this water seeping back into the mines was a constant threat. Pumping was one answer, and in the years before steam power the river itself was harnessed to provide energy to drive the pumps. Huge waterwheels were built and the river diverted along leats to drive them.

The two principal mines in the dale were the Mandale Mine, below Over Haddon, and the Lathkill Mine, a little further upstream. The Lathkill Mine was drained by pumps driven by a 52ft diameter waterwheel, but now only a pit half hidden in the undergrowth shows where the wheel once stood. The ruins at Mandale Mine include the main wall of the engine house beside another wheel pit. The water to drive the pump was supplied by a leat which crossed high above the Lathkill along an aqueduct whose stone pillars, only a third of their former height, still stand. Tunnels or soughs were also dug to drain the water and the Mandale Sough, sometimes dry, is still in good repair.

Now the valley is quiet again, but not deserted, for on busy summer weekends birdwatchers, botanists, industrial archeologists and mere walkers stroll beside the Lathkill, one of the loveliest rivers in the Peak.

ROUTE DESCRIPTION (See map 3.5 page 58)
Meadow Place Grange

From the fountain in the centre of Youlgreave the road by Thimble Hall passes the beautiful seventeenth-century Old Hall Farm and climbs the hill with a grand view of the village below. Leaving the houses behind, fork right along an unsurfaced lane which runs between limestone walls. Crossing a couple of fields the way continues over another road where an insignificant bump to the left is marked Cairn Circle on the OS map. This part of the Peak District has many Bronze Age tumuli and barrows, and the famous Neolithic stone circle of Arbor Low is close by. There are wide views across the dale to the narrow strip fields on the far side in contrast to the earlier large irregular meadows on this side.

As you begin to descend, Meadow Place Grange appears spread out below. This stone-built farm belonged to Leicester Abbey from the twelfth century until the dissolution of the monasteries by Henry VIII in the sixteenth century. The farm buildings partially enclose a central courtyard which was probably the original plan of the medieval monastic grange. Passing through the field gateway follow the signs across the yard and keeping straight on past a barn dated 1851, cross the field to enter Lathkill Dale National Nature Reserve at a gate. Over Haddon village looks so close but inbetween is the deep chasm of Lathkill Dale.

Lathkill Dale

A track slants down to the river doubling back to a grand house, the

Meadow Place Grange

gamekeeper and water bailiff's lodge. Crossing the river by the footbridge beside a ford, go round the old corn mill and follow the river upstream. A notice on a tree proclaims "This footpath is open to visitors except Thursday in Easter week. Toll on that day 1 penny each person." A good path leads up the dale, but half hidden in the undergrowth are signs of a former industry with shafts, levels and ruined buildings.

After passing two trial levels, inviting entrances which only extend for a short way, you enter the wood. Beside the river is the exit of the Mandale sough which drained the Mandale Mine, while to the right are the remains of the 1847 Cornish Beam Engine house and a capped shaft. Caves lead into the mine itself but these are dangerous and should not be entered. Next you pass the ruined pillars of an aqueduct which was constructed in 1840 to carry water to power the mine's waterwheel. At the next bend in the river a manhole covers a shaft beside a ruined powder house, while on the far bank is Batemans House, the home of the mine agent which was built over a 70ft shaft. Stone piers by the river mark an aqueduct to the earlier Lathkill Mine

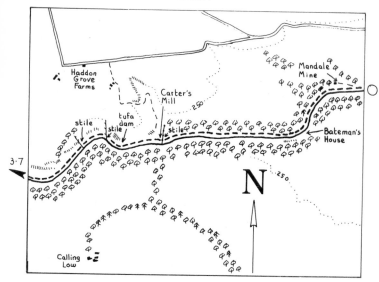

and the pit beside the path held the huge water wheel which, in 1836, was the "second largest in the kingdom". Finally, just before a weir, a slanting rake to the right marks the site of Gank Hole Ochre Mine which was worked in the 1880s. The weir contained Cow Gate pool, the header pool for the leats supplying the water wheels.

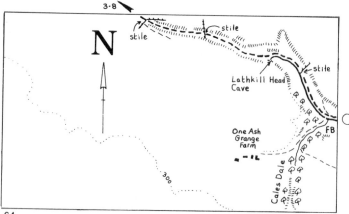

Lathkill Head Cave

Leaving the trees a side valley joins the dale where there is a chert mine, a kind of flint which was used in the pottery and china industries. This is the site of Carter's Mill, an early nineteenth-century corn mill where a pair of millstones remain beside the river. Beyond the mill pond the dam, with its waterfall known as Pudding Springs, is made of tufa, a deposited calcium carbonate which only occurs in very pure limestone streams. The path then winds on below scree slopes and under steep limestone cliffs. Passing the footbridge at the bottom of Cales Dale, the stone walls by the stream partly obscured by vegetation are the remains of a medieval sheepwash built by the monks of One Ash Grange, the farm on the plateau high above. After passing another side dale you reach Lathkill Head Cave from which the River Lathkill pours forth in the winter months. The wide-mouthed cave quickly narrows to a network of branches totalling 2000ft, but accessible only to cavers, while behind a bush on the other side of the path is Crutchlow Cave which has 500ft of passages.

The sides of the dry gorge now close in and flowering here in July is the rare Jacob's Ladder. This pretty little purple flower gets its name from the leaves which have up to twelve pairs of leaflets arranged like the rungs of a ladder. Leaving the nature reserve at a stile, negotiate the huge tumbled blocks of the spoil heaps below Ricklow Quarry which closed in 1900. This decorative form of dark crinoidal limestone was called "grey marble" and now polished smooth by the boots of walkers the fossils in the path show up beautifully. The whole scene has mellowed since Rhodes visited here in 1818. "Neither tree nor shrub find a home in Ricklow Dale, naked crags fence it in on every side and huge fragments torn from the cliffs above lie in disordered masses along the ground. There is scarce a blade of verdure intervenes to soften the general wildness of the scene."

Passing another level, dug in an unsuccessful attempt to drain the Magpie Mine on Sheldon Moor, the initials of the miner Isaac Beresford 1787 can be found carved by the entrance. Continuing on through a gorge which was probably gouged out by glacial melt water, a field is reached where the

Lathkill Dale

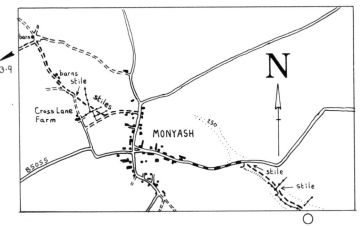

short grass feels pleasant underfoot after the rough stones of the dale. The valley now opens out and the next field leads up to the road, where you turn left into Monyash past the new village hall.

Monyash

The 1619 pub, after a transitory dalliance with fashion when it was re-named the Hobbit Inn, has now reverted to its former name of the Bull's Head. Opposite on the green is a medieval cross which was set up when the village was granted a market charter in 1340. Monyash was once an important mining centre where the Bar Master held a Barmote Court to register the ownership of a new mine. In later years it became the home of a Quaker community and its seventeenth-century Quaker Chapel is now used as a youth centre.

Turning right up Chapel Street where there is an information board, walk past both the Methodist Church and the earlier Quaker Chapel then just before the road starts to go steeply downhill, take the green lane to the left. After 200 yards a footpath cuts over the fields to the right to join Cross Lane. Keep on up this main track past a barn to the little green at its junction with Blackwell Lane. Ahead are the spoil heaps of the Knotlow Mine, once an important lead mine which has some fine coffin levels. Signed public footpath to Hurdlow, follow Hutmoor Butts lane which runs for over a mile heading straight as an arrow for the Bull-i-th' Thorn. The stables near the main road are a donkey sanctuary where up to twenty animals are looked after on a temporary basis. Meeting two being taken for a walk, we were shown the collar of one of them which recorded that 5134 donkeys had so far been cared for here.

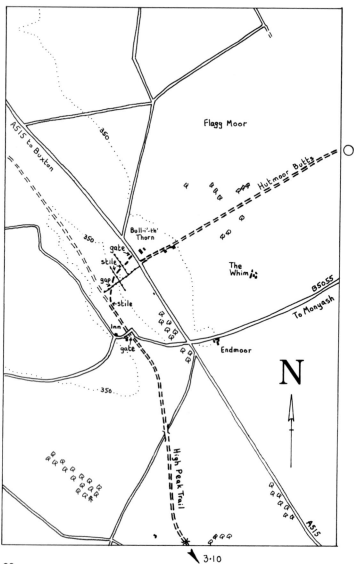

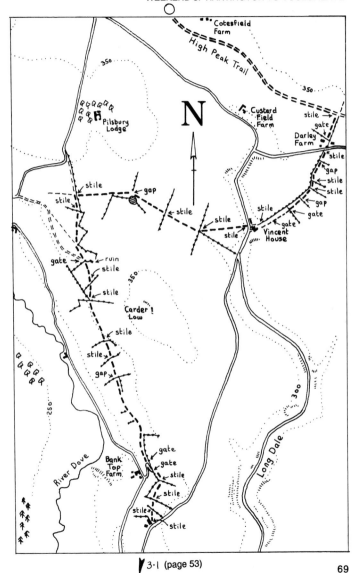

High Peak Trail

At the inn which has three signs carved from solid oak, an eagle, three hounds and the bull in the thorn bush turn right onto the busy main road which follows the route of the Street, an old Roman road, but thankfully leave it almost immediately through the field gate opposite the pub. Cross the fields to the right of a dew pond, then head straight for the Royal Oak at Sparklow to join the High Peak Trail through a kissing gate by an underpass. Turning south for a couple of miles of easy walking go under the road bridge which replaced a level crossing and past the car park on the site of Hurdlow Station. After passing a brick shelter the trail narrows and crosses the next road on a high embankment. Curving round in a grassy cutting and under a bridge, the track then swings across the hillside and through a second cutting. With the buildings of Parsley Hay cycle hire centre 1/4 mile ahead, turn down a flight of steps by a High Peak Trail notice and cross the field by the wall to Darley Farm.

The Dove Valley

The path crosses the road to a stile and continues beside the wall through attractive flower filled meadows. Then passing a small quarry keep to the right of Vincent House Farm to reach another road. Go straight across to a step stile and head up the field to a stile in the opposite corner. Follow the shallow dale gently uphill and at its highest point there is a surprisingly large pond, crossed by two walls, which has been designed to serve four fields. Continuing along the dale to a stile over a wall, the path turns left and climbs steeply towards Hartington.

Sheep and cow pastures run down to the River Dove out of sight below and looking back towards the head of the valley you can see the pointed Chrome Hill and the smaller Parkhouse Hill. The way continues across the fields with little sign of a path over the disturbed ground where a row of depressions marks the line of a rake below the ruined building. Going through a gate the route then continues attractively through the fields along the side of Carder Low above the infant River Dove. Another lead rake is passed with a capped shaft close by the path and on our last visit the next section was waymarked by yellow plastic buckets. A concrete track is joined above Bank Top Farm, which climbs for a short way and then the path continues across the fields and past a last bucket, to join the lane beside a large new barn. Passing Horsecroft, a farm built in 1987, turn off opposite the next house down Wallpit Lane. The grassy track descends to meet Dig Street which is followed into Hartington to arrive in the centre of this pretty little village by the mere.

Hartington Hall

Arriving at Hartington Hall many hostellers must feel there has been some

Hartington Hall

mistake, for surely this fine Jacobean mansion is a stately home rather than their destination for the night. The magnificent building, which is one of the grandest youth hostels in the country, dates from 1350. It was rebuilt in the early seventeenth century by Hugh Bateman and contains some beautiful oak panelling and carving and is possibly the best example of a Yeoman's house in the Peak District. It is also the oldest youth hostel in the Peak, having been opened in 1934.

71

On the night of December 3rd 1745, when his troops were massing in Ashbourne, Bonnie Prince Charlie is reputed to have slept at Hartington Hall on his way to London. By the time Derby was reached the Highland army numbered around 5000 and the *Memoirs of the Rebellion* tells us "they were to be seen, during the whole day, in crowds, before the shops of the cutlers, quarrelling about who should be the first to sharpen and give a proper edge to their swords." London was only four days' march away but 30,000 English troops were waiting for them. The chiefs were not as keen to fight as the men and on December 6th the Highlanders turned back with disappointed troops and a dispirited Charles.

WEEKEND 4: CHATSWORTH, STANTON MOOR AND LATHKILL DALE

DAY 1:	Bakewell to Elton 12 miles
	(Short Route 10½ miles)
STARTING POINT:	(219686) Bakewell Town Bridge
DAY 2:	Elton to Bakewell 11 miles
	(Short Route 9½ miles)
STARTING POINT:	(224609) Elton Youth Hostel
ROUTE SUMMARY:	Chatsworth and the Bronze Age barrows of Stanton Moor lead to Elton while the return route takes in the tranquil lower reaches of Lathkill Dale and the ancient villages of Over Haddon and Sheldon. Undulating countryside with good paths.

DAY 1: BAKEWELL TO ELTON

Bakewell lay below us, invisible in the sea of mist that filled the valley of the

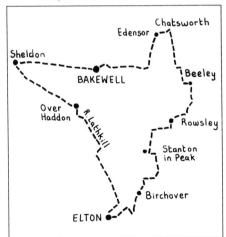

River Derwent as we climbed to cross the track of the old railway that once linked Derby to Manchester. The air was still and fresh and silver threaded cobwebs woven over the dried heads of rosebay willowherb sparkled in the sunshine that was just beginning to break through as we gained height. There were few people about save, as we crossed the golf course, a couple of fanatics teeing up to drive off into the hidden distance. Above on the hillside were the grey ghostly shapes of trees and as we continued to climb they closed about us. Manners Wood is lovely at all times of the year, but especially when gilded with the colours of autumn or as we saw it with shafts of sunlight between the beech trees enchanting the misty depths.

We emerged on the hilltop of Calton Pastures into brilliant sunshine. Long fields stretched down the spine of the hill with sheep resolutely mowing the grass. The limestone of Bakewell was now behind us and this is gritstone country, part of the Chatsworth estate. At the edge of New Piece Wood, whose conifers are a sombre contrast to Manners Wood, is Russian Cottage, the first sign of the influence of the Devonshires and a gift from Tsar Nicholas I in 1855. Then passing through the narrow belt of trees Chatsworth appears ahead. The park is a real gem. While landowners from Scotland to Cornwall are still jealously guarding their property and erecting "Private, Keep Out" notices, the Duke and Duchess of Devonshire have given the public freedom to wander across much of their estate.

Deer roam the park and one day as we sat looking down at them across the open grassland, a pheasant approached. It circled us warily picking up the crumbs we threw, but when our feeding stopped it grew bolder and watching us with its scarlet rimmed eyes stretched out its beautiful russet neck and began to peck at Anne's boots.

Below is the River Derwent. It is thought that before the Ice Age the river, which is now joined by the River Wye at Rowsley to the south, took a different course to the west around the gritstone upland of Calton Pastures. When ice

Pheasant

blocked its former channel a huge lake built up and then as temperatures rose and the lake overflowed, a new channel was rapidly carved through what is now the Chatsworth Estate.

At the foot of the slope is Edensor and as you enter the village it is obvious that it has a strange history with elaborately wrought stone built houses clustered round the tall spire of the church. Each of a different architectural style, these were built in the nineteenth century by the Sixth Duke who had decided to erase the village from its former situation where it spoilt the view from Chatsworth House. The past Dukes of Devonshire and their families lie in a quiet corner of the churchyard, but many visitors come here to visit another grave, that of Kathleen Kennedy, the sister of the late President John Kennedy. She married the present Duke's elder brother though sadly they had only five weeks together before he was killed in action and only four years later she died in an air crash.

On the far side of the busy road that now conveys traffic through the park, a magnificent stand of huge old beech trees conceals the view ahead then suddenly the House comes into view. Backed by woodland reaching up to the moorland above, with a cascade tumbling down the hillside beside it and a fountain which reaches 280ft into the air, this magnificent mansion is set in a landscape designed by that ubiquitous eighteenth-century architect Capability Brown. There was a house on the site as far back as 1552, built by Sir William Cavendish and his celebrated wife Bess of Hardwick, but all that remains from Elizabethan times is the Cavendish Hunting Tower which still stands, rather aloof, high above in the woods overlooking the hall. The present building is basically the creation of the First Duke who between 1686 and 1707 almost entirely rebuilt the house.

The wide, slow moving River Derwent flows sedately south through the grounds and past the small village of Beeley. On the hillside above is Smeltingmill Wood where the industrial past is long gone and the woodland is carpeted with bluebells, while across the valley of the Derwent is the isolated tableland of Stanton Moor. Only just over 1000 feet above sea level, this is a plateau of heather, silver birch and ancient monuments. Cairns and burial mounds lie thickly and as well as the Nine Ladies Stone Circle, over seventy barrows are scattered across the moor. Most were excavated between 1927 and 1950 by J. and J.P.Heathcote who established a private museum at Birchover.

At the western edge of Stanton Moor is a still active quarry and below is the village of Birchover where hidden behind the pub is a fascinating warren of gritstone blocks known as the Druid Stones. The stones were thought at one time to have been the work of ancient man, but the carvings are due to Thomas Eyre, a local vicar who died in 1717. There are caves, tunnels, stairways and even high on the rocks, a stone chair from which to admire the view across the valley towards the River Wye.

To south and west are the attractive villages of Winster and Elton and as you descend to cross the valley and start to climb the fields towards them you leave gritstone behind to return to limestone country.

ROUTE DESCRIPTION
Chatsworth Park

Leaving Bakewell by Town Bridge, one of the oldest bridges in England, fork right then turn along Coombs Road and take the footpath to Outrake Farm opposite the Bakewell Agricultural Showground. Once the largest one day show in England it is now held over two days at the beginning of August. Following the track uphill through the farm gate, keep straight on along an unsurfaced track beside the wall and cross the bridge over the disused railway. Slanting right across the field continue over Bakewell golf course to enter the beautiful Manners Wood.

The path soon rises quite steeply through the trees. Forking left to keep up the hill, kink right to cross another path near the top of the wood and continue climbing past a small stone barn to a ladder stile and out into the fields. Bear right across Calton Pastures on a narrow trod, aiming to the right of a clump of mature trees. Crossing a stile signed Chatsworth, fork left by the pond to another stile just beyond. The path leads down the field to a stile

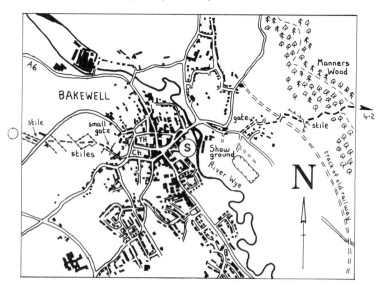

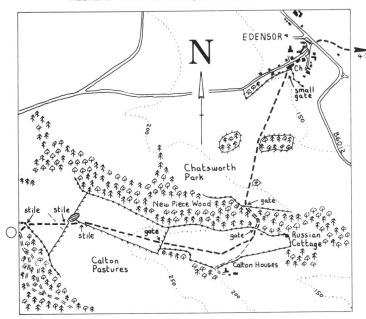

by a gate and continues in the same direction to the junction with the path from Calton Houses near the quaint Russian Cottage. Turning left you enter New Piece Wood at a gritstone step stile by a gate, then follow the track to emerge into Chatsworth Park. Ahead is Chatsworth itself, the finest house in the Peak District with above it, in Stand Wood, the old Elizabethan Hunting Tower.

Short Cut to the River Derwent

To shorten the walk by 1¹/₂ miles, turn right here and follow the edge of the wood down to the river bypassing the village of Edensor.

Edensor

Heading for the spire of Edensor Church, cross the parkland to a small metal gate to the left of the churchyard and at the bottom of the steps turn right into the village. With its hotchpotch of buildings, Edensor has a fairy tale prettiness. The village originally stood in front of Chatsworth House, but it was moved to its present site in 1834. There is a little post office and café and in the churchyard is the grave of Kathleen Kennedy and also of Joseph

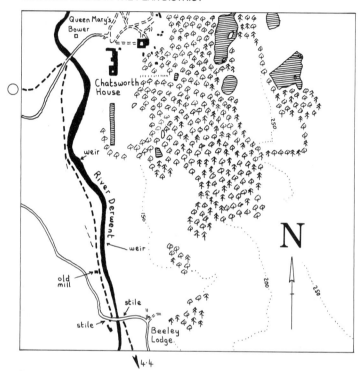

Paxton, the designer of both Edensor village and the Crystal Palace.

Crossing the road, the path opposite passes behind an isolated cottage known as Naboth's Vineyard, the only remaining house of the original village whose owner is reputed to have refused to move. Passing through a stand of mature beech trees, all gold and orange in autumn, the formal gardens come into view with the tumbling waters of the Cascade and the huge waterspout of the fountain, the second highest jet in Europe. This was built by the Sixth Duke to surprise the Tsar who was due stay here in 1844 and though the visit never took place it was called the Emperor Fountain in his honour.

From here you can walk down to the river, but it is worth going as far as the eighteenth-century balustraded bridge for the classic view of the West Front of the house. On the far side of the bridge is the Elizabethan building of Queen Mary's Bower where Mary Queen of Scots is reputed to have taken exercise when she was imprisoned at Chatsworth towards the end of the

Chatsworth

sixteenth century. Certainly her coat of arms can still be seen above the entrance.

River Derwent

Turning downstream a path follows the River Derwent through the park past a couple of weirs and a ruined corn mill which was working until 1952. Keeping beside the river leave the park at a kissing gate to cross One Arch Bridge, the graceful single span bridge which together with the mill was designed in the Chatsworth style by James Paine in the mid eighteenth century. Turn right through another kissing gate where a path leads across a long field to the estate village of Beeley, most of which was rebuilt in 1839 about the same time as Edensor.

Beeley

Crossing the road take the lane past the church into the village then follow it round to the right down to the Devonshire Arms, a seventeenth-century coaching inn. Turn left in front of the pub by Beeley Brook with its pretty little

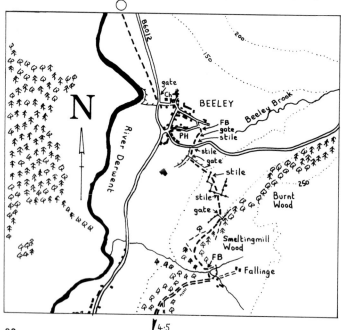

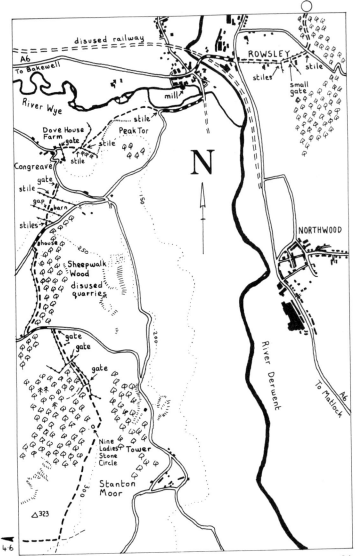

weirs then, taking the path across the stream where the road bends left, climb the hill and cross the field. Going straight over the road continue beside the hedge to the next field gate and then turn up the fence to a stile at the top. The path then cuts across the field corner and continues into Burnt Wood.

Taking the lower path contour round the hillside through the plantation to join a broader path on the edge of a ravine. The path then climbs uphill through the stone abutments of an old tramway by Burntwood Quarry. Though the quarry is now overgrown with a mixture of oak, sycamore and silver birch, two huge moss-covered millstones can be found hidden amongst the trees. Turn right to cross the footbridge over Smeltingmill Brook and then bear right to join the track from Fallinge which is followed down through Rowsley Wood. Crossing the lane take the public footpath to Little Rowsley which runs along the edge of the beautiful and extensive gardens of Woodside, a new house built in 1980. The path then leads down by East Lodge Country House Hotel to the main road.

Rowsley

Keep straight on past the old railway marshalling yard where Paxton's original station stands in splendid isolation. This was the terminus of the Midland railway from Derby when the line was halted in 1849 in its northerly progression towards Manchester by the Duke of Devonshire. After some wrangling with the Duke of Rutland it continued instead westwards towards Buxton in 1860 and was buried in a tunnel through the grounds of Haddon Hall. The house to the left is a later station which was constructed in 1863.

After passing the Grouse and Claret the road cuts through the embankment of the old Midland line. Cross the bridge over the River Derwent which was repaired in 1682, then turn up the road opposite the famous Peacock Hotel, which dates from 1652. By the hotel is a gritstone trough which Rowsley, not wanting to be left out of the well dressing festivities, have been decorating since 1974 on the last Saturday in June. The road passes the village school and a restored water powered corn mill. Caudwell Mill, which is worked by water powered turbines, claims to be the smallest commercial flour mill in the country. It is open to the public and has a refreshment room and shops.

Crossing the River Wye hurrying on its way to join the Derwent, turn right along the road and take the footpath at the bend. Curving away from the river the path climbs uphill across the field to meet a huge raised bank or vallum beneath the hill of Peak Tor, which was possibly an early Celtic settlement. After following the earthwork for a short way leave it and aim over to the corner of the field where there is a stile into the wood. Cutting across the bottom of the bluebell wood the path climbs round the hillside to a farm gate onto a green lane at Dovehouse Farm in the little hamlet of Congreave.

Going left along the road zigzag steeply up the hill and in 300 yards turn through a field gate on the right. Follow the field boundary to a stile then, after passing a barn and a second stile, climb steeply to join the road above. The stone belvedere with a seat and a grand view of Haddon Hall was apparently constructed by the wealthy people of Stanton as a place to stop and rest on their way to church at Rowsley as they got travel sick in their carriages. The right of way opposite has been diverted, so continue past Beighton House and turn up into Sheepwalk Wood just before the field. The path follows the edge of the wood past the gently sloping cricket pitch above the village of Stanton-in-the-Peak whose pub, the Flying Childers, is named after a famous racehorse owned by the Fourth Duke of Devonshire.

Stanton Moor

Follow the lane through the trees to the top of the hill and then turn right on the broad public footpath over the fields where you look across Darley Dale to the woods and moors beyond. A stile by a gate leads onto Stanton Moor, a beautiful spot where the bracken and silver birch soon give way to heather moor. Keep to the main track which, just after bending right, passes the Bronze Age Nine Ladies Stone Circle. The small King Stone close by indicates the stones may have had an astronomical function. Over to the left, standing on the edge of the moor and partly concealed by the trees is the Earl Grey tower, which was built in 1832 to commemorate the passing of the Reform Bill. Continue along the main path across the moor which passes another very obvious stone circle. To the south-east the views towards Matlock are extensive and the twin towered Riber Castle, which is now a zoo, is easily identified above the houses.

At an obvious crossroads turn right and staying up on the moor continue past the Cork Stone. This has eroded carved footholds and iron rungs set into the rock so is comparatively easy to climb. The initials WWM 1864 hidden under the overhang are possibly those of the quarryman who carried out the work and the nearby quarry is a good sheltered picnic spot.

Birchover

Turn left on the road past more old quarries to Ann Twyford Dimensional Stone. This is one of the few quarries which as well as producing building stone, manufactures grindstones for use in engineering, knife sharpening and glass bevelling, and also traditional millstones. Opposite the works a footpath from the far side of the visitors car park leads down through the trees above the houses of Birchover to emerge conveniently opposite the Druid Inn. Rowter Rocks behind the inn has been hollowed out and is a fascinating place to explore.

The lane below the inn leads past the church and the Old Vicarage. Just beyond the track junction turn up the hill along a narrow flagged path across the grass. Rejoining the track, pass in front of Rocking Stone Farm to a

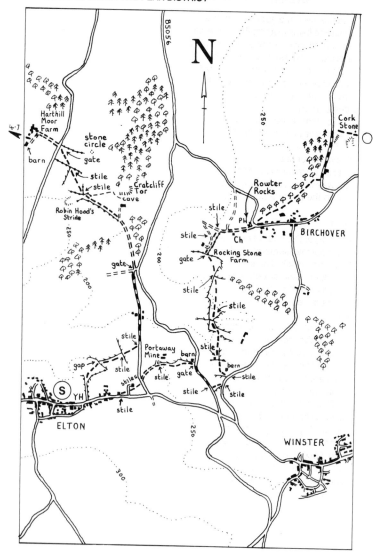

squeezer stile by a gate. The path continues straight on, bending left downhill across the fields to a small gritstone slab over the stream in the valley bottom, then climbs the other side with an occasional waymark for guidance. Pausing for breath by grassy mounds which are the remains of old mine workings, Robin Hood's Stride with its two rocky towers is well seen to the north-west. After passing a couple of ruined barns, join a lane and turn right for a few yards before turning back again into the next field to follow the hedge up to a busier road.

Go right along the road for 250 yards to just past the bend, then by another little barn climb the field to the left up to the fence which encircles the old Portaway Mine. This seventeenth-century lead mine is now being excavated for fluorspar. A path beside the fence leads to the mine road and out to a narrow sunken lane which is the line of the Old Portway, a prehistoric trackway which crossed the Peak District. On the far side of the lane the path goes to the left of a house and joins Winster Lane into Elton.

Elton

Standing at the boundary of gritstone and limestone and built near the site of a Neolithic settlement, the linear village of Elton is mentioned in the Doomsday Book. The solid gritstone Old Hall, built in 1668 at the east end of the long main street, is now the youth hostel, while the present church replaces the chapel of St Margaret, built in Henry II's time, which seems to have been less well constructed as it fell down when its spire collapsed in 1805.

A typical Derbyshire lead mining village, Elton, with its youth hostel, pub and guesthouse fulfils the minimum requirements for a night's rest, but it is not on the tourist trail and most walkers pass it by. The adjacent old market town of Winster is more picturesque with its ancient Market Hall and seventeenth-century houses, but to stay there adds a couple of extra miles walking onto the weekend and there is no youth hostel accommodation.

The area around Elton is rich in Neolithic remains with chambered tombs and the surrounding high limestone plateau was cultivated in a field system over 2000 years ago. In the 1960s the fields to the south-west were the subject of an intensive archaeological investigation with many primitive tools being discovered in the freshly turned earth of the ploughed furrows. Some of the fragments found were stone axes which had been produced at the stone axe factory on the Pike o'Stickle screes of Great Langdale in the Lake District.

Robin Hood's Stride

DAY 2: ELTON TO BAKEWELL

Bakewell lies less than five miles to the north of Elton and given an early start you could be back in time for lunch, but for the walker willing to turn aside, the day fills almost to overflowing with gritstone and limestone scenery, fields, moorland and valley, and history from the Bronze Age to the Industrial Revolution.

As on Stanton Moor to the east, Bronze and Iron Age remains are to be found on Harthill Moor, though here much of the land is under cultivation. The most remarkable feature is the entirely natural Robin Hood's Stride. Why Robin Hood is unclear, though his name is scattered across neighbouring counties, but the two monoliths which top this tor appear from a distance to be the chimneys of a stately home or castle, hence its more popular name of Mock Beggars Hall. Close by is Cratcliff Tor, a popular climbing crag with at its foot a hermit's cave complete with a primitive sculpture in relief.

Soon however the gritstone is left behind as you cross the fields to descend to the limestone rivers of Bradford Dale and Lathkill Dale. At the hamlet of Alport the River Bradford merges into the Lathkill, but within two miles they are swallowed into the Wye and this in turn less than a mile further loses its identity as it joins the Derwent at Rowsley. Although short lived, the Bradford is an attractive river with coots, moorhens, mallards and other less common birds, while the Lathkill is not only longer but even finer, with wide green pools where fish lie still in the depths.

Above the Lathkill is Over Haddon, built on a shelf in the sloping valley side, but the road which bypasses the houses is not the original main street. The village is essentially linear in plan with the houses strung out along a single street unlike those that grew up around a green with a pond.

Villages in limestone country develop where there is a water supply. This can be in a side valley or on a slope as at Over Haddon, where shallow wells can reach the water, or where it is trapped by underlying non-porous rock. But there is no such justification for Sheldon. Perched at over 1000ft on the dry limestone plateau it would have remained a small community unable to expand because of its arid position were it not for the mines. It was lead that caused Sheldon to grow and it was the wealth the mines brought that supplied the village with its own pumped water supply. Over a mile away to the east, down in the valley of the River Wye, is a now tumbled down mill and on the very edge of the river is an even smaller ruin with the remains of a waterwheel. This was the power house where the river was harnessed to drive a pump which supplied not river water, but fresh spring water to Sheldon high above.

On the high limestone plateau mining and farming compete for the land and here stands a stark silhouette, the tall chimneys and empty shell of the Magpie Mine. It is known to have been working in the eighteenth century and is in fact more than one mine with over twenty shafts belonging to three different, but intersecting, workings on the same site. In 1833 rivalry between the companies led to a tragedy when three miners were suffocated underground by fires lit by rivals trying to drive them out. Since then the mine represents, like so many, the triumph of hope over experience with a constant battle against invading water. When in the 1870s steam driven pumps proved too costly with a monthly bill for 300 tons of coal, the decision was taken to drive a sough or drainage channel. Costing the colossal sum of £18,000 it took seven years to dig the mile long tunnel from beside the River Wye to intersect with the mine. As the miners approached the waterlogged shafts they were fearful that the breakthrough would drown them all, for the mine by then was full of water with a pressure at the face of 55 pounds per square inch. Driving a long drill ahead of them to give warning the miners were able to retreat just in time as a violent jet of water burst through.

During the driving of the sough all work in the mine had come to a halt so it was with great ceremony that it re-opened in 1881, but it was too late, the Magpie Mine closed within two years and later operations were on a very small scale with but a handful of workers. The last attempt to re-open the workings was surprisingly recent, in the 1950s, and the buildings from that time, which stand beside the older limestone ones, are the subject of the only known preservation order on corrugated iron.

Modern excavations still scar the land with deep trenches in search of fluorspar, but the workings now last for months rather than decades and afterwards all must be tidied up. Farming has once again gained ascendency over the mines and every April the fields bounce with lambs. Yet the names live on, recalling as you pass Dirtlow Plantation and Dirtlow Farm the lead veins with their abandoned tunnels far beneath the surface.

ROUTE DESCRIPTION (See map 4.6 page 84)
Cratcliff Tor

From the youth hostel at the east end of Elton turn right along Main Street to the footpath beside the Jubilee Field. This leads down across the fields to join Dudwood Lane which follows the line of the Old Saxon Portway. Go steeply downhill to the main road then continue up the track towards the huge gritstone bulk of Cratcliff Tor. As the track bends away towards Cratcliff Cottage at the foot of the rocks, keep straight on up the hill along the Old Portway where a section of old paving remains.

To the left is Robin Hood's Stride, a magnificent rocky pile which gives tempting scrambling. On the opposite side across the field and above the wood is a stile where a path leads round to the Hermit's Cave at the base of Cratcliff Tor. Enclosed by railings and overhung by two yew trees this fourteenth-century shelter has the figure of Christ on the cross carved on the wall.

Returning to the main path the route continues over a stile where a couple of fields away to the right are the four remaining stones of Nine Stones Circle. Go straight over Cliff Lane and take the track to Harthill Moor Farm, rounding it to the left. On the top of the hill behind the buildings but hidden from sight is Castle Ring, an Iron Age hill fort. The path continues across the fields with a lovely view of Youlgreave which looks much bigger than you would expect from here. Crossing the hillside beyond you descend to Bleakley Dike where over to the left are the large grassed over spoil heaps of Mawstone Mine. Lead was mined here from 1878, and in 1882 the

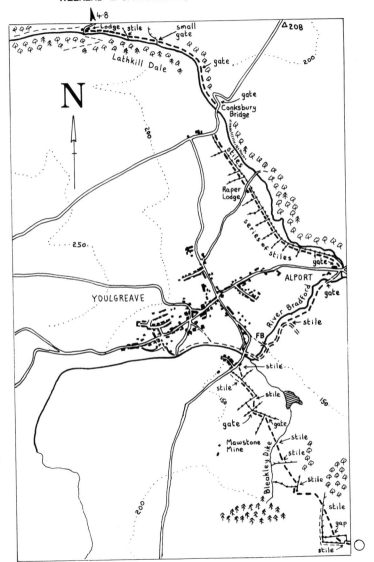

workings were drained by an extension of the Hillcarr Sough into the River Derwent at Darley Dale, 4$^{1}/_{2}$ miles away. Taking 21 years to drive, this was the longest sough in Derbyshire and the mine was worked until 1932 when a gas explosion killed eight people.

Bradford Dale

After more fields the road is joined above a small barn on the outskirts of Youlgreave. The village stands aloof, a little above the valley with only a few houses straggling down to the River Bradford and to visit the shops or the Bull's Head Hotel adds on around half a mile if you are in desperate need of a drink.

Cross the river and turn immediately right on a broad gravelled track to walk beside the river past a pretty little bridge. There is a small cave in the low limestone cliffs just beyond. When the road turns away uphill, take the footpath through the squeezer stile to continue along the river bank and past the smooth vertical 70ft limestone cliff of Rhienstor. How anyone climbs it is beyond the understanding of earthbound mortals, but climb it they do, muscles straining against gravity, clinging to tiny pockmarks in the otherwise unblemished face.

Lathkill Dale

The main road is reached at the eighteenth-century Alport Bridge where the waters of the Bradford join the Lathkill. The old Portway forded the Lathkill here on its way from Castle Ring to the Iron Age hill fort on Mam Tor near Castleton. Alport too is very old with attractive cottages and a saw mill which has the waterwheel still in place.

Cross the road to a stile by a gate and follow the path through innumerable squeezer stiles beside the Lathkill, upstream past Raper Lodge to a narrow lane. There is a fish farm by Coalpit Bridge over which packhorses carried coal from Chesterfield. The path then continues through more stiles to the road at the medieval Conksbury Bridge. Changing to the other bank, continue on a broad made up surface past woodland of wych elm, ash and sycamore above bushes of elder, blackthorn, hawthorn and hazel. The river here is dammed by a series of artificial weirs, known as the Blue Waters, which provide breeding pools for the trout and are popular with herons. Then after climbing a little the dale becomes more wooded and a slippery limestone descent is aided by a handrail. Here there is an extensive area of tufa, a natural porous deposit of calcium carbonate where Bubble Springs the main source of the River Lathkill wells up.

Over Haddon

At the grand white lodge of the Water Bailiff and the ruined sixteenth-century

Raper Lodge

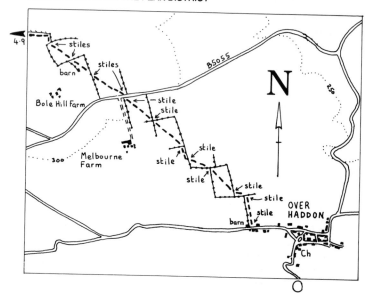

corn mill, the river must be abandoned. A narrow road zigzags its way up out of the valley, past the modern St Anne's church into Over Haddon where many of the houses date from the early eighteenth century. There are a couple of cafés, but the pub is at the other end of the village.

Turn left on the main road for 250 yards then, just after the houses peter out, a footpath beside a corrugated-iron barn climbs the field to the right and then slants diagonally across the fields beyond. The path kinks to follow the wall briefly at the highest point of these bleak pastures before resuming its course towards Sheldon. Paths like this that cross fields rather than following the edge are usually very ancient, predating the stone walls which sprang up around the turn of the eighteenth century with the passing of the Enclosure Acts. Many of the tracks in this part of the Peak District converge on Sheldon for they were made by the lead miners going to work.

On reaching the road the path continues in the same direction, the stile being a few yards to the right with Bole Hill Farm over to the left. The farm is named after the hill above, an exposed position used for smelting lead in a small open hearth or bole. Then again deviating from the straight line, signposts assist in directing you on a somewhat erratic course round the back of the hill across the reclaimed pasture land of the Magshaw or Mogshaw Mine. This very old mine was worked for lead until the nineteenth century and for barytes in the twentieth. Continue to a narrow copse and

92

down past old pits onto the road in Kirk Dale.

On our last visit the Trueblue Mine on the opposite flank of the dale was being opened up to a depth of 60ft by two men with the aid of a JCB, a lorry and a large crane. The search along this old lead rake was for fluorspar, once discarded as worthless by t'owd man, the earlier miners, but now a valuable mineral.

Short Cut Down Kirk Dale

By turning right down the dale the route can be shortened by over a mile leaving the visit to the Magpie Mine and Sheldon for another time.

Magpie Mine

Trueblue Lane opposite climbs the slopes out of Kirk Dale and a path continues towards the Magpie Mine which was worked for over 300 years. When the lane ends keep round the edge of the grassy field from which there is a good view of what are reckoned to be the best surface remains of lead mining in Britain. You can see, looking from left to right, the agent's house and blacksmith's shop, the old square Derbyshire chimney, the headgear, the beam engine house and the round Cornish chimney. There are also the remains of a circular powder house, which was built around 1864 at the same time as the engine house. The whole site, which has been partially restored,

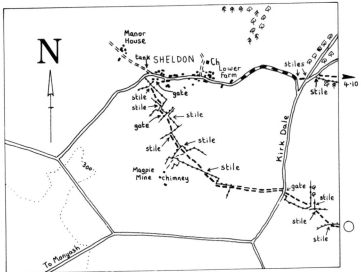

Sheldon

is now preserved as an ancient monument. The footpath leads through a squeezer stile and across the next field to a stile by a gate. A brief diversion from the route can be made over the stile in the corner of this field to the mine which is in the care of the Peak District Mines Historical Society and is being used as a field centre.

Sheldon

The path continues to the corner of the next field then keeping to the left of the houses it squeezes past the bottom of the last garden to appear on the green at the western end of Sheldon. Nearby is the stone base of the tank to which water was pumped from the River Wye in the valley below. "It's being taken over by yuppies" was the view of a local park ranger, and certainly there is no longer a pub in the village. The Devonshire Arms, which served its ale in pottery tankards, closed in 1972. But scenically Sheldon is a very pleasant place, the main street has a tractor or two and chickens scratch about happily in the road.

Walk down the road past Top Farm and the Hartington Memorial Hall. This was the old school given to the people of Sheldon by the Tenth Duke of Devonshire in memory of his son, the Marquess of Hartington, husband of Kathleen Kennedy. Passing the lovely little church which is set a little back from the road continue through the village. The road runs above Little Shacklow Wood, then descending steeply a path shortcuts the corner by the spoil heaps of Kirk Dale mine, which by 1870 had been abandoned.

Kirk Dale

Taking the road opposite which climbs the hill, leave it in 50 yards up a few steps set in the wall. Going over a stile climb steeply up the daleside beside an old lead rake, now covered in mature trees. The wall bounding the old rake is being rebuilt, an expensive undertaking for the Chatsworth Estate, the owner of this land. To the left across the valley of the Wye is Longstone Edge, to the north-east and further away are the Eastern Edges, while straight ahead to the east beyond Bakewell is Manner's Wood.

Keeping above the wall to reach Dirtlow Farm, a small gate to the left of the buildings leads out to the farm drive. Then going through the left-most farm gate opposite, descend diagonally across the field to join the road at the bend.

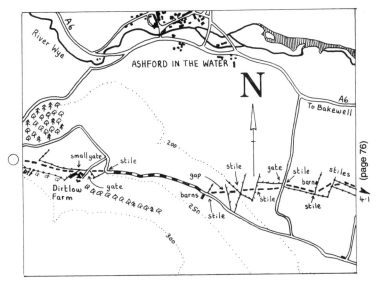

95

About $\frac{1}{2}$ mile of road walking ensues, but it is quiet enough and the lane stays high above the River Wye and the village of Ashford in the Water. On reaching a pair of large modern barns a footpath on the left is taken. Cutting diagonally across the fields through old hedges and over stiles reach a minor road at a stile by a gate. The path beyond follows the wall and then descends leftwards to cross a nameless little grassy dale. Going through a stile waymarked with white paint and along the long thin field past a farm, another minor road is crossed.

The path kinks left, again traversing the fields diagonally, heading straight for Bakewell church spire which appears to sprout from the middle of a field. Descending to a small gate in the field corner to the right of a new house and down an alleyway between high limestone walls, you arrive suddenly in Bakewell beside the thirteenth-century All Saints church.

Bakewell

Bakewell is the largest town within the National Park boundary. Listed in the Doomsday Book as Badequella, after Baedeca's spring, there has been a settlement here since the Iron Age, but the warm springs which attracted the Romans are no longer a feature of the town. The granting of a market charter in 1254 indicates that by then it had become established as a place of some importance, but despite its seventeenth-century Bath House Bakewell did not develop as a spa. Agriculture has been its main preoccupation and its annual show which started in 1843 is widely famed.

Attractively standing on the west bank of the River Wye, Bakewell has an ancient Town Bridge dating from 1300 and a large number of overfed ducks on the riverside path. There is a wide selection of shops including an excellent bookshop and a beautiful old church going back to Saxon times. Bakewell does not pander to the tourist and apart from the information centre which is housed in the seventeenth-century Old Market Hall and a small museum, it makes few concessions to the visitor. Since 1330 market day has been held on a Monday and there is a large cattle market.

In spite of its lack of amenities the little town is very popular, overflowing with visitors in the season and parking can be difficult. Driving home late one afternoon some years ago we were thrilled to see our first book on prominent display in one of the bookshop windows. We circled the roundabout and drew up behind a line of cars in front of the shops. After a brief but glorious spell of narcissism we returned to our vehicle to find it standing by the kerb in splendid isolation and sporting a parking ticket. Our drive home was somewhat marred by calculating how many books we would have to sell in order to pay the fine.

WEEKEND 5: CHEE DALE AND TWO DEEP DALES

DAY 1:
STARTING POINT:
Miller's Dale to Longnor 9½ miles
(138733) Miller's Dale Station car
park 2 miles south of Tideswell

DAY 2:
STARTING POINT:
Longnor to Miller's Dale 11½ miles
(089649) The centre of Longnor

ROUTE SUMMARY:
The gorges of the River Wye and
Deep Dale lead to the tranquil valley
of the upper Dove with a return over
limestone meadows visiting the
village of Flagg and a second Deep
Dale. Rough underfoot in the dales,
then the walking is easy.

NOTE: Chee Dale may flood after heavy rain making it impassable,
but it can be avoided by taking the path through Wormhill.

DAY 1: MILLER'S DALE TO LONGNOR

Following the River Wye upstream from Miller's Dale, gradually the sides of the valley close in, rock walls rise steeply on either hand and after vainly trying to escape, the path descends again to the water's edge over moss covered tree roots and down smooth polished limestone steps. This is the Rishi Ganga, the secret gorge of the Peak District.

As you penetrate deeper into the unknown the vegetation becomes lusher and greener, the

97

walls drip with mosses, liverworts and ferns and a hazy light shines through the mist that hangs over the water. The cliffs now overhang the narrowing river bank and the sides press in even closer until the land comes to an end and rock rises sheer from the black surface of the water. The only way onward is to take to the river on stepping stones set in its bed and balance upstream, hands brushing the perpendicular rock wall for reassurance and support.

Above the river, crossing and recrossing on high viaducts, diving into tunnels only to emerge again into daylight, the railway forces its way up the dale. It is disused now, converted to the Monsal Trail and the tunnels which once were fun to walk through have been closed.

Gradually the valley opens out a little, just enough to reveal the full 270ft of Plum Buttress and crossing the footbridge, the only access to Railway Cottages, you walk beside the Wye under the towering viaducts of the now silent railway. Silent? But surely that was a train overhead? And indeed it is, for though the line down Chee Dale was closed in 1968, the branch to ICI's Tunstead Quarry is still open with wagons rumbling up the track towards Buxton. This, the largest working rock face in the country, stretches for over three miles and was at one time the longest quarry face in Europe.

Ahead is Topley Pike Quarry which is well screened from the road and only some old machinery and the rather dusty white appearance of the trees hint at the workings concealed from view. Then you climb up the steep slope past the settling ponds into unspoilt Deep Dale beyond. But don't rush too quickly past the quarry because for all its ugliness on one hand, there is on the other a bank of flowers, orchids and cowslips among them. In the rocky gorge of Deep Dale, meadow sweet fills the air with scent, the massed flowers of greater willowherb hide the tiny stream and you pick your way up the stony valley not minding the slow progress as you stop to look at butterflies or consult a wild flower book to check your latest discovery.

If rain makes progress slower than usual and you are tired of wet limestone, slippery as ice, there is Thirst House Cave to look forward to. In the dry, seated on the rock shelf under the protective roof with a flask of coffee, life as a caveman doesn't seem too bad after all. And if you care for a little further exploration with a torch, a descent over the mud slope at the back of the cave will bring you into a second chamber.

Deep Dale gradually eases out into Horseshoe Dale, where there is a good expanse of the meadow saxifrage every spring, and then No Man's Land is approached. When the Peak National Park was first proposed, the limestone quarries were a problem. Great Rocks Dale was bad enough, but south-east of Buxton ran a line of gaunt open eyesores which were quite incompatible with the ethos of natural beauty and the National Park. The answer was that where the quarries had taken a great bite out of the landscape, a corresponding bite should be taken out of the National Park and so the boundary, the thin green line on the map, skirts round Buxton and then extends in a long narrow corridor of land in which lie the extensive tiered excavations of Dowlow and Hindlow Quarries.

Separated from the green pastures to the east by this huge limestone trench, Longnor and the valleys of the Dove and the Manifold seem impossibly out of reach beyond. But a narrow strip of land, a green bridge, brings you safe across to follow a flower filled lane on the lip of the abyss before descending to Earl Sterndale and the Quiet Woman.

While the stone from the quarries is blasted out and measured by the ton, the rocks to the west are valued for their scenery. Here the dramatic limestone reef knolls of Chrome Hill and Parkhouse Hill look down on the valley of the upper Dove and across to the little village of Longnor. In 1971 Granada Television featured the inhabitants of this isolated community in a documentary on giving up smoking. Some twenty years later we asked the barmaid in the pub if it had been successful. "Only five of them still aren't smoking," she answered, "and two of them are dead and they died young." After a brief moment of fame Longnor slumbers on.

ROUTE DESCRIPTION
Miller's Dale

From Miller's Dale car park follow the disused railway line past the station buildings and then at the end of the old platform turn down the flight of steps which descend to the River Wye. Heading upstream through the trees the

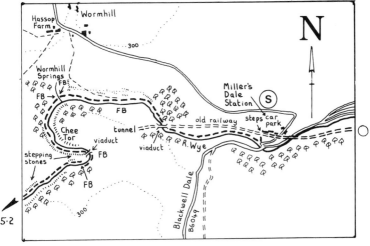

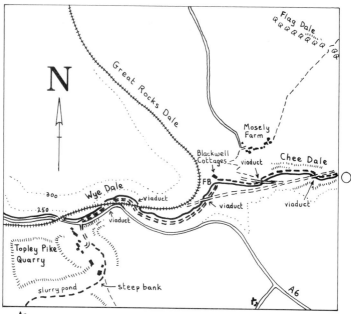

5.3

path is sandwiched between the river and the railway embankment until it passes under a high viaduct where, on our last visit, young would-be cavers were practising ladder climbing techniques. The valley briefly becomes more open as you pass a footbridge to the village of Blackwell, situated high above the dale. The path then descends over polished limestone rocks to reach Wormhill Springs whose crystal waters bubble up beside the path. At the river edge is an extensive area of the yellow monkey flower and a huge mass of watercress which grows abundantly in the better aerated mud of the calcareous springs.

Chee Dale

Crossing two footbridges over often dry resurgences at the end of Flag Dale the way continues into the narrowing gorge between high cliffs and over highly polished, slippery limestone and down to the muddy valley floor. The massive 200ft cliffs of Chee Tor, whose summit earthworks show it was the site of an early settlement, deflect the river in a long semicircular loop before it continues its eastward progress. Passing beneath a huge overhanging

Anne at the stepping stones, Chee Dale

Plum Buttress, Chee Dale

wall, often festooned with climbers, strategically placed stepping stones negotiate the next section of the dale where the cliffs come straight down to the water.

A footbridge crosses the Wye beneath the railway which emerges from a tunnel to keep company with the river again all the way to Buxton. The path climbs a little and you can join the disused track, signed "Concession Path to Trail", as an easier alternative to staying beside the winding river, especially if the path is muddy and slippery.

Taking the riverside option the path recrosses the river at another footbridge and then goes over more stepping stones before curving back under the railway. A flight of steps here leads up to the old track. In late summer the vegetation is dense with marsh thistle, greater willowherb and meadow sweet overhanging the path. The railway again crosses overhead beside another footbridge, but staying on the right bank a much improved path leads to Blackwell Cottages. Standing on the site of a medieval mill at the junction of Chee Dale with Great Rocks Dale and surrounded by railway lines, these cottages were built for railway workers. They even had their own tiny railway station, Blackwell Halt, with an up and a down platform, just long enough for one railway carriage.

A broad footbridge, the only access to the cottages, leads over the river and the track stays by the riverside, passing under three more viaducts before reaching the busy A6. The main road follows the line of the old Buxton to Ashford turnpike which was built in 1810 cutting through the limestone of Topley Pike to provide an easy gradient for coaches.

Deep Dale

Taking the dusty quarry road opposite enter the huge scar of Topley Pike Quarry which is well screened by its narrow entrance. The public footpath to Chelmorton keeps to the left of the dale, passing close by settling ponds and ugly buildings covered in a film of white powder. Because of the absence of

sheep the steep grassy slopes to the left are a botanists' delight, covered with a wide variety of lime loving plants at their best in spring and early summer. After the quarry the way up Deep Dale is not obvious and the route does not go up the short dale ahead, but instead turns right to

Grass of Parnassus

scramble up the steep grassy bank below the power lines. This end of the dale has been dammed to provide a deep slurry pond, which smells faintly of wet plaster, but to the left the hillside is rich in flowers. Even in August when many of the other species have finished there is still a profusion of harebells, St John's wort, marjoram, scabious, the delicate fairy flax and the rare grass of Parnassus with its lilac veined white petals.

The route returns to the original valley floor and continues up the now untouched and very lovely Deep Dale. It is quite slow going on the narrow and rather rough path which leads up the steep sided valley across patches of scree formed by the action of rain and frost on the limestone. In about a mile Thirst House Cave is reached. The large entrance soon drops to a wide passage with a muddy slide to a second chamber and the cave has been excavated yielding a large collection of Romano-British relics. The rough stony path continues a little further then emerging from the trees the going becomes easier.

Horseshoe Dale

Rounding a bend by Raven's Tor the dale becomes less deep and divides. Back Dale is to the right while the path follows Priest's Way up the grassy Horseshoe Dale straight ahead. Now the walking is easy for the rest of the weekend. Nearing the head of the dale there is the huge chasm of an old lead rake in the side valley of Bullhay Dale and then the A5270 is reached at farm buildings. Crossing to a hidden stile behind a fence there is no sign of a path across the field where one cloudy September afternoon we saw a fox watching us from amongst the cows. The route doesn't follow the valley, but climbs steeply out to a stile by the gate silhouetted on the skyline. Aim diagonally across the next field towards the trees where the racetrack of the A515 is crossed to Brierlow Grange.

Hindlow

The farm road leads straight past the front of the farm and through the gates to turn left at the T-junction by the wood. The track which briefly follows the route of an old railway line through a cutting, curves right to cross the newer mineral railway which now serves the quarries. Turning immediately right through a gate, go up the side of the field to a derelict wooden shelter. Keeping to the edge of the fields in the narrow corridor of countryside which divides the quarries, follow the perimeter of Hindlow Quarry round past another shelter to a green lane. The sudden view ahead is breath-taking with Chrome Hill and the smaller, but no less dramatic Parkhouse Hill, both remnants of coral reefs that once stood on the bottom of the sea, rising splendidly from the valley floor.

A notice warns of the danger of blasting and tells you to take cover in the shelter provided, a concrete igloo. Gateways which once led to pasture land

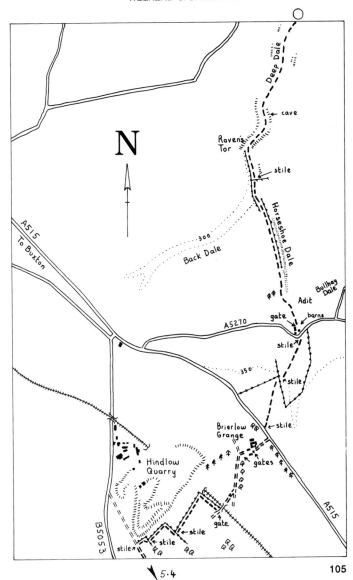

5.4

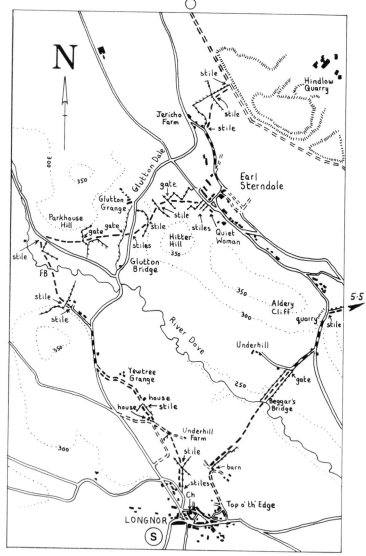

Earl Sterndale

are now wired shut on the edge of the vertical plunge to the quarry floor and the old lane follows the lip of the quarry for a third of a mile to a second igloo where you turn right to Earl Sterndale.

Earl Sterndale

Cutting across the corner of the field to a stile by a gate you look down upon the village and the valley of the River Dove. The path then goes steeply downhill to a stile to the left of a house and through a beautiful rockery which took the owners eight years to build. Turning left past an old quarry the road leads down into Earl Sterndale and by the church to the village green. The fine tree in the centre has grown around its memorial stone which commemorates the coronation of King Edward VII, while a sapling nearby marks the Silver Jubilee of Queen Elizabeth II.

The public footpath to Hollinsclough passes in front of the Quiet Woman, whose signboard depicts a headless female figure, then through the ducks and hens and over a stile behind the cottage. Heading across the fields of Hitter Hill towards Parkhouse Hill, which looks most impressive from this angle, the path then goes steeply downhill to cross the road below Glutton

Parkhouse Hill

Grange. Dated 1675 this was once a monastic farm.

Parkhouse Hill

Continuing over the fields at the foot of Parkhouse Hill cross the tarmac lane to a stile. A detour of a few steps up the road gives a good view towards Dowel Dale and of the Sugarloaf, the isolated limestone pinnacle on Parkhouse Hill. A footbridge erected in 1980 marks the line of the little trodden route which goes up to the right of Dove Bank Farm to a stile under the power lines. In a few yards another stile is crossed to join the farm drive and then on reaching the road, turn right past a house and then left to Yewtree Grange. Bypassing the grange follow the track to the next house and pass it on the right where a stile leads into the boggy field. The route passes below the next house then you join the track to Underhill Farm. Go through the gate and turn up a footpath across the field with fine views back across the upper Dove to High Wheeldon. At the top of the hill cross the field, keeping to the right of the wall heading for Longnor church, then passing behind the new bungalows join the lane down into the village.

Longnor

Tucked down behind a fold of the hills between the Dove and the Manifold with only its church tower peeping over the ridge, the miniature market town of Longnor has become a quiet backwater, quaintly old fashioned and still living at the gentler pace of former times.

One sunny September Sunday we set off from the market square looking forward to our return, as the tea room and all the pubs temptingly advertised afternoon teas. Turning homewards later in the day we strode resolutely past the Quiet Woman at Earl Sterndale, refusing its offers of mugs of tea and coffee, and pressed on. Visions of buttered scones with jam and cream, home made cakes and huge pots of tea beckoned encouragingly as we climbed the last hill and panted into the town. What a disappointment, not one was open! A few visitors read the tea signs hopefully and loitered about the square consuming ice creams bought from the post office cum Information Centre, but this and the Longnor Craft Centre in the Market Hall were the only signs of life in this sleepy little place. No coachloads of sightseers cluttered its quiet streets and were it not for the parked cars that disfigured the square, you could imagine yourself a century or two back in time.

Longnor once had hopes of becoming an important town. As long ago as the early fourteenth century there was a market, but by the end of the Middle Ages it was no longer flourishing. Reviving briefly with the coming of the turnpikes, when it stood on an important crossroads on the road from Buxton to London, there was a brief building boom; then, even though it had a fine eighteenth-century church, a grand 1873 Market Hall, and four good pubs, the town failed to grow. The coming of the railway spelt prosperity for neighbouring Buxton, Leek and Ashbourne, but with the nearest station the far side of the River Dove, Longnor's remoteness spelt its decline.

DAY 2: LONGNOR TO MILLER'S DALE

Almost 1000 years have passed since the recorders of the Domesday Book made the entry "Flagun", the village that we know today as Flagg. Up here on the high windswept limestone plateau, farming and mining have formed the landscape of green fields surrounded by a network of white walls stretching into the distance and lines of grass covered depressions mark where the miners left no ground unturned in their search for lead.

While the lands to the south of Lathkill Dale were monastic settlements owned by the Abbeys of Leicestershire, Yorkshire and Cheshire, the plateau to the north was of villages surrounded by fields with beyond them the rough tumbled ground of the miners. The earliest fields were on the fringe of the villages, higgledy piggledy walls with never a straight line between them which fit together like a complex jigsaw. Walls like these were built as early as the thirteenth century though the bulk are probably sixteenth and seventeenth century. The linear walls enclosing a narrow strip of land date from the Enclosure Acts and the open moor was also enclosed around this time. Until then the right to a portion of the common field had provided many people with independence, but when the local Lord of the Manor together with a few wealthy farmers enclosed and re-allocated the common land, the poor man, unable to meet the enclosure costs was dispossessed and forced into labouring for others.

While many a Peakland wall now lies in ruins with the gaps filled by post and wire fencing or all too often by whatever comes to hand, a well built "stone fence" will last for several generations. A wall sits on its foundations and when these go it slips and subsides, but a certain amount of movement is allowed for when it is built and a good one will withstand the inevitable settling. A wall with capstones set in cement is though seen all too often and as the stones gradually sit more comfortably upon one another the rigid top layer cannot move and so cracks leaving a gap beneath. While wallers were at one time a vanishing breed there has been a revival in the past few years with grants available from the National Park Authority for repair and renewal.

The words "mine disused" now pepper the map, but for 400 years mines were worked on the moorland beyond the enclosures which ringed the villages of Sheldon, Monyash, Over Haddon, Chelmorton and Flagg. To the east of Flagg the map records High Low. This strange contradiction is only one of the many Peak District "lows". The word means hill or mound, often burial mound, and there are over sixty places in the Peak which include this reference. Hurdlow beside the High Peak Trail means the treasure mound and marks a Bronze Age burial.

Crossing the high moorland, beyond is a second Deep Dale which leads down to the valley of the River Wye. This is the pastoral Deep Dale and although in its floor there are mine shafts, one of which until a few years ago gaped open to trap the inattentive walker, it is a quiet peaceful dale with cowslips and meadow saxifrage, thyme and harebells.

It was getting late as we crossed the busy A6 to climb the slopes of Brushfield above the River Wye and passing through the yard of Brushfield Hough Farm we continued across the fields. The route was familiar, we had come this way often and it was a surprise to see a bull in the field, by itself and between us and the open gateway. It stopped and looked at us. The law appears to think that a bull, if it is not of a dairy breed, and provided it is with cows, is quite safe. However many farm workers and others with long experience of having actually to deal with the beasts are more cautious. No bull, they say, is safe. Slowly a second animal ambled into view, but to our amazement this too was a bull. They both stood and looked at us. We looked at them. Then making a wide sweep we gained the wall and a stile and climbed into the next field to join the cows. A few minutes later we passed through the farmyard where the farmer was mending his tractor. "Two bulls?", we queried, "They must be very well behaved". "Aye," he said, "We've given them a good talking to. Mind you," he added, "Whether they take any notice or not I can't say."

ROUTE DESCRIPTION (See map 5.4 page 106)
High Wheeldon

From the old coaching inn of the Crewe and Harpur Arms in the centre of the village leave Longnor past the Cheshire Cheese, then just after Town Head cottages at the end of the village a lane turns left to Top o' th' Edge. At the cottages the bridleway forks right and immediately goes steeply downhill to the corner. Leaving the track go round the side of the barn, then continue across the wide grassy field. To the left is the notched Parkhouse Hill and the higher Chrome Hill, and ahead is the whalebacked High Wheeldon with its trig point on top. Beggar's Bridge crosses the infant River Dove then the grassy track of Green Lane joins a tarmac lane which leads out to the road.

Turning left uphill to the old quarry of Aldery Cliff, a popular spot with rock climbers, opposite is a stile and a path around High Wheeldon. The hill was

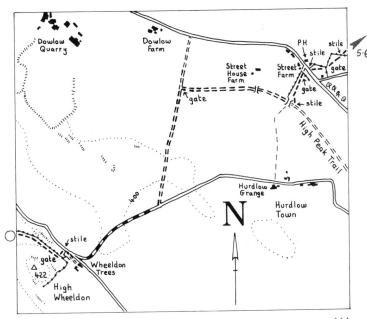

given to the National Trust as a memorial to the men of Derbyshire and Staffordshire who fell in the Second World War. The energetic can climb straight up the nose of the hill, where near the top is Fox Hole, a cave with a locked gate barring the passage to its two chambers which have been archaeologically excavated. The resulting finds of human habitation are in Buxton Museum. A much easier route is to follow the path by the wall up to a gate, from which the summit is an optional extra. A little trod leads up behind the National Trust notice easily to the top where the stone and concrete trig point carries a memorial plaque. There are extensive views in all directions. To the north beyond the quarries lies the distant hill of Chelmorton Low, to the south is the hamlet of Crowdecote with Longnor tucked down behind the hill, to the west Chrome Hill towers over the diminutive Parkhouse Hill while to the east the conical hills of Dove Dale rise beyond Hartington.

High Peak Trail

To continue the walk, return to the gate at the side of the hill where a path leads out to a stile onto the road by Wheeldon Trees Farm. Turning right, straightway fork left up the minor road which has a narrow ribbon of tarmac running between wide grassy verges. After half a mile turn up a wide green lane whose end was fenced off on our last visit by an ingenious contraption consisting of two bits of wood, an old tractor tyre and four lengths of string. The tips to the left are the outposts of Dowlow Quarry and stone walls show the original line of the 1831 track bed. A gate on the right marks the end of the High Peak Trail. This section of the line was opened in 1869 to bypass

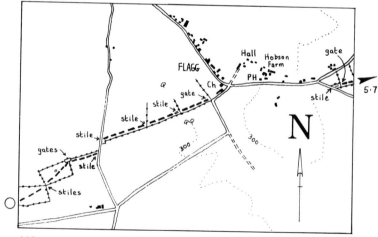

the steep Hurdlow Incline. The Cromford and High Peak Railway which linked the Cromford Canal with the Peak Forest Canal closed in 1967, though the last six miles which run west of here to Buxton serve the working quarries.

After ¹/₂ mile of easy walking along the disused railway line to just past the second bridge, a stile leads to a footpath coming from the grandly named Hurdlow Town, whose Grange and Hall are now all that remain of the former medieval settlement. Keeping along the edge of the field to the main road, pass Street Farm, which stands on the line of The Street, the Roman Road which ran from Derby to Buxton.

Flagg

A path to the right of the Duke of York car park cuts across the patchwork of open fields passing a dew pond and an enclosure where Pasture Barn once stood, to reach a tarmac lane after ³/₄ of a mile. Crossing a stile in the dip to the left, continue over the fields staying beside the wall to join a second lane at a bend. Turning towards the houses of Flagg, a Viking settlement, next go right towards Monyash and Taddington at the crossroads by the nineteenth-century Methodist Church.

Passing the Elizabethan Flagg Hall, the Plough Inn and the Foy Society children's holiday centre, fork right towards Monyash at the next road junction and in 100 yards turn across the fields at a stile under a tree. After four fields the path dips to cross a road in a dry valley and then climbs up the hill towards Sheldon. With increasing signs of mining activities a line of stiles,

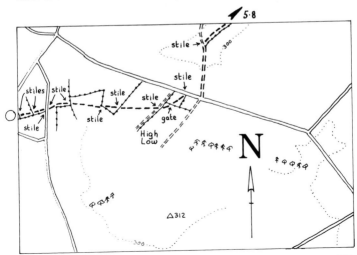

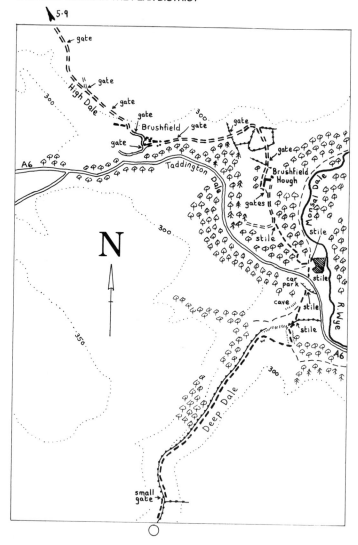

many with good examples of crinoidal limestone, lead to another road where you go right to a bridleway. The broad old way to Taddington, unusually for limestone country, has patches of heather on its banks where the surface soil has been leached of lime.

Deep Dale

At the bottom of the hill a stile leads down into Deep Dale. Crossing to the other side of the wall at a metal gate, the path passes an old mine with recent signs of excavations by cavers. In wet conditions water flows from the mine, flooding the path before it seeps back underground. The typical dry limestone dale has steep grassy sides with earth slip ridges and is a beautiful flower garden in spring and early summer. Near the bottom of the dale the path veers right across the hillside, which in spring is white as new fallen snow with hawthorn blossom and a carpet of meadow saxifrage. At a three way junction the path to White Lodge picnic site goes down a pretty little limestone gorge. Then passing below Taddington Dale Resurgence Cave, which also has a stream in wet weather, the path crosses a field to the car park.

Monsal Dale

Continuing through a stile on the other side of the busy A6, descend to Monsal Dale where patches of yellow monkey flower bloom beside another stile. Just beyond turn left at a signpost taking the higher path up the hill to Brushfield. A newly stepped way zigzags up through woodland above the River Wye and near the top the path comes out into the open onto a rocky limestone bluff with grand views down into the densely wooded Taddington Dale.

Brushfield

Climbing a step stile into the field follow the track up towards Brushfield Hough Farm which occupies a marvellous position looking down upon the River Wye and across at Fin Cop whose summit is the site of an Iron Age fort. Go through the gate on the left by the barns and then round the back of the buildings to a farm track. The route then leads through the fields above Taddington Dale to Brushfield. Going through the yard at Lower Farm turn right along the road to Priestcliffe to pass Middle and Top farms, then keep to the gated lane above High Dale for another half mile to the right angle bend.

A stile leads into Priestcliffe Lees Nature Reserve where the path follows a wide strip of grassy field past the disturbed ground of old lead mine workings. Follow the L-shaped field down round the corner to a stile and then go steeply downhill past more old workings. Descending through scrubland, the disused railway line is joined at a bridge where you turn left along the track. After half a mile a flight of steps leads down to Ravenstor Youth Hostel, but the hamlet of Miller's Dale is a further mile along the railway passing some

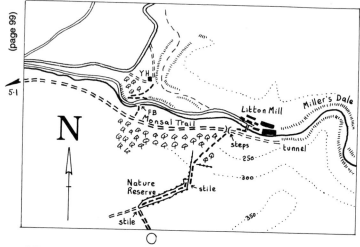

old lime kilns which are well worth visiting, before crossing the double viaduct to the old station car park.

Ravenstor

Nearly forty years ago Ravenstor Youth Hostel was the scene of a conversion almost religious in its enthusiasm and impact. A technician working there with a group of botany students became so fascinated by the colour and variety of the plants in Miller's Dale that a lifelong passion for flowers was born. As he began to study them more closely he discovered that, almost without conscious effort, he had memorised the Latin names of the plants. Studies and the examination system which had been abandoned were resumed and Dr David Bellamy went on to become not only a Professor at Durham University but also an author, film maker and television personality. We were delighted to discover that the botany lecturer with whom we have studied was, together with Dr Bellamy's future wife, one of those students at Ravenstor in 1954.

Ravenstor Youth Hostel stands in its own grounds high above the junction of Tideswell Dale and Miller's Dale. Built in 1907 for the owner of Litton Mill, the house and the surrounding land was presented to the National Trust only 30 years later by Alderman J.G.Graves of Sheffield and it is leased by the YHA. The hostel is in the middle of an area which is one of the richest parts of Britain for the variety and colour of its wild flowers. Many of the plants in these dales, including some of the mosses and lichens, only grow on Carboniferous limestone and are nationally rare.

116

WEEKEND 6: THE FLOWERING DALES, MILLER'S DALE TO CASTLETON

DAY 1:
STARTING POINT:

Miller's Dale to Castleton 8½ miles (138733) Miller's Dale Station car park 2 miles south of Tideswell

DAY 2:
STARTING POINT:

Castleton to Miller's Dale 12½ miles (150828) The centre of Castleton by the Youth Hostel

ROUTE SUMMARY:

The flower-filled valleys of Monk's Dale and Peter Dale are followed by high moorland, with a return over Bradwell Edge to finish down the lovely Ravensdale. Monk's Dale for a short way is awkward walking over limestone blocks, but the rest is easy.

DAY 1: MILLER'S DALE TO CASTLETON

We climbed over the stile and headed up Peter Dale. The morning was cool

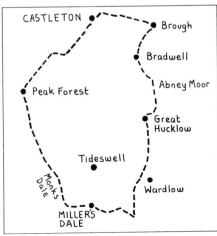

and fresh, and already the sun was up in a clear blue sky. It was the perfect day for a walk, but after an hour we had progressed no more than 200 yards. The problem was the flowers, or rather us stopping to look at them. In spring and summer there are more flowers per square yard in these limestone dales than practically anywhere else in the country. The floor of the dale, the steeply sloping sides and every rock

Early purple orchid

ledge is a rippling, changing, glorious pattern of colour. In spring there are the brilliant spikes of the early purple orchid, the nodding golden yellow heads of cowslips and beneath them large deep blue dog violets, all perfectly complemented by the white flowers of wood anemone, cuckoo flower, wood sorrel and the lovely meadow saxifrage. When we last did this walk we counted over 100 different species.

Before Peter Dale comes Monk's Dale. This too has a wealth of flowers including the rare herb Paris, but it is not just stopping to examine the flora that slows progress, it is simply not possible to hurry. At first the way is easy enough, then as you enter the woodland the path becomes a polished maze of limestone blocks, not too difficult when dry, but in wet weather a place where each footstep requires careful thought.

Beyond the dales continue; through the upper reaches of Peter Dale, a meadow flanked by low limestone cliffs, then Hay Dale and finally Dam Dale, where the gorge-like valley opens out, the view expands and the white limestone walls creep down into the valley bottom. Farmland now dominates with herds of cows slowly eying the passing stranger. Then astride the A623 is the hamlet of Peak Forest where there is a pub, and the even smaller hamlet of Old Dam where there isn't.

Peak Forest gets its name from the Royal Forest of the Peak which once stretched from Glossop in the north to Buxton in the south and to the east as far as Hathersage. The village itself grew around the house of the Forest Ranger who was appointed in the sixteenth century to manage the deer, but long before that, by the mid thirteenth century, the forest was no longer exclusively a preserved chase. It came under attack from all sides by villagers felling the trees and by the encroachment of moorland vegetation. By 1579 there were only thirty deer left. The ranger, who managed an enclosed area of some four square miles, seems to have been very successful with the numbers growing to over 120, but by the mid seventeenth century the forest was no more and wild deer have long been a distant memory.

Peak Forest church which was founded by the Countess of Devonshire in 1657, was established by a royal grant and as it was under its own jurisdiction, the vicar was able to issue marriage licences. This brought him in a regular income of a £100 a year. The "Gretna Green" of the Peak became so popular that in 1753 parliament enacted a new law to bring it under control, but the practice continued until it was finally stopped in 1804.

Beyond Peak Forest is Old Moor where pasture gives way to moorland, cows to sheep, and among the clumps of rough grass are the signs of long abandoned lead mines with occasional fences ringing still open shafts. The more modern scars are opencast excavations in search of barytes and fluorspar, the gangue minerals of the old lead mines, discarded as worthless by the old miners, but now valued for their use in the steel and chemical industries.

Across the moor to the west is the quarry on Eldon Hill. After many years of devouring the hill, it is due to close in 1997. On its slopes lies the fearsome Eldon Hole, over 180ft deep and the deepest pot hole in the Peak District. Then, leaving the moor, the path funnels down into Cave Dale where the steep walls are of gleaming white limestone. The inviting entrances on either hand turn out on close investigation to be only surface scratchings and the caves are small and hidden, but right on the edge of the cliffs are the ruins

of Peveril Castle, a stronghold of William Peveril. Beneath the castle the valley narrows, the cliffs close in and you squeeze between them to emerge suddenly, right in the middle of the little medieval town of Castleton.

ROUTE DESCRIPTION
Monk's Dale

From the station car park walk a few yards up the road to the whitewashed Glebe Farm where you turn right over a stile to enter the National Nature Reserve of Monk's Dale at a little gate. Descending into the dale the path turns left, joining one from the church, and continues up the dale to cross a footbridge. The path

Cowslips

119

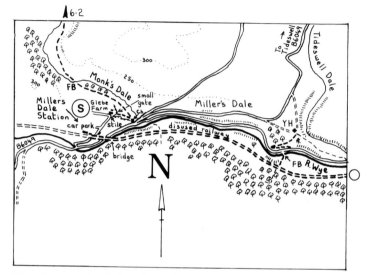

keeps in the valley bottom then climbs to reach a little rocky eminence decorated in May with the yellow flowers of the spring cinquefoil and then for ¼ mile follows the hillside up the dale before descending to enter the wood. The next section through the woodland shade is awkward over smooth limestone rocks which are slippery when wet. After coming briefly out of the trees by a patch of scree, the path improves with only the occasional relapse until you leave the reserve and enter a field where the walking is pleasantly easy after the struggle along the valley bottom.

Peter Dale

Leaving Monk's Dale cross a narrow lane to enter Peter Dale, where the first section of the dale is also part of the National Nature Reserve. After crossing a grassy field the dale narrows to pass through a little gorge, a natural rock garden at its best in spring and early summer. The steep valley sides, though not very high, are lightly wooded and the grassy path gives easy walking. After widening briefly the dale closes in again and becomes quite rocky with cliffs of up to 30ft on either side. The white meadow saxifrage is the most noticeable flower here in early summer along with the pink of the red campion and the yellow of the crosswort. The dale widens to another field where black and white cows graze peacefully and then crosses an even narrower lane below a bungalow, grandly named Curlew Lodge, to continue up the more open Hay Dale.

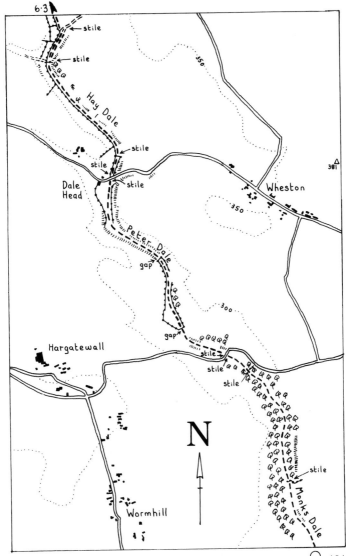

6·3

stile

stile

Hay Dale

stile

stile

stile

Dale Head

stile

Wheston

381

350

Peter Dale

gap

300

gap

Hargatewall

gap

stile

stile

stile

N

stile

Monks Dale

Wormhill

○ 121

Hay Dale

The cliffs now give way to gentler, less rocky slopes which flank the grassy floor of the dale. In ½ mile the greened over spoil heap of an old lead mine is reached where a rocky cutting and a few railway sleepers lead to the mine entrance while a couple of rusty bits of corrugated iron are all that remain of the mine buildings. An avenue of fine witch hazel with an occasional oak and ash, now lines the path down the dale.

Dam Dale

The next lane to cross the dale is unsurfaced. Turn right onto it for only a short way then go left over a stile with a crinoidal limestone step to stay down in the valley. Dam Dale, the shallowest of the three dales is more pastoral, with small fields enclosed by a multitude of walls. It has an empty look after the closeness of the steep sided wooded lower dales. Keep straight on past Dam Dale Farm which unusually sits right on the valley bottom. The valley was crossed here by the Roman Batham Gate, the road to the bath which ran from Navio, the Roman fort at Brough, to Buxton Spa. Looking to the south-west you can see where cars speed past a small wood on the skyline along a metalled section of this old road.

Curving round the hill slope across the field, the path leads to Mill Cottage and a stile to its right. Passing a sheepwash, cross the track which traverses the old dam. This was built to contain and conserve small seasonal streams caused by a layer of impervious volcanic rock or "toadstone". The perched water-table level has fallen in recent years due to nearby quarrying, so the dam is now dry.

Peak Forest

Continue straight on across the fields to reach the main A623. To the left is the village of Peak Forest. The original church which saw so many runaway marriages was replaced in 1877 with the present church of Charles King and Martyr. On the opposite side of the road is the Devonshire Arms, where we took refuge from the rain and dripped in a corner while the rest of the bar watched the Cup Final. Going past or through the pub turn right at the crossroads along Church Lane for a quarter of a mile of road walking to the village of Old Dam, where the dam after which the village was named lies to the right of the lane.

Eldon Hill

Keeping straight on, go up the No Through Road to the left of the modern bungalow. At Conies Farm the lane ends and the path continues across the fields, climbing gently to the left of Conies Dale up the slopes of Eldon Hill. Go through the upper gateway and then across a series of stiles to old mine

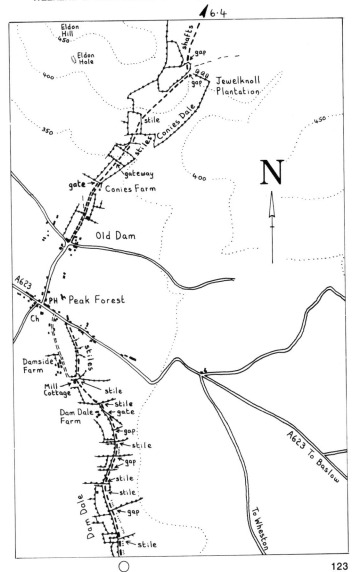

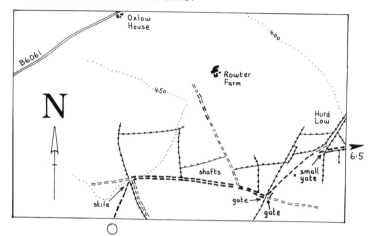

workings above, where there is an extensive view down into the dale and back over Peak Forest to the hills beyond. The spoil heaps are covered in early summer with the small white flowers of the spring sandwort, *Minuartia verna*, known locally as "leadwort". It is one of the few flowers that can flourish on lead spoil though the pretty yellow mountain pansy seems to like it here as well. From the narrow belt of trees, grandly entitled Jewelknoll Plantation, the path winds across the open moor. Some of the many depressions on either side hide open shafts so take care.

The path leads to a gate and a signpost at a junction. The track to the right goes down to the Portway Mine. Marked disused on the OS map, the spoil heaps are now being reworked for fluorspar. Taking the level track, head east towards the re-opened Hollandtwine Mine, past grassy spoil heaps bright with little yellow pansies. The high hills of the eastern edges appear ahead and then the bridleway joins another track coming in from the left. After passing through a gate turn left at a five-way junction on the public bridleway to Castleton.

Cave Dale

The broad grassy path veers away from the wall to pass between a dew pond and two old railway carriages now functioning as sheds, heading straight for Win Hill the little cone shaped peak on the skyline. At the dip in the field follow the dale down to the right to a little metal gate. There are more traces of old workings here on the line of Slack Hole Rake. A gentle descent to another metal gate follows, then after a third metal gate by a wood, suddenly Peveril Castle is seen towering over Cave Dale. This impressive dry gorge once

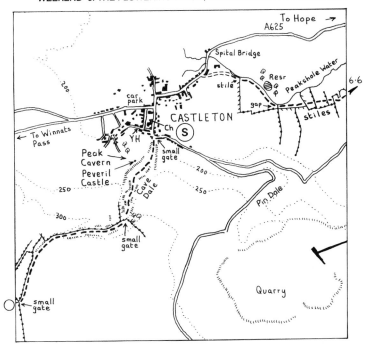

thought to have been formed by the collapse of a former cave system was more likely gouged out by torrents of melt water at the end of the Ice Age. Just after the gorge narrows to a rocky gateway there is a tempting cave entrance to the right. Disappointingly this doesn't go anywhere, though the one just a little further down and round the corner to the left has a thin rift which leads down into the roof of the Orchestra Chamber of Peak Cavern show cave, though it is now blocked with concrete. There are more caves high up under the castle and at the bottom, on the left under overhanging rock by the entrance to the dale, is an old mine level. A gate by a stile, a rocky cleft, and there you are in the centre of Castleton with only a few steps to the youth hostel which stands by the square.

Castleton

"Castleton is one of the most interesting villages in Derbyshire, presenting to the mineralogist and geologist, as well as to the antiquary and lover of nature, an assemblage of objects of curiosity and attraction such as few other

Peveril Castle from Cave Dale

places can show." The words written by James Croston in 1876 are just as true today.

A medieval new town first recorded in 1196 and still surrounded by a ditch, Castleton was planned, rather than merely growing into existence like most mining settlements. The church was probably built around the same time, but the town ceased to prosper in the fourteenth century when the castle lost its importance. Many of the houses are seventeenth century though Castleton Hall in the village square, now a youth hostel, dates from 1410.

Lying on a geological junction of shale and limestone Castleton is famous for its show caves and for the mineral Blue John which is only found here. The name probably derives from the French *bleu-jaune*, meaning blue yellow. It is a form of coloured fluorspar from which small ornaments and jewellery are made though in the past large pieces were used to produce vases and even a famous candelabra.

Peveril Castle is the only surviving stone built castle in the Peak District. Perched in a commanding position above the village, the original wooden structure was built around 1080 by William Peveril, the bailiff and illegitimate son of William the Conqueror. An imposing stone rectangular keep and gateway were added in 1176 by Henry II and a dry ditch separates the castle yard from the rest of the hilltop. The castle was used as a fortified hunting lodge in the royal Peak Forest until 1250 and then became a prison, though by the seventeenth century it was ruined. Beloved of the Victorians, it features briefly in Sir Walter Scott's novel *Peveril of the Peak* and the view from the castle is worth the effort of the climb.

DAY 2: CASTLETON TO MILLER'S DALE

Peakshole Water, which issues from the huge mouth of Peak Cavern, flows east down the Hope Valley meandering past the villages of Hope and Brough to join the Derwent. Walking through these valley fields, the view to north, east and west is of the hills, a long high skyline of gritstone moorland, but to the south defiantly facing Hope is the chimney. You can't get away from it. There is simply no way of landscaping, screening with trees, or otherwise concealing a chimney 439 feet high. The cement works, constructed long before the National Park was conceived, is sited at a geological junction with limestone to the west and shale to the east, the essential ingredients of cement. This is the largest manufacturing unit and the biggest employer in the Peak with a workforce of around 500 people.

Brough is overlooked by the remains of a Roman fort but there is very little to be seen now and if it wasn't so plainly marked on the map no-one but the experts would notice the grass covered bank above the village. This was the principal administrative centre when Romans ruled the High Peak and it was linked by roads to other strategic forts such as Melandra Castle near Glossop.

Beyond, a series of small fields leads to Bradwell, meaning not a well but the broad stream on which the village stands. Rising steeply above the village is Bradwell Edge where the sky on most weekends is filled with hang gliders wheeling and turning in the up currents above the scarp slope. It is a steep climb to the edge where brilliantly coloured sails of orange, green and white are spread out on the short turf. Now we are out of the limestone and onto the gritstone moor. Rough dark walls of millstone grit divide the fields and underfoot the pretty four petalled yellow tormentil and the sweet scented heath bedstraw speckle the grass. This moorland, cousin of the much more extensive heaths to the north, is an isolated fragment, cut off by the River Derwent and encircled by the limestone of the White Peak. Above, the hang gliders give way to soaring sailplanes which are winched into the air at Great Hucklow on the edge of the escarpment. As the gliders reach the end of their steep ascent, they wriggle like fish to disgorge the hook and trailing a tiny parachute the long towline floats gently down.

Descending through the village of Great Hucklow and the adjacent hamlet of Grindlow there is a handy pub. Beyond is Silly Dale. Nothing to do with foolishness or too convivial a lunch at the inn for the name means happy. Certainly attractive, a limestone walled lane is lined in summer with the large blue flowers of the meadow cranesbill, but the best is yet to come.

Reaching Wardlow Mires, once as its name suggests a boggy area where underlying rocks prevent the surface water from draining away, you enter Ravensdale or Cressbrook Dale, it has two names. This is the loveliest of all the dales for its rock garden of flowers. Other valleys have finer gorges, cliffs and pinnacles, but Ravensdale has the best of the flowers, from the springtime early purple orchids and yellow cowslips, through summer when the valley slopes are covered in scented purple thyme, golden rock roses, dog roses in pink and white and the sweet smelling fragrant orchid. On the spoil heaps grow mossy saxifrage, spring sandwort, a sure sign of lead mining, while on the moorland edge is the mountain pansy.

At the head of Ravensdale is Peter's Stone, an isolated turret of limestone whose striking profile is immediately in view as you walk down the dale. At first sight it appears impregnable with vertical limestone sides, but a steep gully cleaves the rock providing an easy scramble to the top. On a recent visit, scattered in various stages of exhaustion on its slopes, were a party of French schoolchildren. Two of them on the summit of Peter's Stone when addressed haltingly in their native language enquired with great tact if we too were French!

Beyond Peter's Stone the path continues down the dale past beds of yellow flowered silverweed and then climbs steeply to the very lip before falling back into the valley bottom. It may seem an arduous ascent, but the grassed over old mine workings on the valley sides are host to saxifrages and sandworts, while the descent is through a rock garden of orchids, thyme, the yellow rock roses and the large deep red flowers of the bloody cranesbill. Descending through the scrub woodland, the cliffs of Raven's Tor appear high on the skyline to the left. An impressive cliff when seen from below, it is even more impressive from the standpoint of a rock climber on one of the narrow ledges with vertical rock above and below.

In the valley bottom beneath the cliffs is a small group of cottages built for workers at Cressbrook Mill. The owner of the mill, which now stands crumbling into ruins at the foot of the dale beside the River Wye, was a staunch Methodist who built Trinity House, the church in Cressbrook village. The local Anglicans were obliged to worship beyond the bounds of the parish in the Curates Room to which a curate travelled on Sundays from Tideswell and the Anglican church was not built until 1902, still outside the parish boundary.

Above the Wye meandering in its narrow gorge, the chimney on the hillside marks the position of Litton Mill. Miller's Dale village is dominated by this derelict and dismal mill which at present is empty and a proposal for a time-share development was recently refused. The gloom of the buildings is darkened further by their history, one of the most notorious exploitations of child labour.

It is a relief to leave the mill behind and follow the road past the youth hostel. Beside the road are dozens of different wild flowers including the bloody cranesbill and the Nottingham catchfly with its curled back white petals. Rather than continuing along the road, a short climb brings you to the track of the disused Manchester to Derby Midland Railway. In the twenty years since its closure the railway has blossomed and it is now a delightful way where you will find another garden of flowers to complete one of the best walks in the White Peak.

ROUTE DESCRIPTION (See map 6.5 page 125)
Brough

From the square in the centre of Castleton walk past the church then follow the main road to Hope through the village for ¼ mile till you are nearly out of the houses. Just before Spital Bridge a track to the right is the beginning of the public footpath to Hope which after passing a ruined mill enters the fields. The path follows Peakshole Water past a reservoir heading straight for Hope Cement Works with its high chimney. After crossing a branch railway line, which supplies the works with around 3000 tons of coal a week, the chimney is left behind and the path wanders pleasantly along beside the river under the beech trees to a lane where you go left towards Hope village and then right in a few yards on Eccles Lane.

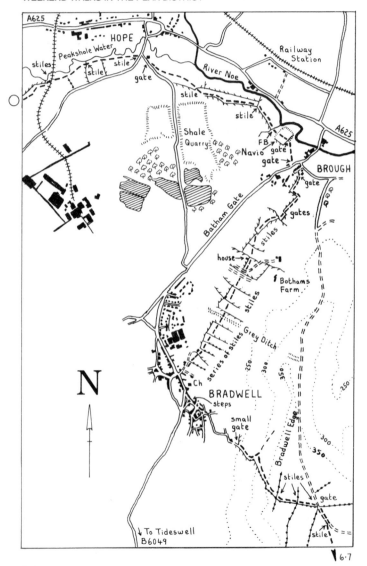

Walk uphill for a short way past a house then turn off to the left into the fields on the footpath to Brough. The broad grassy track climbs gently to a stile, through some hawthorn bushes and out into the open again following a belt of trees concealing quarry workings. After crossing a footbridge you pass the Roman fort of Navio. Built around AD 158 on the site of an earlier fort it was only small by Roman standards, covering about 2 acres and would have held a garrison of less than 500 men. Though this is the most important Roman site in the Peak District, standing at the junction of three Roman roads, there is little to be seen today. Then it is downhill to join the B6049, the old Roman road of Batham Gate. Turn left over the stream and then right onto the end of Brough Lane going right again past St Ann's Well and in front of the cottages.

Bradwell

Taking the public footpath to Bradwell follow round the edge of the field to a signpost. Half concealed under the trees is an old stone-walled smelt mill flue which doubles back along a parallel course. The path crosses the fields passing to the left of a cottage then over a track and on to the Grey Ditch, which can easily be mistaken for the line of an old hedgerow. No one knows why this massive earthwork is here but it was probably constructed to repel invaders after the Romans left. Continuing through meadows of mowing grass bright in June with white and red clover, buttercups, daisies and the more unusual yellow rattle, join Soft Water Lane by Bradwell Brook, which is a mass of water crowfoot. If you are passing through Bradwell on the first Sunday in August you will find this quiet little village surprisingly busy with the well dressing. We can recommend a visit to Bradwell's Ice Cream Manufacturers.

Turn left by the bridge along Church Street, then leaving the main road at the bend go up the steps to Bessie Lane. Fork left and then right rising across the hillside on the lane which ends at a gate and a stile. The large field on the other side of the valley is the landing field of the Sheffield Hang Gliding Club who fly from the top of the ridge and the members are fined if they land in any other field. The wide grassy track climbs steeply, quickly gaining height and after a zigzag continues uphill in the same direction to a stile. On reaching Bradwell Edge there is a bird's-eye view of Bradwell. It is only from here that you realise the full extent of the industrial area that is set right in the middle of the Peak District.

Abney Moor

The path crosses a couple of fields past the site of Robin Hood's Cross, a medieval marker stone at the junction of three parishes. Though we have searched diligently on several occasions, we have been unable to find any trace of it. Turn right on the track through a gate where the fields end and the open moor begins, then branch right over a stile in 100 yards on the footpath to Great Hucklow. It is a mile across Abney Moor, an open expanse of mat grass and bracken with larks high above and higher still gliders circling silently. Ahead, beyond the valley of Bretton Clough, a tall radio mast marks Sir William Hill.

After passing a memorial seat turn right onto the lane, then in a few yards go left over a stile by the track from Abney Grange which once belonged to Welbeck Abbey. This footpath short cuts across the fields dipping into a side valley and then into the head of Bretton Clough by a disused pumping station. Looking down the deep clough you can see many grassy hillocks which were formed by landslips. Climb to the road by a fenced-in reservoir and turn left. This is a good spot from which to watch the gliders taking off and landing at the Derbyshire and Lancashire Gliding Club, which was formed in 1935. The gliders are towed by a winch to around 1000ft and there can be as many as thirty in the air at once. In a few yards fork right into the wood to an old marker stone where you meet the main track and go down past the school into Great Hucklow.

Great Hucklow

The Queen Anne pub and the major part of the village are to the right but we go almost straight across, past the Unitarian Holiday Centre, and then left beside the Old Unitarian Chapel. Follow the line of stiles across the fields to end with an awkward squeeze through into a private garden. Turn left onto the lane then right at the T-junction in Grindlow village.

Passing Chapel House Farm the road leads in ¼ mile to a T-junction where you go straight across past a bungalow down a green lane which leads above the strangely named Silly Dale. Joining another old trackway turn right, then after Stanley House Farm go left at the lane corner over a stile into the field. Cutting across the field keep to the left of the wall which runs down to the next farm. Negotiating the farm buildings the busy main road is met at Wardlow Mires by the old fashioned Three Stags' Heads pub.

Cressbrook Dale

Cross the minor road to Wardlow and going in front of the cottage take the grassy track down Cressbrook Dale. This National Nature Reserve is one of the loveliest of the limestone dales and our favourite for the wide variety of beautiful flowers it contains. Though this is usually a dry valley we came one winter to find the whole of the upper portion one enormous lake. Rounding the corner Peter's Stone comes into view guarding the end of the dale. It looks unassailable but by climbing left there is an easy scramble to the top. There is a gruesome tale connected with this spot for in 1815 a murderer was executed and his body left hanging from a gibbet on the rock.

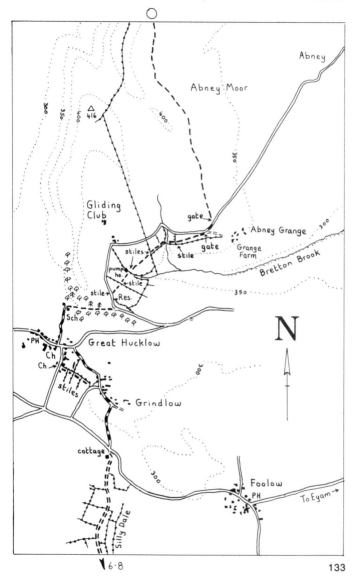

6·9

The good path continues down the dale where there are masses of early purple orchids in the spring, then after passing the end of Tansley Dale it slants left uphill forking right near the top to meet the wall corner with grand views both back up the dale and down into the semi-natural ash woodland. The path first follows the valley rim then drops down a rocky staircase and into the woodland where the sweet smelling lily of the valley can be found.

After crossing a footbridge follow the path beside the usually dry stream bed through the wood and past Ravensdale Cottages which were built for mill workers. Above the houses towers Raven's Buttress where the limestone cliffs are over 150ft high. The tarmac lane climbs to join a road which leads down to Cressbrook Mill, an alternative way to Litton Mill through Water cum Jolly Dale.

Cressbrook

Cross the road and continue up the rough track to a higher road where you

Ravensdale Cottages

turn right for a few yards then take the walled path which climbs between the houses. The route now follows the quiet road through Cressbrook, another and larger group of mill cottages built by the owner of Cressbrook Mill. The houses are soon left behind and there are lovely views down into Water cum Jolly Dale and over towards Brushfield. After passing the isolated church of St John the Evangelist an old lane descends to Litton Mill and Miller's Dale. The grassy track zigzags down past a mill chimney, built to carry the smoke away from the valley, to enter Miller's Dale from the rear. The cottage to the right has an unusual chimney separate from the house. Once a ruin the

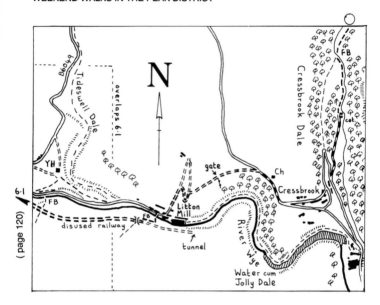

owner has been renovating it for twenty years and the chimney is all that remains of a former smelt mill.

Litton Mill

Joining the road end by Litton Mill, an old cotton mill where the apprentices were cruelly mistreated, turn right past the row of cottages and the Village Shop which serves refreshments. Ravenstor Youth Hostel is half a mile down the road, but for Miller's Dale Station cross the river by a footbridge and climb up to the disused Buxton to Matlock railway line. This closed in 1968 and is now the Monsal Trail. The embankments and cuttings are covered in vegetation and many of the plants so carefully protected in the nature reserves now grow here in profusion.

After a mile following the old railway line high above the valley there is an interesting series of old lime kilns which were built in 1878, then, crossing the spectacular viaduct over the road and the River Wye, Miller's Dale car park is reached and the start of the walk.

Miller's Dale

The hamlet of Miller's Dale is little more than a cluster of houses at the junction of Monk's Dale with the River Wye. There is a pub, St Anne's Church and a scattering of cottages and farms just a few yards up the road from the massive viaducts of the former Midland Railway which linked London to Manchester.

The line through the Peak District which opened in 1863 was built like an alpine railway, tunnelling through the hillside and criss-crossing the river on huge metal viaducts. Although at first Miller's Dale station had only the southern viaduct, this was an important junction for Buxton so a second bridge was built in 1905 and two extra platforms were added. In 1968 the line was closed and the track converted to the Monsal Trail. Walking through the tunnels with the aid of a torch made an exciting trip until they were blocked off in 1980 for safety reasons.

At Miller's Dale three of the platforms and some of the station buildings remain. These are used as a Peak Ranger Centre. There is a large car park, toilets, the remains of old lime kilns and the rangers have established a small wild flower garden. Maybe one day trains will run here again as Peak Rail has plans to open the line as a single track railway. Based in Buxton, the Society hope to run steam trains along the old Midland line down the Wye Valley to Rowsley and on to Matlock.

LONG WEEKEND 7: BAKEWELL, EYAM & TIDESWELL

DAY 1:	Tideswell Dale to Bakewell 8½ miles
STARTING POINT:	(154743) Tideswell Dale car park 1 mile south of Tideswell
DAY 2:	Bakewell to Eyam 9 miles
STARTING POINT:	(219686) Bakewell Town Bridge
DAY 3:	Eyam to Bakewell 7½ miles
STARTING POINT:	(221765) The square in the centre of Eyam
ROUTE SUMMARY:	The first day follows the River Wye down to Ashford in the Water and Bakewell while the second visits Great Longstone on the way to the plague village of Eyam. Finally crossing limestone pastureland to Foolow, lovely Ravensdale brings you back to Litton and Tideswell. Three easy days on good paths.

DAY 1: TIDESWELL DALE TO BAKEWELL

The great double S-bend in the River Wye that is known as Miller's Dale is now a peaceful scene. Moorhens and coots potter about its wide slow flowing reaches, busy making their nests in tangled swamps of willow, bulrush and horsetail. On either side rise limestone cliffs, some with the river lapping at their feet, some defended by steep scree slopes, while others overhang the dale like a wave frozen at the moment of breaking.

Jammed into the valley the eponymous mills stand empty, one at either end. Litton Mill survived until the 1970s, gradually getting more and more dilapidated and now with windows smashed awaits its fate. Cressbrook Mill is even further gone, the once stately building rotted and supported both inside and out by props, we expect one day to find it has given up hope and expired in a pile of rubble.

There must have been many workers in the nineteenth century who gave up hope, for both mills were extensive users of child labour. Long hours, six days a week, were considered normal for young orphans brought here from the poorhouses of London. E. Rhodes speaks of "These boys and girls,

deserted by their natural protectors, and thrown, like waifs, upon the world's wide waste, without a being to shew them kindness". We were fascinated with the account which illustrates how people at the time thought about this philanthropic treatment, "I felt assured that these friendless children were confided to the care of an indulgent master". Perhaps it wasn't so bad at Cressbrook. They had a few hours off on a Sunday, even if it was to walk to church and thank God for their situation. But at Litton Mill the conditions were so bad that many children died, so many in fact that the bodies were taken to adjacent parishes for burial to avoid any possibility of scandal.

It is because of the industry that the valley appears as we see it today. The wide lagoons are the result of dams which provided a head of water for the mills and when recently the weir was breached, large mudflats were exposed and the river appeared little more than a stream. Fortunately the dam has been restored and once more the millpool fills the valley.

This section of the valley is also known as Water cum Jolly Dale. Until about ten years ago the overhanging cliffs resounded to the clang of hammers on metal pegs, but modern rock climbers with chalk bags, special "sticky" boots, rainbow coloured tights and multicoloured ropes are now able to climb these smooth overleaning walls. It isn't magic, there are holds there if you go and look, but for most people even to leave the ground at all is impossible!

Beyond Cressbrook Mill the Wye straightens out with only minor meanderings for the next mile and though the valley sides are still steep it is no longer a gorge. High on the southern side runs the track of the old Midland Railway. Unable to twist and turn a way through Miller's Dale the engineers were forced to tunnel through the limestone and at the eastern end of this section, where the Wye has to be crossed high above the river, they built the Monsal Viaduct.

Many guidebooks quote John Ruskin's diatribe against the railway builders for "Heaping thousands of tons of shale into its lovely stream - now the valley is gone and the gods with it", but James Croston accuses Ruskin "Of forgetting apparently that the Arcadian god and his associates must long before have been scared from their haunts by the rattle of the Derby coach and the tootling of the guard's bugle". Now the railway is gone and the trains with it, but the viaduct is preserved as an ancient monument and beside the old track, once the main line from London to Manchester, cowslips flourish, orchids colour the verges and with the summer come the golden flowers of hawkbit, great white ox-eye daisies and the yellow stars of St John's wort.

Beyond the viaduct the Wye nearly doubles back on itself to round Fin Cop. Crowned by an Iron Age hill fort and on three sides spectacularly steep, Fin Cop is really only a spur of the limestone plateau, a harder rock which was left behind as the river cut its way down. From here to Bakewell the main A6 road runs in tandem with the river, but by climbing to Great Shacklow Wood the traffic is left behind for a while before you descend again through the sycamore, beech and oak to join the banks of the Wye and so on to Ashford in the Water.

The medieval Sheepwash Bridge over which the walker enters "Aisseford", for that is the name of Ashford in the Domesday Book, was built where the Portway, an ancient road, forded the river. The stone enclosures beside the bridge are sheep pens and it is only recently that the river has been forsaken in favour of the less aesthetic, but more effective chemical sheep dips. The houses and cottages, built predominantly of limestone, make Ashford one of the most attractive Peakland villages and as the lead mining drew to a close at the end of the nineteenth century it was limestone that continued the industry. Just off the main road, a little to the west of the village and now overgrown with trees, is the Ashford Black Marble quarry. The rock which when polished attains a black lustre was used as a background for coloured inlays for everything from jewellery to furniture.

Bakewell, downstream from Ashford, has not only harnessed the Wye but diverted it too and the changing course of the river illustrates the history of local industry. Now the mill leat is filled with rushes while turbines power the factory, a waterwheel slumps rusting beside Victoria Mill and as the day started with mills, so it comes to an end and you enter Bakewell through the old industrial quarter.

ROUTE DESCRIPTION
Miller's Dale

From the Tideswell Dale car park the track leads beneath an old quarry which was worked until the 1950s. Staying in the valley the path divides then rejoins again by a footbridge and continues between high limestone cliffs partly concealed by dense vegetation. Soon after a second footbridge Tideswell

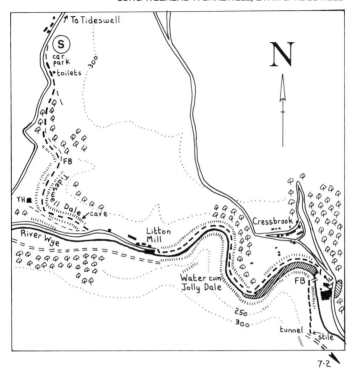

7.2

Dale Cave is passed, an old resurgence cave with a narrow 100ft passage leading to a small chamber. Just beyond, the road is met in Miller's Dale, where up a flight of steps to the right is Ravenstor Youth Hostel.

Turn left down the road beside the River Wye to the cottages by Litton Mill, where there is a pottery and a café. This old cotton mill which opened in 1782, though most of the present buildings are nineteenth century, was notorious in the past for the treatment of its apprentices. The mill's future is uncertain, with plans for a timeshare and leisure complex recently turned down.

Water Cum Jolly Dale

Passing through the mill gates by the old apprentices' house, walk between the mill buildings. Turning across the leat then proceed with the stream beneath high limestone cliffs into Water cum Jolly Dale, which is as lovely as

141

Monsal viaduct and Upperdale

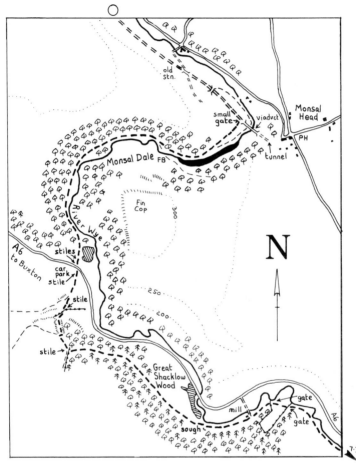

its name. The concession path continues through the wooded dale and after passing the remains of a waterwheel which pumped drinking water from a spring to the village of Cressbrook, the valley broadens and the river widens to form a mill pond. Walking under the overhanging cliffs of Rubicon Wall, a good place on a wet day, go through a tall metal gate and the route continues to the right over the footbridge which spans the weir. Diverting a few steps to look at Cressbrook Mill you pass a gothic folly which was probably used

143

as a chapel at the end of Apprentices Row. Urgent repair work has been carried out, but this imposing mill is rapidly falling into an unsafe and derelict condition.

Monsal Dale

Returning to the yard near the iron gate, cross the new footbridge which was constructed by the Territorial Army Royal Engineers. Climbing a flight of limestone steps, follow the path along the hillside to join the disused railway line by the 471 yard Cressbrook Tunnel where there is an information board about the mill. Beyond the disused Monsal Dale station there is a railway hut which has been made into a shelter, then passing the entrance to an old lead mine, the line enters a deep cutting. On reaching the 80ft high Monsal Head Viaduct and before turning right through a little gate to join the path beside the River Wye, stroll out onto the bridge where there is an interesting information plaque and a grand view both up and down the river. The line now continues on its way through the sealed 533 yard Headstone Tunnel to Bakewell.

The path follows the river which soon widens to a pond fringed with bulrushes above a curved weir and you pass a footbridge to enter the trees and scrubland below the flat topped Fin Cop. The sound of the river is a companion with its tranquil sections interrupted by little waterfalls. The steep slopes to the right are typical limestone ash woodland and the hawthorns of the valley floor are a mass of blossom in the spring. Reaching a wooden ladder stile over a small stream, climb up the field to a step stile and squeezer onto the busy A6.

Great Shacklow Wood

Cross the main road to a stile on the far side of White Lodge car park and take the path through the fields across the hillside to enter a narrow limestone valley. Ignoring the rocky gorge to the right, go over the stile and keep straight on, climbing gradually to a path junction. Taking the footpath to Ashford and Sheldon climb the flower covered hillside to enter the trees where a stile leads over the wall into Great Shacklow Wood. This was planted by the Fifth Duke of Rutland at the beginning of the nineteenth century.

The path ambles along high above the valley and then descends gently past a fishpool to the river and the Magpie Mine sough. On 23 April 1966 water pent up by a blockage in this drainage channel burst out and the resultant explosion gouged a chunk out of the hillside above. We were once startled to see a black-suited frogman emerging from the sough which was driven in 1873 and is navigable by boat. The buildings a little downstream, originally a bone mill but later used as a saw mill, are being carefully restored and the waterwheels are still in place. The smaller ruined building by the river pumped spring water to Sheldon village on the dry limestone plateau above,

Mill, Great Shacklow Wood

while the less attractive modern building monitors the flow of water.

Continuing through the meadows beside the river fringed with forget-me-nots, huge banks of watercress and the yellow monkey flower, join the lane at a gate and turn left past a repaired bridge which leads to the site of the Black Marble Mill. The adjacent ruins are of a later nineteenth-century mill which made combs from tortoiseshell. To the right is the overgrown Arrock Quarry which was worked until 1905 for decorative limestone and there are a few bits of this black marble in the limestone wall beside the road.

Ashford in the Water

Turning right along the main road for a short way, cross over the busy A6 to the three arched Sheepwash Bridge where an information plaque beside the roofed Parish Pump tells much of the history of the attractive village of Ashford in the Water. The nineteenth-century Holy Trinity church contains a table with a top inlaid with pieces of Ashford Marble and a memorial to Henry

145

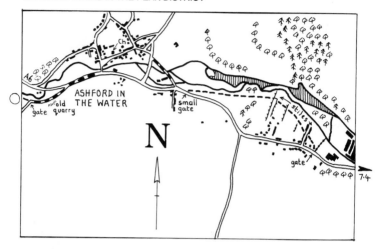

Watson who established the marble works in 1748. Continue along Church Street past the Bull's Head and then rounding the Ashford Hotel cross the new road to the right of the beech fringed cricket ground. Follow the old road over a bridge inscribed 1664. This is not the year of its construction but a memorial to the Rev M.Hyde, Vicar of Bakewell, who was thrown from his horse and drowned. Cross a second bridge over an old mill leat where just upstream is Ashford's oldest building, the corn mill mentioned in the Domesday Book.

Holme Bridge

A kissing gate leads to a path through the fields beside the Wye. The weirs and pools beside the river were built to provide the mills of Bakewell with an improved water supply and the original course of the river has been much altered. Passing a weir below a reservoir built in a bend of the river, continue over a series of stiles. The path then goes through a gap between the houses and crosses a road to the next field where the A6 is joined at a squeezer stile by a field gate.

The main road leads into Bakewell past modern factories and the older Lumford Mill, which was built on the site of Arkwright's third spinning mill. The river divides to form a leat and to the left is Holme Bridge, a lovely old packhorse bridge with an information board about the river's history. Continuing down the main road into Bakewell turn left after Victoria Mill, an old corn mill which has a dilapidated waterwheel still in place. Millford Lane leads beside the mill leat to the end of Castle Street where the smart gritstone

Ashford in the Water

façade of its terraced houses conceals the cheaper limestone at the back. Joining Bridge Street you arrive in the centre of Bakewell by the splendid Town Bridge whose five arched span replaced a ford around 1300.

Bakewell

Bakewell is home to two important institutions. The first is the Peak Park Joint Planning Board which manages the Peak National Park. The headquarters of this august body are at Aldern House on the outskirts of the town. In April 1951 the Peak District was the first National Park to be designated in Great

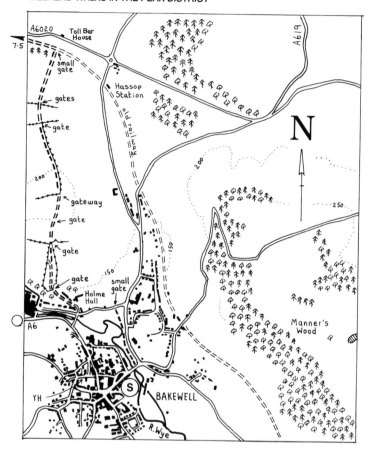

Britain and the board is responsible for achieving the difficult balance between the needs of both the visitors and the local people. Mineral working and industry must be managed as well as problems of visitor accommodation, access and rights of way. As over half the population of Britain lives within 60 miles of the Peak District this is a mammoth task.

The second is Bakewell Pudding. Not the common or garden tart as produced by Mr Kipling but a somewhat more solid pudding. Tradition says that the original version was produced in error by the cook at the Rutland

Arms in the nineteenth century. Local shops sell their own versions but the original recipe is a closely guarded secret. A copy of *Model Cookery and Housekeeping,* which belonged to an elderly aunt, as well as being a helpful guide to the duties of servants gives the following recipe for the pudding.

> Line a dish with puff paste, and put in it raspberry or any other preserve, about half an inch thick. Mix with a quarter of a pound of sifted sugar the grated peel and juice of two lemons; then stir in the yolks of eight and the whites of two eggs well-beaten, and lastly four ounces of butter, which only requires melting and pouring off clear. Stir all together until it is thoroughly mixed, then pour it over the preserve, and bake in a quick oven. Half the quantity will make five or six puddings, baked in buttered saucers lined with puff paste.

DAY 2: BAKEWELL TO EYAM

While a journey by road from Bakewell to Eyam would take you from the valley of the River Wye to the Derwent round the high limestone plateau, the traveller on foot can climb to look down on the valleys and hillsides and see the land spread out as a giant map.

The high spot is Longstone Edge which looks down on the valley of the River Wye in its narrow gorge to the west while to the east, in a much broader valley, flows the River Derwent. With bracken covered slopes, patches of heather, heathland vegetation and even the place name Bleaklow, the moor evokes the feel of the high land to the north, but this is not a gritstone moor for the underlying rock is hard white limestone.

It is the limestone that holds the secret of the hill for along the summit ridge runs a scar, a deep trench torn across the land and from its depths is dredged the mineral fluorspar. Scattered on the map are the names Watersaw Rake, White Rake, Dirty Rake, and on the hilltop itself High Rake and Deep Rake, once the sites of lead mines where t'owd man scoured the land in search of wealth. Strung out in a long line across the fields, depressions and hummocks are evidence of workings that go back to the eleventh century and beyond. It is thought that the Romans mined here, though remains of their activities have long vanished, but in early days once the surface workings were exhausted the miners moved on. It wasn't until the sixteenth century that techniques improved through the expertise of Agricola. This was the latinised name of the German mining expert whose book on mines *De re Metallica,* published in 1556, was to remain the standard work for over 200 years. Now shafts and levels could be dug and when the mines were taken below the water table, pumps were introduced and soughs or drainage tunnels driven. Towards the close of the seventeenth-century gunpowder was introduced and in 1715 the first steam engine appeared in a Peak District mine. The eighteenth and nineteenth centuries saw the mines flourish, and Waterhole Mine on Longstone Edge near Rowland was one of the very productive ones.

This age too has passed and now the gangue minerals, once discarded as worthless by the old miners, are considered valuable. Fluorspar, barytes and calcite have taken over from lead, but few tunnels or shafts are laboriously excavated these days and instead the hillside is ripped apart and what once took years of toil can now be won in a matter of days.

At the foot of the southern slopes of Longstone Moor, where the bracken covered hillside gives way to green pastures, are Little Longstone and Great Longstone. Unlike the villages of the Derwent Valley which grew up beside the river, those of the White Peak are higher up the slope, nearer the good agricultural land on the plateau top. The settlements are astride a geological junction, where limestone beds join the underlying shales and where the water, percolating down through the soluble rock, emerges to provide springs and wells. While on gritstone there is plenty of water and houses and hamlets lie scattered freely across the land, the relative scarcity on limestone concentrated habitation around such water sources.

The little hamlet of Rowland is an isolated instance of a Scandinavian place name and though in 1570 this was a collection of some ten farms, by the seventeenth century it had almost disappeared, the land being depopulated to make way for sheep by the wealthy Eyre family. Its present form is due to a scattered community which made a living from a mixture of farming and mining on the hill above.

Crossing the top of Longstone Edge you look down into the black depths of a narrow cleft and then descend to the valley beyond. Because sheep are kept away from dangerous workings these limestone quarries and mines are often, despite their ravages of the landscape, some of the best places in the Peak for flowers. In the upper part of Coombs Dale is the still active Sallet Hole Mine that tunnels beneath Deep Rake to reach the rich vein of fluorspar. An engineer showed us the plans of the mine, we admired the deafening compressors that drove the drills, learned about ore yields and peered down the long black tunnel, a fascinating hour.

In Coombs Dale ancient ashwoods cling to the slope and the banks of the dale are covered in flowers, some of them among the rarest in the country. This is one of the Peak District's SSSIs (Sites of Special Scientific Interest). There are 28 such sites in the Peak which have been selected for their rare botanical interest and a further 29 where the geology is sufficiently unusual to warrant protection. A quick check when compiling this book showed that between them the walks visit at least half of these SSSIs.

Beyond Coombs Dale is Stoney Middleton. Though its limestone crags are noted for a particular coral fossil and feature as an SSSI, and are also greatly prized by rock climbers, the gorge itself is still too closely linked with modern quarrying to be attractive. The village is a pleasing contrast, with a reputed Roman bath, an unusual octagonal church and a matching toll house built in 1840. The road avoids the steep climb out of the valley over Middleton Moor, but there is no avoiding the final ascent of the day to the attractive village of Eyam through meadows filled with thyme and the golden flowers of the hawkbit.

ROUTE DESCRIPTION (See map 7.4 page 148)
Monsal Trail

Crossing over Town Bridge in Bakewell take the footpath to the left across the meadow called Scot's Garden. Briefly join the road past Holme Hall which was built in 1626 then at the seventeenth-century Holme Bridge turn up the lane to the right. Following this important old packhorse way uphill past a disused quarry housing a stoneyard, go through a farm gate and continue up the hill. Keep straight on when the track turns off into a quarry and the old way

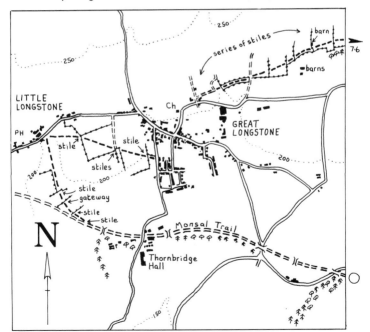

continues as a green lane between limestone walls. Looking back Bakewell lies spread out below in the wide valley of the Wye while to the east is Manners Wood.

At the top of the hill the lane terminates in a field with a fine prospect ahead of Longstone Edge. Soon becoming enclosed again the path then descends to the disused railway, now the Monsal Trail. Opposite is the pink painted Rowdale tollhouse with its bell and gate symbol which stands where the old packhorse way crosses the much later Ashford to Baslow turnpike.

About ¼ mile to the right are the remains of Hassop Station which was constructed in 1863 for the sole use of the Duke of Devonshire, only a mile from the Duke of Rutland's station at Bakewell. Neither of the Dukes wanted the railway to run through their estates. The Duke of Rutland finally allowed it to pass underground behind Haddon Hall, but as they could not agree on the site of the station they had one each. Hassop Station buildings are now used as a bookshop.

Turning left, the track passes over two roads and under three bridges before reaching Longstone Station, a private house. This was built next to the imposing Victorian mansion of Thornbridge Hall which for a time was an education centre for Sheffield.

Great Longstone

After going through a cutting, turn off to the right towards Little Longstone. The path follows beside the line for a short way, then veers away through the fields to meet the road at three farm gates and two step stiles. From here it is a only few paces off the route to the Packhorse Inn and the village of Little Longstone whose cottage gardens along the single street are among the prettiest in Derbyshire.

Turning back into the fields take the footpath to Great Longstone across the park-like meadows. At the road go left past the Methodist chapel to the medieval cross on the village green by the Crispin pub. Opposite is the ugly Longstone Hall, a piece of extravagance constructed in red brick in 1747 to distinguish the house from its stonebuilt neighbours.

Walking through the village which originally consisted simply of one long street, turn left up Church Lane, then on rounding the bend after St Giles' church which dates from the thirteenth century, you are suddenly in a quiet country road. A footpath leads off an unsurfaced lane after a modern bungalow and cuts across the field corner to the adjoining walled pathway. When the lane bends away keep straight on over the fields, across another narrow lane and continue through a series of stiles over more fields and past a two storied stone barn. To the left is the ridge of Longstone Edge and ahead lie the houses of Rowland.

Longstone Edge

Turning left along the road, the lane deteriorates to an unsurfaced track after the last farm and passes the dome of a reservoir screened with a limestone wall. Heading straight on up the hill ignoring turnings to the left, cross a cattle grid and keep along the main track. The old opencast workings have been grassed over and the whole area is covered with a wealth of lime-loving wild flowers in the spring and summer. The view expands to the right towards Chatsworth Park and the little village of Baslow nestling beneath the gritstone outcrops of the eastern edges. Below is the wooded Hassop valley which is thought to have been the course of the River Derwent before the Ice Age when a major glacier in the region of Bakewell formed the present river channel.

Taking the left fork at the top of the hill, cut across the corner to a stile on the far side of a broad track. The path joins another track which crosses the abyss of the appropriately named Deep Rake which is still being mined

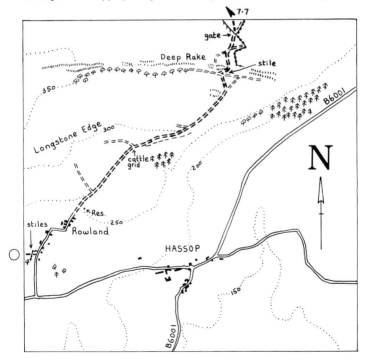

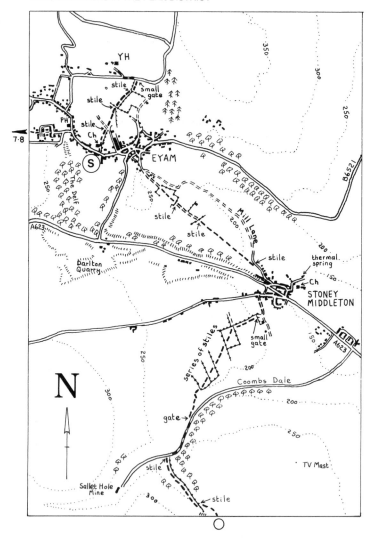

by Laporte, no longer for lead but for fluorspar. Fortunately this part of the rake is not being excavated and there are good views down into the old mine workings which have mellowed with time. Keeping straight on across the network of tracks, descend into the valley at a stile by a gate.

Coombs Dale

Turning down the steep sided dry dale, whose grassy slopes have occasional outcrops of limestone, cross the wall at a stile half way down. The valley sides are carpeted with thyme, eyebright, golden rock roses and blue and purple milkworts. Joining the metalled road in Coombs Dale turn downhill for 300 yards. Here in early autumn, when the trees were just beginning to change colour, we found the nettle-leaved bellflower still blooming. Resembling a garden delphinium this is one of the more unusual wild flowers in the woods of the Peak District. Crossing the stream to a field gate and a stile hidden in the vegetation, the path climbs to a rocky bluff. Here two more unusual plants can be found, the fleshy leaved orpine and the mallow which was first introduced into Britain by the Romans for flavouring food. Keeping above the trees to a stile the path leads across the fields with the cliffs of Froggatt Edge on the skyline, while to the left Sir William Hill with its tall mast comes into view.

Stoney Middleton

At the signpost turn down the wall and staying on its right, go through a mesh gate at the end of a garden. Turn left onto Vicarage Lane then go down High Street into Stoney Middleton where a steep path beside the school leads to the busy main road. Take the road opposite behind the old eight sided toll house, but before turning left up Mill Lane it is well worth detouring to the right to visit the unusual octagonal church. The seats inside all face into the centre and there is only one other in the country like it. Further down the lane is a thermal spring which was possibly the site of a Roman bath where the stone buildings erected around 1815 "for the accommodation of bathers" have recently been restored. The two wells in the square nearby are dressed on the first Saturday in August. The custom, originally a pagan ritual in thanksgiving for the vital water, was adopted by the church and was revived here in 1936.

Mill Lane, which was once the main road to Eyam, leads uphill and just past the old quarry a public footpath crosses the fields. The path climbs up the flower filled meadow, passing the Boundary Stone at the top of the hill. Here, in order to isolate the village at the time of the plague, money to buy food was left soaking in vinegar. After a narrow drystone walled lane, a track crosses the fields joining Mill Lane down into Eyam. Reaching the Square in the centre of the village by the Miner's Arms, which was built in 1630, there is an iron ring for bull baiting. Although this was a cruel sport the baiting was thought to tenderise the meat before the animal was slaughtered.

To reach the youth hostel follow Church Street and take the churchyard footpath past the site of Glebe Mine, climbing up the field to Edge Road and the hostel.

Eyam

Though backed by gritstone moorland, Eyam is very much a village of the limestone Peak. Picturesque houses and cottages line the street from Town End past the church and up to Town Head, and it is a surprise to find that until recently a major lead mine thrived at the bottom of the churchyard.

Eyam is famous as the plague village. Not simply because so many of the inhabitants died from bubonic plague in 1666, but because of the self sacrifice of the villagers who led by their rector William Mompesson cut themselves off completely to limit the spread of the infection. Of the 350 inhabitants, 257 died and the victims included Mompesson's own wife Catherine of whom he wrote on September 1st 1666 "This is the saddest news that ever my pen could write. The destroying Angel having taken up his quarters within my habitation, my dearest wife is gone to her eternal rest, and is invested with a crown of righteousness, having made a happy end." Many of the cottages carry a plaque recording the death of the occupants during that dreadful year.

To limit infection people were buried close to their homes. Next to Lydgate Cottage near the Square are the graves of George Darby and his daughter Mary, while on the hillside towards Hathersage are the Riley Graves. Here the mother of the Hancock family buried her husband and six children in an open field as one after another they all died.

Every year on the anniversary of Catherine's death, a commemoration service is held at Cucklett Delf. This rocky outcrop in a little valley is where Mompesson himself held services out of

Celtic Cross, Eyam Church

doors in order to minimise the risk of infection. The local well dressing is also held on this day, Plague Sunday, the last Sunday in August.

As well as the many items of interest within the church including wall paintings in the nave, Mompesson's Chair and the Plague Register, the churchyard contains an unusual sundial, the tomb of Catherine Mompesson and a magnificent carved Celtic Cross. The lead mine, the once flourishing silk mills and boot and shoe factories are now all gone and today's main industry is tourism.

DAY 3: EYAM TO TIDESWELL DALE

Following a briefly energetic departure as you climb from Eyam, a series of fields too numerous to trace brings you, after a gentle perambulation, to Foolow just at opening time where the Lazy Landlord, the pub that is, not mine host, is worth a visit. Foolow is an attractive village set out round a central green complete with pond and ducks and overlooked by an ancient cross.

Today could be a glorified pub crawl as, taking a suitably devious path, the route zigzags across the centre of the White Peak to visit the hostelries of Wardlow, Litton and finally Tideswell before a gentle stroll back down to Tideswell Dale.

The deviousness is not just to visit all the pubs on route, but to see the villages and also to avoid Cavendish Mill which is planted four-square in the centre of Middleton Moor. The enormous lakes, which look so attractive on the map, are settling ponds where slurry, a by-product of the fluorspar processing, gradually congeals. The heavy lorries seen trundling across the moor carry ore from mines and opencast pits to the mill, but this industry is only a distant smudge on the landscape as you follow the ancient way across the moor past Castlegate Farm. Here the path crosses all the fields diagonally, but this apparent perversity is because the path pre-dates the walls which are themselves over 200 years old.

Wardlow, ignored by most authors, is dismissed in one line by the rest and were it not for E.Rhodes we might never have learnt the lurid history of the last man to hang in these parts, strung on a gibbet at Wardlow Mires in 1815.

"One would suppose that there was little on these bleak hills and plains to excite the cupidity of the robber or to induce the commission of the crime of murder, particularly amongst a people whose wants are necessarily as circumscribed as their means; but even here, at a little distance on the left of the road, we observed a man suspended on a gibbet, which was but newly erected. He had entered the cottage of a poor woman who kept the toll gate at Wardlow-Mears, and for the paltry consideration of a few shillings, he had violated the law of God and man, which says 'thou shalt not kill'. He then, with an inconsiderate infatuation which often attends the commission of enormous offences, gave the shoes of the woman he had just murdered to another who resided near, a circumstance which led to his immediate detection."

Beyond Wardlow you descend into Cressbrook Dale past old mine workings, long abandoned and now covered in flowers. This is a mere flirtation with one of the most floriferous dales in the Peak District and the glimpse in late spring of the early purple orchids, golden yellow cowslips and on the valley rim the lovely mountain pansies, will tempt you back for more.

Litton, with its houses set out spaciously along the main street and its pub fronted by the village green, complete with stocks and an old gritstone cross, is a quiet genteel sort of place. Keeping aloof from the vulgar commercial mill in the dale below, which in the nineteenth century became notorious for exploitation of child labour, most days seems like Sunday, and on hot summer afternoons the patrons of the inn emerge from its smoky interior to recline on the village green.

It is only a short walk up the country road and then you look down on Tideswell and its church. Tideswell had by the thirteenth century become an important centre in the Peak with a thriving trade in lead and wool and its church, built over a period of only 50 years from 1320, is the finest in the whole area. Known as "The Cathedral of the Peak" it has an eight pinnacled tower, interesting windows, brasses and monuments, and is the most complete medieval church in the Peak District. Though still a village it is the largest of those visited and has today an air of, if not affluence, at least friendly community, while if your visit coincides with the annual well dressing the streets are full to overflowing. Well dressing, thought to be originally an ancient pagan custom, was sanctified by the church several hundred years ago and then, more recently, commercialised by some villages. But Tideswell's tradition is firmly rooted. The wells are decorated for a week every summer, each with a large pictorial display on a religious theme and made from moss, leaves and tens of thousands of flower petals.

ROUTE DESCRIPTION (See map 7.7 page 154)
Foolow

From the Square in the centre of Eyam follow Church Street past the church and the seventeenth century Plague Cottages where the first victim of the plague lived. Opposite Eyam Hall which was rebuilt in 1676, there is a little green with the village stocks and an information plaque. Turn left before the Rose and Crown along New Close and keep straight on through the housing estate. Crossing a lane and a triangle of grass to another lane, a narrow hedge-lined path squeezes between more houses to reach the fields.

Foolow

Climbing past a roofless barn, continue over a complex network of fields whose limestone walls are composed of the fossilised remains of ancient sea creatures. There is much evidence of mining with the humps and hollows and boarded over climbing shafts of Middlefield Rake. On the skyline of Eyam Edge to the right is the Barrel Inn and below it are the buildings of Black Hole Mine, while the tall mast marks Sir William Hill. Navigating from stile to stile dip down to cross Linen Dale finally going right to join the main road into the next village. Foolow is everything a village should be. With its duckpond on the green fed by a walled spring, its ancient cross and bullbaiting stone, church, chapel and manor house, it has a picture postcard prettiness.

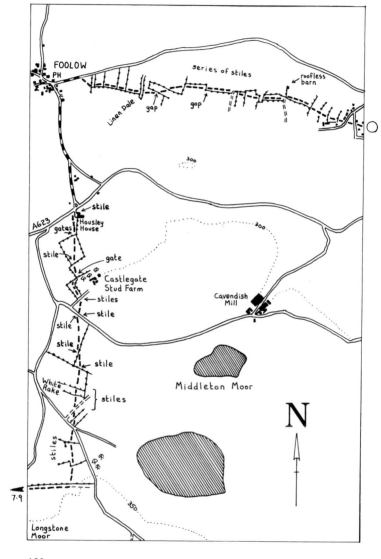

Longstone Moor

Leaving the village by the lane opposite the Lazy Landlord, half a mile of roadside walking follows, forking right at Housley, the site of the Watergrove Mine which was worked from the beginning of the eighteenth century. Crossing the A623, take the path by Housley Cottage over the wall and past the duckpond. After the first field slant right across the fields to the curving wall which encloses the screening belt of trees at Castlegate Farm. Perhaps the farm was named after this old way to Castleton.

Crossing the farm track and a lane, continue in the same direction with a lovely view over nearly 180 degrees of surrounding countryside, a complex pattern of limestone walls which march over the fields dividing the rolling plateau into an interlocking jigsaw of tiny squares and rectangles.

After the reclaimed land of White Rake cross a track to another lane and continue south over more fields and through more old workings of Blagden Great Vein. A final stile leads onto Longstone Moor near the site of the strangely named Cackle Mackle Mine.

Cressbrook Dale

Turning right beside the wall, follow it to the road then continue straight across and down to Wardlow past more shafts and spoil heaps to join the main road at a farm gate. Go right towards the houses and past Hall Farm, then before you reach the Bull's Head turn up the public footpath to Ravensdale. The path runs between stone walls, passing the flanks of Wardlow Hay Cop to arrive on the lip of Cressbrook Dale at a stile. A

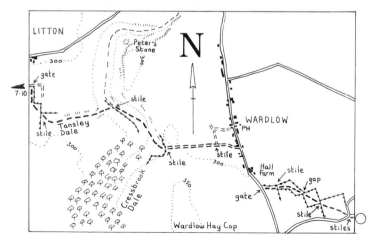

marvellous view appears of the dale below and to the village of Litton high on the far side. Here we met a breathless party of walkers who had just climbed out of the valley under the mistaken impression that they were heading for Litton.

Descending into the dale, the grassy path slants down to the right past mounds of old mine spoil covered in the spring with the white stars of the leadwort. Turn up the valley bottom beside the wall for a few yards and then cross a stile into the side valley of Tansley Dale. Near the top of the dale the path climbs out to the right, crossing a stile into the field. Arriving back on the limestone plateau where the meadow saxifrage blooms in early summer, follow the field round to the right. A step stile by a gate leads onto an old

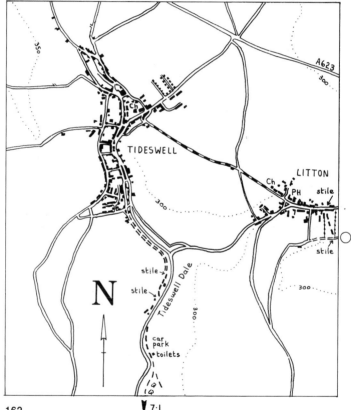

7·1

unsurfaced lane then a few steps to the left at the corner of the next field a path crosses diagonally into Litton.

Litton

Turn left through this attractive village and passing the Red Lion, take the road heading slightly uphill past some new bungalows and a church. Over to the right is Litton Edge. Keeping straight on at the junction, Church Lane leads down after a mile of easy road walking into Tideswell, with the magnificent Cathedral of the Peak framed straight ahead. A footpath between the houses cuts off the last corner and you emerge in the centre of the village, opposite the church.

Tideswell Dale

Tideswell is a delightful village. Larger than most of its neighbours it has a reasonable complement of shops, with many small cottages, narrow streets and interesting corners to explore. Walking left by the National Westminster Bank keep on down the main street, past Cherry Tree Square, then to avoid more road walking fork right in front of the Horse and Jockey. Keeping straight on past South View Farm, the track continues, terminating at a farm gate beneath ancient beech trees. Turning left through a stile, a little path descends gradually into Tideswell Dale, finally going down a field to a stile onto the road. Walk 200 yards down the road then cross over to follow a line of beech trees down into Tideswell Dale car park.

Tideswell

"Though Tideswell ranks amongst the market-towns of Derbyshire, yet, with the exception of the church, it is but a humble looking place. The houses are low, irregularly situated, and ill built, and there is altogether an air of poverty and meanness about it, with a want of cleanliness and comfort in its general appearance." So wrote E.Rhodes in the early nineteenth century in *Peak Scenery* which we discovered among a pile of musty journals and ancient volumes when staying in a converted silk mill at Tideswell.

The village now has a far more prosperous air and is busy with both locals and visitors especially for the famous annual well dressing which takes place on the Saturday nearest June 24th. The long main street zigzags past the magnificent fourteenth-century church, the Cathedral of the Peak, and from it a maze of little lanes spreads up towards the old lead workings on the hillside above. Solidly built limestone houses, cottages and shops line the streets and there is a feeling, sometimes missing in the commuter swamped villages, that this is a living community.

Fortunately no main road passes through this large village so it has remained mostly unspoilt, though a small modern industrial area provides

St John the Baptist, Tideswell

local employment. The original settlement was long and narrow and situated at the top of Tideswell Dale in a sheltered hollow in the high limestone plateau. The site was chosen because of the springs which occurred here. Although one is an ebbing and flowing well, the village was not named after this tidal well as was once thought, but after a local inhabitant called Tid, who was probably buried nearby at Tideslow.

WEEKEND 8: THE EASTERN EDGES

DAY 1:	Baslow to Hathersage 12½ miles
	(Short Route 10 miles)
STARTING POINT:	(258722) Nether End, Baslow
DAY 2:	Hathersage to Baslow 13½ miles
STARTING POINT:	(231815) The centre of Hathersage
ROUTE SUMMARY:	After climbing to reach Nelson's and
	Wellington's Monuments, the
	gritstone edges are followed, while
	the day ends beside the River
	Derwent. The second day follows the
	same pattern, climbing to Stanage
	Edge before descending again to the
	Derwent through Padley Gorge.
	Straightforward walking along good
	paths.

DAY 1: BASLOW TO HATHERSAGE

For over 12 miles, from Derwent Edge above the Ladybower Reservoir in the north to Chatsworth in the south, a series of steep walls of gritstone stand blackly against the sky. This marks the eastern edge of the Dark Peak, with the moor beyond dropping quickly to the outskirts of Sheffield. Stanage Edge is followed by the escarpments of Burbage, Froggatt, Curbar, Baslow, and finally Birchen Edge where Nelson's Monument, perched on the very brink, looks down on the valley of the River Derwent.

The Edges and the northern moors are all that remain of the Peak District's gritstone cap. Once the area was covered by a shallow sea in which lived tiny creatures whose fossil remains make up a band of limestone up to 200ft thick. This limestone was covered by sand which coalesced to form hard gritstone, but as wind and rain get to work on the stone it gradually crumbles again into sand. After the gritstone covered the Peak, earth movements lifted up the area into a dome and as erosion wore down the land the limestone core was exposed in the centre, surrounded by a tonsure of gritstone.

This coarse and very rough rock was used to make millstones for grinding corn and also the grindstones on which the cutlery industry of

166

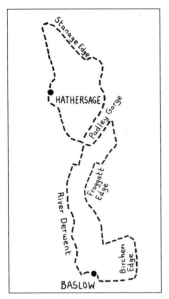

Sheffield was based. Many of these stones can be found beneath the Edges and near Surprise View above Grindleford are lines of finished millstones stacked ready in rows. Their manufacture, which was carried out by hand, must have been exceedingly hard work. The millstone was first trimmed to an octagonal shape and then rounded. Its opposing faces were flattened and finally the hole in the middle was hewn. The bottom fell out of the market in the nineteenth century when imported stones were found to be more hard wearing and cheaper. Local labourers were furious and formed gangs which attacked the mills breaking the stones, but soon little remained of the industry except the great quarry faces and millstones lying scattered on the hillside waiting for a collection that will never come.

Facing each other across the valley of Bar Brook and the busy A621 with its stream of traffic heading for Sheffield are the monuments to Nelson and to Wellington. Nelson's Monument came first in 1810, erected by John Brightman from Baslow, though the stone mason was reported to be Sampson Savage who lived at Robin Hood. Many years ago the column was topped by a stone ball, but this was thrown down by vandals and no doubt it was even earlier vandals who carved the date 1865 on the face. Set a little back from the edge three great tors, once known as the Wain Stones, were rechristened after the ships of Nelson's fleet. Carved on their prows are the names Victory, Defiance and Royal Soverin, the last misspelling apparently proving to the experts that the work was not supervised by an educated man, but then not all educated men can spell!

Wellington's Monument was put up nearly sixty years later and some 14 years after the Great Duke's death. The inscription "Erected 1866 by E.M.Wrench late 34th Reg'mt" implies a military tribute and indeed Dr Wrench served in the Indian army, but it was as Baslow's respected doctor that he led the erection of this and several other local memorials.

At Curbar Gap, where the packhorse route to Chesterfield zigzagged its way up to the edge, a jagger's guidepost is carefully marked on all four faces and also signed and dated 1709. Understandably the supervisor wanted there to be no doubt that he had complied with the 1702 Act of Parliament

Wellington's Monument

requiring all such junctions to be marked. The guidestone on the far side of Eaglestone Flat goes to the other extreme with only one face inscribed CHESTE RFEILD ROADE. The tall pole at the entrance to the Longshaw Estate is another guidepost which once marked the Dronfield to Tideswell packhorse track, though the pole itself is a recent replacement. The estate now belongs to the National Trust and at the imposing Longshaw Lodge, built as a shooting lodge for the Duke of Rutland, there is an information centre and an exceptionally good teashop.

Yarncliff Wood on the western edge of the Longshaw Estate descends steeply towards the River Derwent and the village of Upper Padley where the trains from Sheffield emerge once again into daylight after their 3½ mile journey beneath Totley Moor. Close by is the Roman Catholic Padley Chapel which was once the private chapel of Padley Hall and in 1588 two Jesuit priests who were found hiding there were executed at Derby. The chapel was re-dedicated in 1933 and an annual pilgrimage in July marks their memory.

A little way beyond Padley Chapel and easily passed without noticing it, an incline now covered in trees comes down from the hill above. Less than a century ago Bole Hill quarries were the source of over a million tons of stone used to build the great dams of Derwent and Howden in the Derwent Valley. The stone was loaded onto waggons and then lowered down the incline to join the railway and as the trucks used were of standard gauge they could be transferred immediately to the main line.

The railway is still very active and since the closure of the Woodhead route is now the main line between Sheffield and Manchester. Busy Sprinter trains shuttle to and fro and if the final couple of miles through riverside meadows are too much to face, it would be perfectly possible to finish the day in style by descending to the station at Grindleford to arrive in Hathersage by train.

ROUTE DESCRIPTION
Short Cut to Wellington's Monument

By climbing straight to Wellington's Monument, Chatsworth Park and Nelson's Monument are omitted. From opposite the Devonshire Arms at Nether End take Eton Hill road which rises to the junction with Bar Road. Turning right the road soon becomes unsurfaced and the old packhorse way climbs past the water trough of Lady Well to Bar Quarry, from which the stone for many of the houses in Baslow was obtained. On reaching Eaglestone Flat moor the Main Route is joined by turning right to Wellington's Monument.

Chatsworth Park

From Nether End, take the lane to the right of the Devonshire Arms, then after the bridge turn right on the track which leads in front of the cottages. Entering

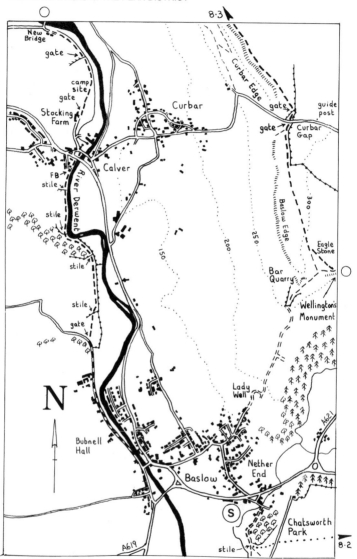

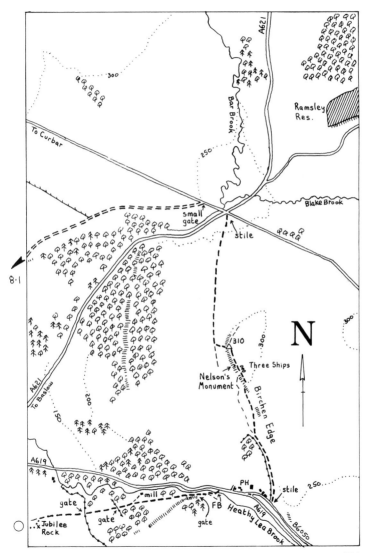

Chatsworth Park at a tall metal kissing gate, fork left on the concessionary footpath to Robin Hood. There is at first no sign of a path, but head eastwards across the short turf uphill to the prominent rock which commemorates Queen Victoria's Golden Jubilee. Continuing in the same direction a faint grassy track is joined which leads to a gritstone step stile over the high wall beside a farm gate. Following the track to another tall stile, continue above Heathy Lee, an old saw mill which was working until the end of the First World War and past a high gritstone escarpment to a third stile. A path 100 yards beyond turns off left down a few steps to a footbridge over Heathy Lea Brook then goes up a steep flight of steps to the busy A619.

A few yards up the road is the entrance to the Eric Byne Campsite, a memorial to the climber, guidebook writer and member of the Climber's Club who died in 1967. Pass the Robin Hood Inn then after a house a concealed stile over the wall leads onto the National Park's Eastern Moors Estate.

Nelson's Monument

Following the path gently uphill with a little golf course below, fork right after $\frac{1}{3}$ mile into the silver birches. The path climbs to below the cliffs and then taking one of the scrambly routes you emerge onto the top of Birchen Edge beside Nelson's Monument, which is known locally as Nelson's Pole. This was erected in 1810, some 30 years before its more famous London namesake and is sometimes used by climbers as a convenient belay point. Close by are three huge gritstone tors inscribed with the names of the three ships which gained fame and glory at the battle of Trafalgar during which Lord Nelson was killed. There are fine views back across the Chatsworth Estate of the chequerboard pattern of the fields below, and to the north-west is the white ribbon of path snaking up Curbar Edge.

Stay by the edge along to the trig point with its adjacent gritstone windshelter and then descend steeply through the heather to join a good path. Crossing the moor of heather, rushes and scattered silver birch, the road is joined at a ladder stile by the crossroads. Continue up Curbar Lane, the old 1759 turnpike road to Calver which crosses Bar Brook, then turn left through a little gate onto a rough track. Passing an old guide post which originally stood on the turnpike and is marked unusually on one face only, the track climbs almost imperceptibly to reach Wellington's Monument.

Wellington's Monument

This was erected by Dr Wrench of Baslow and faces the tiny finger of Nelson's Monument beyond Gardom's Edge. Turning away from the edge, take the path which goes by the Eagle Stone. A doubtful story says the bachelors of Baslow were required to climb to the top of this before they could marry. They must have been very agile for the huge gritstone block is no easy scramble even for a rock climber. The path heads off across the heather towards the high cliffs of Curbar Edge ahead and crosses the road at Curbar Gap where another old guide stone stands just beyond the car park.

Curbar and Froggatt Edges

The broad path now traverses the heathery moor to run along Curbar Edge. To the right is the higher parallel escarpment of White Edge while to the left the ground drops away steeply to the village of Curbar and the River Derwent. The high cliffs are continuous, but after about a mile, and past an

8·4

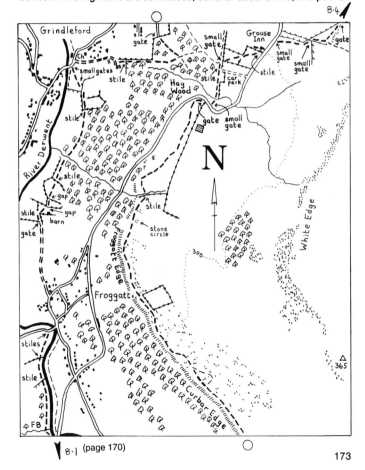

8·1 (page 170)

old stone walled enclosure, the escarpment changes direction and becomes Froggatt Edge. Beyond and to the east of the path is Stoke Flat Stone Circle which in summer almost disappears in waist high bracken. After a narrowly proportioned kissing gate by a stream the silvery path wanders on through the trees.

White Edge Lodge

Crossing the road to the National Trust Longshaw Estate at Hay Wood, the path dips to cross a stream before climbing to a well screened car park. Continue through the trees for a few yards and then take the gate into the fields and the path to the Grouse Inn. Just past the inn cross the road to another little gate and go over the field to the opposite corner. Following the path, turn left on the bridleway across White Edge Moor which is one of the most recent additions to the Longshaw Estate. The 124 acres of moorland

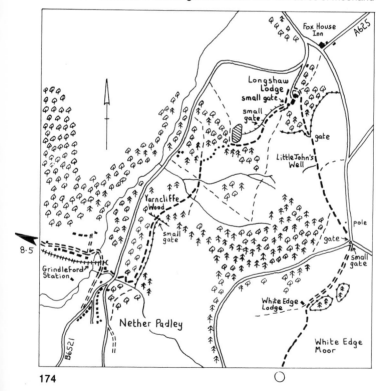

174

were bought in 1974 from the Water Board. The path passes to the right of the box shaped White Edge Lodge and joins a track which brings you to a small gate at a busy road junction.

Longshaw Lodge

Crossing the B-road to enter the parkland by the Wooden Pole, a modern replica of a guidepost, follow the grassy track along the raised embankment. This was the old Holmesfield Turnpike which led from Tideswell to Dronfield. Just after passing some stone steps up the hillside which lead to a viewpoint constructed by the Duke of Rutland, another flight of gritstone steps goes down to the stone trough of Little John's Well. This was the water source for the bathing pool at Longshaw Lodge, but now it supplies Yarncliffe Lodge with water. The well was probably originally a watering place for stock being driven along the old turnpike road. At a large white gate enter the wood and follow the drive to Longshaw Lodge.

Arriving at the back of the buildings, loop round the National Trust Visitors Centre, shop and restaurant and take the footpath in front of the house which though built as a shooting lodge around 1827 is now converted into flats. Turn right beneath the yew trees and walk beside the rhododendrons to a pool which was made in 1830. Here you leave the path to continue in the same direction across the grass and through the bracken for about 200 yards to a main green track. Turning left cross a stream, then fork right to a kissing gate. A slender path leads by the edge with a bird's-eye view of Grindleford Station, then keeping right, gritstone steps descend through Yarncliffe Wood to the main road.

Grindleford Station

The tarmac way opposite leads down to Grindleford Station Café which serves pint mugs of tea and enormous platefuls of chips. Crossing the railway line by the Totley Tunnel, which was constructed in 1893 and is the second longest railway tunnel in Britain, the track continues past Padley Chapel. This former gatehouse is all that remains of the fourteenth-century home of the Eyre family. Two Roman Catholic priests found hiding here on Christmas Day in 1588 were hung, drawn and quartered in Derby. The chapel, which was once used as a cowshed and then housed the navvies who built the Totley Tunnel, is now listed as an ancient monument. Just beyond a cattle grid, and hidden in the trees, is an overgrown old tramway. This was used to lower stone from Bole Hill Quarry to the railway below for transportation to the Derwent and Howden Reservoir dams whose construction began in 1905.

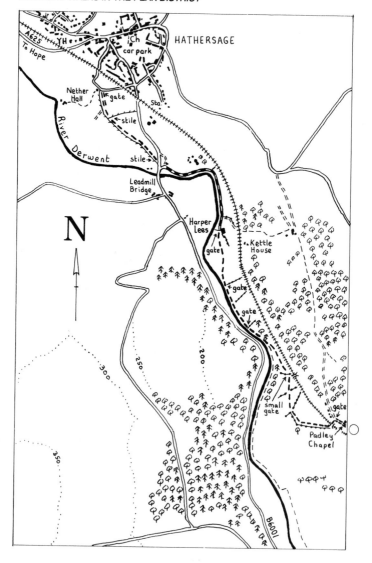

River Derwent

Going immediately left through a kissing gate and over the railway, the path crosses the fields to enter Coppice Wood through a small gate by another railway bridge. The path then goes down through the trees to the slow flowing River Derwent where it joins a broad way along the bank.

The river meanders away and the path crosses the fields to Harper Lees where the Derwent is rejoined and the route continues along a private tarmac road beside the river to Leadmill, whose lovely old bridge was widened in 1928. The mill on the far side of the road is now a private house, though the leat remains.

Going straight over the B6001 take the field path to the nineteenth-century lodge of Nether Hall. Turn left and follow the road into Hathersage under the railway past the tall chimney of the Barnfield Works, which once made needles and pins.

Hathersage

Modern Hathersage is an upmarket village. Only 12 miles from Sheffield it is well within the commuter belt and there is little to remind one of this former industrial centre where "numerous manufactories" once made steel wire and needles. In the main street a large Outdoor Pursuits shop rubs shoulders with the usual tourist gift shops and as well as an outdoor swimming pool there are a number of hotels, pubs and cafés to cater for the visitors. The youth hostel is a Victorian Gothic building, while the large imposing bank is testimony to its prosperity.

This is Robin Hood country for although Nottingham is over 30 miles away, Hathersage is on the western fringe of the old Sherwood Forest. With Robin Hood's Picking Rods, Stoup, Stride, Inn and Cross, the Peak District is steeped in associations with the outlaw. On Stanage Edge high above the village an unusual chamber hollowed in the gritstone cliff is known as Robin Hood's Cave while Longshaw Park boasts not only his well, but also one for Little John.

Local legend says that Little John is buried in Hathersage churchyard and to the south of the church is a suitably large grave 10ft long, flanked by two yew trees and surrounded by a low railing. Croston relates meeting an aged widow who tenanted the nearby cottage in which John Nailor alias Little John was said to have been born and to which he returned to die, She placed implicit faith in the whole tradition and in her youth, which would have been around the 1780s, she saw "Little John's green cap suspended by a chain in Hathersage Church". She also remembered his grave being opened when a thigh bone, measuring 32 inches in length, was dug up. In 1652 Little John's bow was also in the church but the *Derbyshire Times* stated that this was later moved to Cannon Hall in Barnsley where it remained for over 100 years.

Hathersage also has literary associations with Charlotte Brontë who

177

came to stay with her friend Ellen Nussey at the Parsonage in 1845. The church has many memorials to the Eyre family and it was from here Charlotte acquired the name of her most famous novel. Jane Eyre alighted from her coach at the Fox House Inn, went to stay at Thornfield Hall (North Lees Hall) and ran away to Morton (Hathersage).

DAY 2: HATHERSAGE TO BASLOW

Of all the gritstone edges which line the eastern rim of the Derwent Valley, the longest and most continuously steep is Stanage. From Stanage End in the north where the rocks peter out into Moscar Moor, an almost continuous wall of crags nearly 4 miles long stretches to the trig point which looks down on the scattered millstones at the southern end.

Below the rocks are bracken and rough moorland, while in the upcurrents above the edge soar the brilliantly coloured sails of hang gliders and paragliders. Teetering on the brink, rock climbers shout instruction to those on the face below, walkers and Sunday strollers follow the path along the top and beyond is the open heather moor.

The naturally steep cliffs, which quarrying has made even steeper, have been for much of this century one of the most popular climbing grounds in England. The rocks are not particularly high, but they present every standard of technical difficulty from easy slabs and cracks, on which one may learn the techniques of climbing, to fearsome vertical walls and overhangs to test the ablest of rock athletes. Gritstone climbing relies on friction, where the tiniest ripple in the rock is sufficient toehold for the expert, and on jamming. First perfected on gritstone this is the art of inserting hand or fist, foot or toe, into a crack and then by twisting forming a hold. Holds like this are among the most secure possible and smooth vertical cracks can be climbed with ease, well with at least not too much desperation!

During the depression of the 1920s many young men out of work and unable to afford the travel to Scotland, Wales or the Lakes, pushed climbing to very high standards, and subsequent generations have continued progress with Joe Brown and the late Don Whillans achieving in the 1950s perhaps the biggest individual leap forward. Nowadays on some of the modern routes serious training in a gymnasium is necessary even to leave the ground at all, while soloing, that is climbing without ropes or any form of security, is often seen.

To the south of Stanage and facing Burbage Edge across the valley of Burbage Brook are Higger Tor and Carl Wark. These outcrops of hard gritstone standing proud of the surrounding moor have been left behind as the encircling softer rock has worn away. Although the process continues today it must have been more rapid towards the end of the Ice Age with successive freeze and thaw and the harsh effect of sand windblown from the

Packhorse bridge, Burbage Brook

bare rocky surfaces.

Carl Wark, with steep slopes on three sides, is defended on the fourth by a wall of massive blocks. It was obviously a fort, though whether it was Iron Age as some people suggest, or post Roman is less clear, but it must have been a good defensive position and is a superb vantage point looking down on Burbage Brook and the valley below.

Burbage Brook flows south to Toad's Mouth where the resemblance of a rock to that amphibian has been improved by the addition of an eye. The brook side beyond is a favourite spot in summer for families with young children out for the day from Sheffield. On a recent visit after many weeks of drought the usually sparkling clear stream had shrunk to a trickle and the pools dammed by the children were little more than liquid mud. Upturned parental faces turned pink in the scorching sun, dogs and children churned the muddy water, a thoroughly good time was being had by all and among several hundred people not one single radio could be heard.

As the hillside steepens, Burbage Brook tumbles over waterfalls into the steep sided ravine below. This is Padley Gorge, one of the Peak District gems where the ancient woodland survives and which despite its popularity retains its charm. It is oak woodland, sessile oak, one of Britain's two native oaks and easily distinguished from the pedunculate oak because the acorns are stalkless. The woods have been coppiced, that is repeatedly cut,and the stumps allowed to grow again. The trees, which provided fuel for the iron and leather industry, were last coppiced in 1870. The gorge has been designated an SSSI and the National Trust, by fencing off the wood from the voracious sheep, is encouraging the natural regeneration of the oak trees.

The Edges are accompanied throughout by the Derwent which rises on Bleaklow to the north. Having fulfilled its duty to the thirsty people of Sheffield by filling the reservoirs of Howden, Derwent and Ladybower, it escapes down past Bamford where it is joined by the River Noe. The river is now broad, slow flowing, sombre and sedate as it meanders south through Hathersage and beneath the gritstone edges.

Walking back beside the Derwent towards Baslow at the end of the day we stopped for a leisurely tea in the fields. On the far bank of the stream half a dozen ducks pottered happily about, up-ending periodically to inspect the river bottom. Then, as we opened our few remaining sandwiches, we were noticed. A flotilla of bright eyed mallards were heading in our direction. They reached the river bank. They climbed out. Green headed drakes and their mottled brown companions waddled purposefully towards us. This was no town park, simply the middle of the countryside, but they knew a sandwich when they saw one. For a few minutes we tossed them crumbs, then as they came even closer Anne offered the boldest a hand held titbit. A quick peck and it was gone and the others crowded round us, but where we had expected to feel the sharp pinch of their beaks, it was with almost a caress that they took the food and the final crumbs were sucked from our hands by beaks that swallowed our outstretched fingers.

ROUTE DESCRIPTION
Green's House

Besom Lane in the centre of Hathersage cuts the corner behind the National Westminster Bank to join Baulk Lane, then in 100 yards a "Dry Weather" footpath leads up to the church. The path through the churchyard passes Little John's Grave, then going through the lych gate turn left to the road bend. Take the footpath to the right and in a few yards turn left down an unsigned path to cross the stream. Keeping to the right of the hedge continue through the fields to join the track, but before Cowclose Farm is reached a footpath forks left passing Brookfield Manor which is now a training centre.

Half hidden in the trees is the medieval castellated tower of the home of the Derbyshire Eyre family, the sixteenth-century North Lees Hall, which

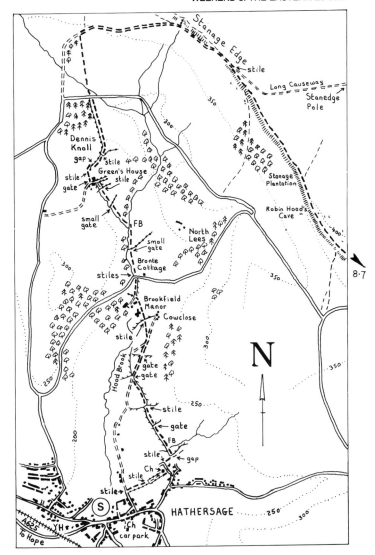

Charlotte Brontë used as the inspiration for Thornfield Hall, Mr Rochester's house in Jane Eyre. "It was three stories high, of proportions not vast, though considerable: a gentleman's manorhouse, not a nobleman's seat: battlements round the top gave it a picturesque look."

Crossing Birley Lane by Brontë Cottage, take the footpath to a little gate on the far side of the field, then go through the trees beside the stream to a footbridge. Climbing through more fields to Green's House, which was once a paper mill, turn left between the buildings and then right through a gate up a grassy track. Narrowing to a path through the bracken, it crosses to the other side of the wall and then a high gritstone step stile leads into another field where attempts are being made to eradicate the bracken. Continuing beside the wall past the plantation at Dennis Knoll, cross the road by a cattle grid, then keeping straight on, a minor path short cuts across the moor passing to the right of another little plantation to join the main track up onto Stanage Edge.

Stanage Edge

The track climbs gently uphill towards the long skyline of cliffs. There is a large abandoned millstone beside this old way which was probably constructed for the transport of these stones. Reaching the top of the edge, leave the Long Causeway which heads off across the open moor to Stanedge Pole and as you follow the edge of the cliffs this ancient guidepost comes into view away to the left.

The moor is at its best in late summer, a sea of purple heather stretching into the distance. In about a mile a temporary fence encloses a small area in order to "improve the vegetation by reducing sheep grazing for a limited period" and it has certainly made a dramatic increase in the proportion of grasses to heather. Below the lip of the cliffs and opposite the enclosure is Robin Hood's Cave, a surprisingly large wind-eroded opening with two entrances and a balcony with a balustrade. The whole area is immensely popular with climbers for there is a choice of over 500 routes. One hot September Sunday we counted 75 cars strung along the verge of the road below, but in spite of this there were few people walking along the path on the top.

The edge climbs gradually to a concrete OS trig point where at the foot of the cliffs lies a group of abandoned millstones. The escarpment beyond peters out and the path goes down across the moor to Upper Burbage Bridge where there is usually a welcome refreshment van.

Higger Tor and Carl Wark

The path follows the valley rim keeping high above Burbage Brook and climbs a newly constructed flight of steps to the isolated rocky knoll of Higger Tor. From the southern end of the rock strewn top the path picks its way down

Stanage Edge

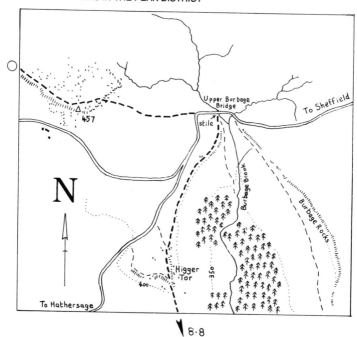

through the jumbled boulders. Ahead is the Iron Age hill fort of Carl Wark with its defensive wall. There is an information plaque round to the right by a gritstone trough. Just before the end of the rocky top turn down a minor path towards the end of the plantation where a little packhorse bridge spans Burbage Brook, then follow the stream to join the main track to the busy A625.

Padley Gorge

Crossing straight over the road enter Longshaw Park and turn right down the grassy track beside the wall to cross the brook at a footbridge. Keep beside the stream, a playground for Sheffield on hot summer afternoons, until you enter the tree covered Padley Gorge. This is one of the few places in the Peak District where the original ancient woodland still survives. The main path stays high above the stream and after about half a mile climbs briefly before finally turning down again, past a waterworks building, to a gate onto a rough track. At the bottom turn left past Padley Mill, Totley Tunnel and the station café for the second time, then go left up the footpath and cross the main road.

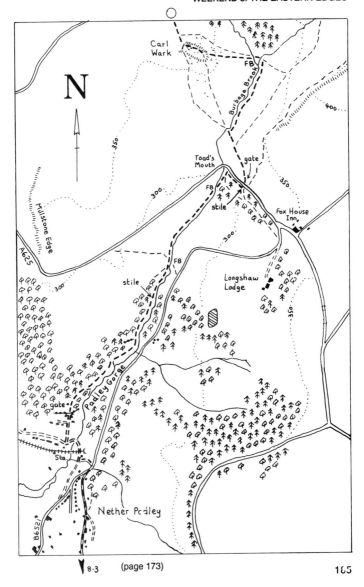

N

Carl Wark

FB

Burbage Brook

400

350

Toad's Mouth

gate

FB

350

stile

Fox House Inn

Millstone Edge

300

300

FB

Longshaw Lodge

A625

300

stile

350

Padley Gorge

gate

Sta.

Nether Padley

B6521

8·3 (page 173)

Grindleford

Follow Tedgness Road to its end, past the villas and the smart new houses, then entering Hay Wood the path climbs a little for the last time before turning right downhill at a junction. At the bottom of the wood turn right on the track and join the main road by St Helen's Church, Grindleford. Opposite is Toll Bar Cottage which has a rounded bay and adjacent is a fine bridge over the River Derwent which has been spoilt by the ugly modern footbridge beside it.

Froggatt

Turning back into the fields on the public footpath to Froggatt, Curbar, Calver, Baslow and Chatsworth, the way crosses the meadows to a wood where in places the old gritstone paving slabs remain. The path then continues through more fields, and beyond another section of the original paving between gritstone walls, it becomes Spooner Lane and enters Froggatt village. Turn right along Hollowgate on a raised walkway then cross Froggatt Bridge and go down the steps to walk beside the wide River Derwent where pink purslane grows beneath the trees.

Calver

After a footbridge over a tributary stream the road is reached at New Bridge, another fine bridge which was built in 1781. Continuing down the track opposite which runs beside the Goit, an old mill race, pass through the fields and campsite by Stocking Farm where the bell turret on the roof shows it was once used as a school. The path passes Calver Mill which was built in 1803 by Arkwright. The former textile mill now makes stainless steel sinks and it was used in the filming of the BBC series Colditz. This part of the village was named after the narrow eighteenth-century Calver Bridge which was bypassed by the main road in 1974.

Crossing over the minor road near the Derbyshire Craft Centre and café, go under the modern road bridge and continue beside the river. Entering the fields over a stream, which drains the disused lead mines above, you can see a few yards to the right below a house the sough tail of Calver Sough mine. This mine ceased working in 1868 and its Cornish beam engine was sold to the Magpie Mine at Sheldon.

Bubnell

The path crosses the fields with the cliffs of the gritstone edges on the skyline. Joining Bubnell Lane a walk of ¾ mile down this quiet road past the grand Bubnell Hall with its well manicured lawns brings you to the three arched stone bridge. Built in 1603 to replace an earlier wooden one, it has a tiny watchman's house just big enough for one person at the far end. This was the original settlement of Bridge End and is the oldest part of Baslow. The main road leads past the church, with its unusual clock face, to the roundabout, then continues round to the left gently uphill to the start of the walk at Nether End.

Baslow

The three settlements of Bridge End, Nether End and Over End which make up the village of Baslow have changed little since the middle of the nineteenth century when Croston describes "a pretty little rural village, consisting of a few irregular groups of cottages standing on the slope of a hill that rises from the eastern bank of the Derwent". Bridge End was the original village, but Nether End grew with Chatsworth when in 1823 it became the northern entrance to the estate, while residential development in the later nineteenth century is centred at Over End on the hillside above.

At one time Baslow had hoped to be as grand as nearby Bakewell and a Hydro was built in 1881 but it never became established as a spa. As the building needed a great deal of money spending on it after the First World War and this was never done, the Hydro was demolished in the 1930s.

Dr Wrench, born in 1833 and for 50 years the local doctor, was Baslow's most famous son. Something of a philanthropist he took a great interest in the welfare of the local people and forsaw that one day a National Health Service would be established. He was also given to making speeches at appropriate moments and never missed an opportunity for creating suitable memorials. His monument to the Iron Duke is a prominent landmark and was erected in 1866 after Wellington had been to stay with the Duke of Rutland who owned these moors. It was probably inspired as a companion to Nelson's Monument which had stood on the opposite hillside for around 50 years.

To celebrate Queen Victoria's Golden Jubilee, Dr Wrench had an inscription carved on the Elephant Stone in Chatsworth Park and this was unveiled on Jubilee Day 1887 with a ceremony at which all the local children were present. He was also responsible for the Jubilee clock on St Anne's Parish Church which instead of numerals has VICTORIA1897 on the face.

Baslow has not forgotten Dr Wrench and his own memorial is a stained glass window in the church.

187

WEEKEND 9: THE ROACHES AND SHUTLINGSLOE

DAY 1:	Buxton to Gradbach 12½ miles (Short Route 6½ miles)
STARTING POINT:	(048720) Grin Low car park, 2 miles south-west of Buxton. If starting from Buxton the route can be joined at Burbage
DAY 2:	Gradbach to Buxton 11½ miles (Short Route 8½ miles)
STARTING POINT:	(993660) Gradbach Youth Hostel, 2 miles south of Wildboarclough.
ROUTE SUMMARY:	Wild moors, a hidden watersmeet and the dramatic rock scenery of the Roaches bring you to the tiny hamlet of Gradbach. The following day climbs Shutlingsloe, passes the second highest inn in England then follows an old turnpike. Fairly energetic walking on good paths.

DAY 1: BUXTON TO GRADBACH

As the sun sinks across the Cheshire Plain the Roaches are thrown into sharp relief, a long line of gaunt black buttresses against the evening sky. In the distance is the scarp silhouette of Bosley Cloud, on the skyline the sentinel finger of a tower marks Croker Hill, while far below is the silver gleam of Tittesworth Reservoir. The heather, bilberry and gritstone remind one of the quiet beauty of the Eastern Moors, yet so close to the road are the Roaches that every evening in summer the rocks are alive with climbers enjoying some of the longest routes in the Peak District.

Almost at the highest point is Doxey Pool whose dark waters are set amid heather fringed with peat and silver sand. Little waves lap and break on the shore while in winter it freezes to a solid block of ice. The pool is named after the beautiful daughter of Bess Bowyer who was herself the daughter of a highwayman and lived at Rock Hall, the gritstone house built against the rocks of the lower tier. The girl, it is reported, was carried off by "strange men" of whom there have been many apart from the climbers. Rock Hall until

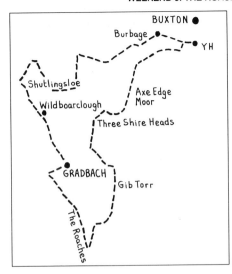

recently was inhabited as a private house. Deluded into thinking the Roaches a quiet place, which it can be in mid-week, Doug Moller, self-styled Lord of the Roaches, led a reclusive existence here for eleven years with his wife Anne, Rock Hall cottage is now the Don Whillans Memorial Hut for climbers.

While modern rock gymnasts tiptoe up smooth slabs at the absolute limit of achievable friction, or jam and bridge up impossibly overhanging rock, others are content with climbs first ascended before the First World War. When you read the name Stanley Jeffcoat on the memorial plaque on the summit of Great Gable in the Lake District, it is the same who gave his name to Jeffcoat's Chimney, one of the most delightful of the Roaches' easy climbs. But some of these early climbs are far from easy. Bachelor's Buttress with its very delicate step about 40 feet above the ground is entirely unprotected and a mistake would be fatal. It was misnamed, said Morley Wood in 1921, as married men were more used to taking risks than bachelors.

The Roaches ridge reaches its highest point of 1658ft towards the northern end. Though not very high, it feels a worthy objective and is an excellent viewpoint especially on one of the cold clear days in winter. We were once persuaded by our local orienteering club to help with mapping the area. The contours had already been drawn and all we had to do was to plot accurately the position of the boulders. A simple enough task, but not only did all the boulders look alike, they also moved about. Again and again we would sight along the compass only to find that this contradicted some previous measurement. In the end the chief mapper left most of them off, he said they were too small to bother about anyway.

To the north the ridge drops to Roach End and then continues undulating gently along towards Macclesfield Forest in the distance, with closer at hand the trees of Back Forest fringing the River Dane. Back Forest conceals

189

another of the Roaches surprises in Lud's Church. At one time this was quite hard to find, its entrance concealed by a block of gritstone fallen across a narrow gap in the rocks. There were no signposts then, the trees grew thick about and it was easy to imagine Squire Trafford at full gallop coming to the chasm, and unable to stop, spurring his horse to leap. Some of the mystery has gone, the fallen block has been removed, signposts have been erected and then, because so many people can now find it, a well meaning group has slashed down the lovely silver birch trees in an attempt to channel walkers onto approved routes. It is still well worth a visit though, down narrow steps into the shadowed chasm whose vertical walls drip with moss and ferns. Named after Walter de Ludauk it was a fourteenth-century refuge for the Lollards who worshipped here. It is also thought to be the site of the legendary Green Chapel in the early medieval poem of Sir Gawain and the Green Knight.

The great rift of Lud's Church was caused, long before man roamed the valley, by the entire hillside slipping down towards the River Dane, one of the most attractive of the Peak District's rivers. The Dane like the Dove, rises on Axe Edge Moor where coal pits, still in use in 1926 have now disappeared beneath the heather. Rapidly growing as it gathers the waters of the moor the river flows down past disused gritstone quarries until it arrives at Three Shire Heads with its lovely old packhorse bridge. Here packhorse trains rested beside Panniers Pool at the junction of the three counties of Staffordshire, Cheshire and Derbyshire. This was also a route of escape for the eighteenth-century entrepreneurs of Flash who were able to move from the jurisdiction of one county to another after long winter evenings spent counterfeiting coins, hence the term "Flash Money".

The Dane which began the day also brings it to an end. As you descend from Lud's Church through the pine trees, larch and silver birch the river is met again where it joins Black Brook and you walk the final few yards beside it to the youth hostel at Gradbach Mill.

ROUTE DESCRIPTION
Axe Edge Moor

From Grin Low car park follow the tarmac road over the brow of the hill. A little way downhill a stile to the right leads into a plantation, then joining a track you turn left out to the road junction. Keeping straight on along Leek Road a farm track here is all that remains of the Cromford and High Peak Railway which opened in 1831. A public footpath goes right into the field and climbs past an underground reservoir to a field gate. Passing below Terret Plantation an old road is joined and this is followed to meet the busy Macclesfield Road.

A ¼ mile up the road, most of which can be avoided by a path on the far side, a track strikes off left across Axe Edge Moor at a gate. The highest point

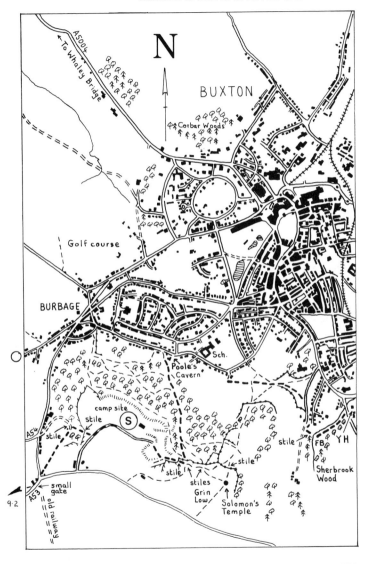

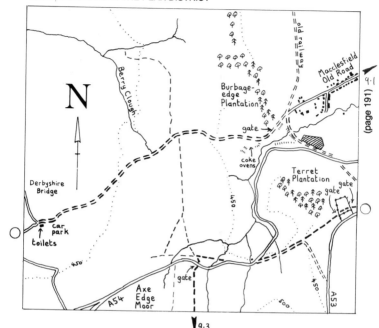

(page 191)

of the moor is the Ordnance Survey trig point on the skyline to the left where the first Ordnance Sappers "Saw from hence the signals exhibited on Lincoln Cathedral and the top of Snowdon at the same time, though the distance between is more than 150 miles". After passing a fenced air shaft a faint path goes left to the site of the old Axe Edge Colliery, the earliest workings on these moors, but staying on the main track continue past spoil heaps to the road at Dane Head.

Three Shire Heads

Kinking right along the unfenced road, pick up the continuation of the path across Cheeks Hill. Crossing the infant River Dane, which has a 22mile journey before it joins the River Weaver at Northwich, the path continues to the wall corner and the county boundary. A stile leads from Derbyshire into Staffordshire and the grassy path then goes downhill to join a main track. This was made when the numerous coalmine shafts alongside were capped with concrete.

The track follows the stream in its steep sided clough to join the track from Orchard Farm, then when it becomes tarmac, fork right staying in the
192

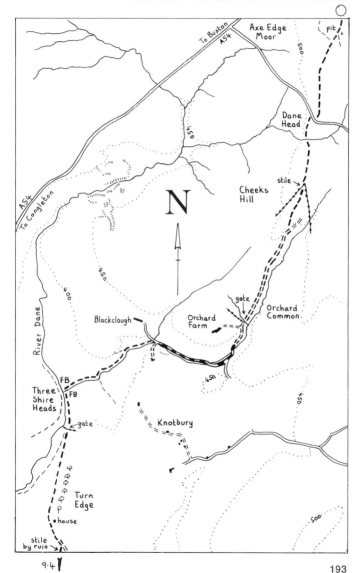

Three Shire Heads

clough on the gated road. At the crossroads where the metalled surface climbs to Blackclough Farm, keep by the stream and continue down past a little packhorse bridge to Three Shire Heads. Four packhorse ways met here so it must at one time have been a busy place. All good guidebooks tell you to look under the old bridge to see where it has been widened to accommodate an increase in traffic or perhaps to carry carts. It is a pretty little spot, the steep hillsides are covered in bracken and a few trees stand near the watersmeet.

Staying on this side of the river cross the smaller bridge and follow the sandy track along the hillside high above the river. Far below is a deep pool beneath a waterfall. At the gate keep to the higher path under Turn Edge then, just after the track is joined by the drive from the house above, turn right through a gateway. The path goes round below a ruined house to a stile in the far corner of the field. Follow the wall down into the next field and across to a high ladder stile. Turning left along the grassy track, dip into the valley to where a footbridge spans the stream and climb up the other side past a barn to the road.

Short Cut to Gradbach

In bad weather the road can be followed down to the right, turning right again at the next junction. The road leads along the valley bottom past a small bridge then a track forks left beside the stream to Gradbach Mill Youth Hostel.

194

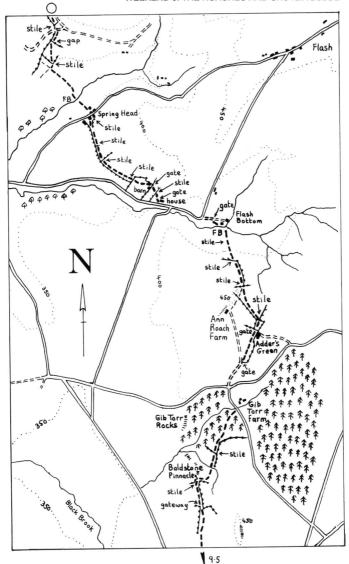

Flash Bottom

Crossing over the road take the path round the left of Spring Head Farm. The waymarked route contours round the hill through the fields to a barn where a signpost points the way over a stile to a farm gate, but the house beyond is hidden till the last moment as it is tucked in under a little rocky cliff. Turn left up the hill along the road then keep straight on at the bend down the track to Flash Bottom.

Fork right to the stream which is crossed at Flash Brook Farm. The old way climbs following the wall and looking back Flash is seen on the opposite hillside. At 1518ft this is the highest village in Britain. Cresting the rise fork left in the next field to a stile by the gates in the corner. Ahead you can now see on the skyline a sharp scarp slope rising above the forest and a lower ridge of jagged rocks, the Baldstones. The path goes to the right of Adder's Green Farm then joins the track from Ann Roach Farm which is followed out to the road near the striking rocky outcrop of Gib Torr.

Baldstones

Continue straight on down the road opposite and turn right immediately after the stream by Gib Torr Farm. A grassy path leads up through the plantation and out onto the moor, crossing the ridge to the left of Baldstone Pinnacle. Following the ridge along on the far side of the wall you look across the valley of Black Brook to a high heather moor which is the back of the Roaches. After crossing a stile by a gate, pass under the rocky buttress of Newstones to Corner House and go down the lane opposite, past Hazel Barrow Fish Farm.

The Roaches

Fork right at the next junction by a humpy field with traces of old bell pits where thin seams of coal were mined. The road goes across heathery moorland then after $1/2$ mile of tarmac turn left up the farm track with the strikingly serrated ridge of Ramshaw Rocks to the left. The track forks right at a stile by a farm gate to enter the Roaches Estate, then when it bends left to Summerhill Farm, keep straight on over a stile and continue through the heather. After passing below a ruined cottage the old way, which dates from at least the middle of the eighteenth century, passes between Hen Cloud and the end of the Roaches and Tittesworth Reservoir appears ahead.

Leave the track turning right to pass in front of Rock Hall cottage. Derelict for three years after the Mollers were rehoused at Knotbury End in 1989, the cottage has now been converted to a hut in memory of the late Don Whillans. A flight of steps leads up beside Raven Rock to the upper tier of cliffs. To the left on the very edge of the drop is a stone seat carved to commemorate the visit of the Prince and Princess of Tek in 1872. The Princess was Queen Mary's mother. The path passes along the terrace under the high cliffs and

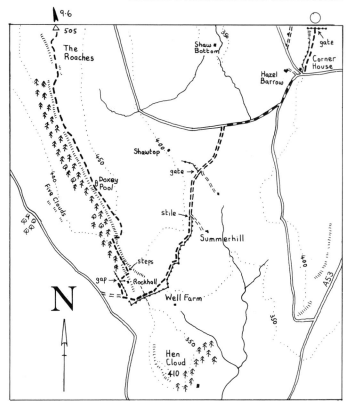

then turns up to gain the ridge. Turning left follow the edge along above the pine trees and at almost the top of the ridge you come to Doxey Pool. The wavy rim of the shelf far below marks the top of the Five Clouds, a long rock face which is divided into five sections by gullies.

It is another ½ mile to the highest point where just before the final ascent two rocking stones can be found balanced near the edge. An Ordnance Survey trig column stands on the summit which is a good viewpoint with a far skyline of hills. Eastwards is Gib Torr and the moorlands beyond Morridge, to the south gleams Tittesworth Reservoir, to the north-west is the steep asymmetrical cone of Shutlingsloe while across the Cheshire Plain rises the scarp slope of Bosley Cloud which we can see from our bedroom window.

The Roaches

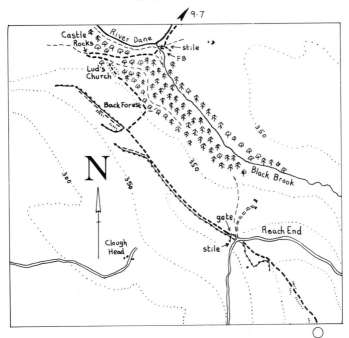

Lud's Church

The path then descends by more weirdly shaped boulders for another ½ mile to Roach End. Crossing the road continue along the ridge by the stone wall which was rebuilt by Len Page in 1991. After ¾ mile and just before a stile, turn right down a concession path. This descends to a wood where you turn left to reach the top end of Lud's Church. The path goes through the ravine which is a deep natural cleft and not a collapsed cave, though it is marked as one on the OS map.

Turn left for 300 yards to Castle Cliff Rocks, also the result of a landslip, then hairpin back downhill through the trees. At the bottom, go down to the confluence of Black Brook and the River Dane and cross the footbridge which replaces the former Casters Bridge, named after a nearby forge. Climbing a little to a stile, the path by the river is then followed to Gradbach Mill Youth Hostel.

Gradbach

It is difficult to imagine as you walk through Gradbach that this was once a

199

busy industrial centre. The large youth hostel was a silk mill employing 200 people and the narrow track leading up the hillside a major packhorse route. A school and many cottages were built principally for the mill workers but apart from the 1849 Methodist Chapel which still stands a little further up the valley, all have vanished without trace.

Gradbach Mill was first built in 1640, but was restored after a fire in 1785. The two storied gritstone building is supported by internal cast-iron columns and until the 1950s the remains of the 38ft diameter waterwheel could be seen at the end of the mill where the entrance now is. The mill was first used for flax spinning, but in the eighteenth century it changed to silk production, which in turn gave way to carpet manufacture around 1871 and the building finished its working life as a saw mill. In later years watercress was cultivated in beds upstream from the mill for sale at Macclesfield market. The farm above the hostel belongs to the Buxton and District Scouts and the surrounding fields are often full of their tents.

The house opposite the hostel belonged to the mill owner and the extension housed a doctors' surgery and more recently a tea room where walkers sat round one huge table and queued outside for the earth closet. Electricity was late coming to Gradbach. For many years the houses were lit by gas but in the 1960s television as well as electric light came to remote farms and cottages. Though outside lavatories are now a thing of the past, mains water has still got no nearer than Flash and the hostel and the surrounding farms have their own reliable wells or springs.

DAY 2: GRADBACH TO BUXTON

The old packhorse way to Wildboarclough climbs steeply from the valley of the River Dane past stone troughs where the horses rested, on by the Eagle and Child, then as you reach the moorland top, ahead appears Shutlingsloe. Reaching the summit at the end of a summer's day, the long shadows of the mountain cast an evening shade over Wildboarclough, the orange glow of the sun catches the moorland beyond, the Roaches appear in black outline and the sun sinks beyond the sentinel tower on Croker Hill.

Although by mountain standards Shutlingsloe at 1659ft is not very high, its distinctive outline rising above Macclesfield Forest and the surrounding lower hills is one which catches the imagination. Really little more than the high point of a ridge which half encircles the forest below, the view end on gives the peak far greater appeal than many a hill of much higher status in terms of altitude while its side view, a flat topped profile, is instantly recognisable from afar.

Long before there was a right of way to the top, pilgrims had trodden a path. Although it was private and the landowner vainly attempted to exclude walkers from the peak, this was a losing battle for Shutlingsloe is a summit that has to be climbed. Eventually the right was won and you can now stand beside the trig point with full legal approval.

The summit is not only a magnet for ramblers for in Alan Garner's *The Weirdstone of Brisingamen* here was the final battle with the dark forces that sought the stone. "They came above the forest on to a bleak shelf of moorland; and out of the far side of the plateau, half a mile distant, the last two hundred feet of Shutlingslow reared black against the paling night." As the witches and warlocks were disguised as hikers there is always a slight unease as you gain the flat summit to find another figure there and some doubt as to the purpose of their visit!

At the foot of the eastern slopes is the hamlet of Wildboarclough which though once an industrial centre with three mills, is now a quiet backwater. The first of the mills was built in the mid-eighteenth century and James Brindley, an unknown at the time who went on to become a famous engineer, worked here on the construction of machinery which was modelled on a mill in Manchester. Brindley, who could not read, walked to Manchester one Sunday, memorised the details and then walked back. The mills which employed 600 workers were originally silk mills and later carpet mills, but in 1958 they were demolished leaving only the imposing administrative block which until 1979 was the largest sub-post office in the country.

On May 24th 1989 a torrential rainstorm was concentrated upon the valley with several weeks' rain falling in as many hours. The stream swollen to a river was suddenly blocked by a landslide and a wall of water, now out of control, tore through the valley smashing down walls and bridges and further down the road thundered by the cottages level with the bedroom windows. For days all roads into the valley were closed, then the rebuilding began and today the only signs of the disaster are the clean new walls which contrast strangely with the crumbling boundaries on adjacent hillsides.

Between Wildboarclough, tucked in its sheltered valley, and Buxton, rise the moors of Danethorn Hollow and Danebower Hollow. The streams which drain these upland valleys flow east to join the infant River Dane, while on the opposite slopes of the moor facing Shutlingsloe is Cumberland Brook whose waters also join the Dane, but flow west to Folly Mill. Crossing the moor, roads from Congleton and Macclesfield join on these windswept heights before descending to Buxton and here at the wildest and remotest spot stands the Cat and Fiddle Inn, 31ft higher than the summit of Shutlingsloe itself and the second highest inn in England. In summer this popular hostelry is surrounded by cars, high heels, leather jackets and motor bikes, but when winter winds drive the snow across the moors the inn is a place of refuge for stranded motorists.

One weekend after a night of heavy snow and when the snowplough had just cleared a narrow path, two friends drove up to the moors for a day on their cross country skis. After five hours energetic exercise they returned, tired and happy to find a problem. The snow had drifted, it was getting dark and their car was irretrievably stuck, so again strapping on their skis they skied down through the forest and into Macclesfield where they caught a train home!

The busy A537 which passes in front of the inn, follows the line of the new turnpike opened in 1821, but the first road across the moors from Macclesfield was built just over half a century earlier. This passed behind the Cat and Fiddle, before the small building which was to be the inn appeared on the moors, and then descended into the Goyt Valley at Derbyshire Bridge. The early route is however a more scenic one and while the first part is metalled, it is the rough surface of this old turnpike which you follow as you climb for the last time out of the Goyt Valley before descending to day's end at Burbage on the outskirts of Buxton.

ROUTE DESCRIPTION
Wildboarclough

Crossing the modern footbridge beside Gradbach Mill Youth Hostel take the narrow packhorse way which climbs steeply up the hillside bending left at a fourfold horse trough. The path bypasses Goosetree Farm staying in the very stony field to join the track above. Cross straight over the road and up the old way opposite, past the eighteenth-century Eagle and Child. This former inn belonged to Lord Derby and the arms of the Stanley's can still be seen over the front door. Since the 1920s it has been owned by the Kirkham family whose afternoon teas were famed for miles around till EEC regulations forced them to close in 1991.

The old road climbs gradually over the fields for ¾ mile then passes above Heild End Farm with a fine view of Shutlingsloe ahead. Briefly joining the farm track, leave it at the hairpin bend and descend to a stile to cross the A54. Continue over the fields past a large gritstone barn and then round the end of the plantation. After a step stile an old walled track goes downhill by the side of a wood and you look down upon the Crag Inn, which shelters in the valley bottom beneath the slopes of Shutlingsloe.

Entering a field the path forks left joining another old trackway to a stile and then goes down the edge of the wood. Cross the new footbridge where Clough Brook flows through a narrow rocky ravine and join the road in Wildboarclough by the Crag Inn. Turning right for only a yard or two fork left uphill on the tarmac lane. Across the brook is the site of Crag Mills and as you climb you can see the former agent's house and the administrative block through the trees in the valley below. Above them the stately Crag Hall, which belongs to Lord Derby, soon comes into view. Reaching the gate the weather will probably be the deciding factor for the route choice.

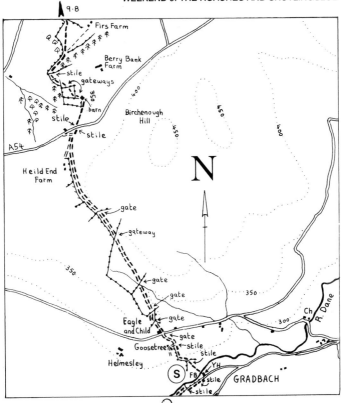

Short Cut to Cumberland Clough

If you are omitting the summit of Shutlingsloe the way continues along the hillside to Banktop Cottage then after a gritstone barn descends gently above a larch plantation to an immensely tall stile onto the road. Cross the new footbridge and the field to a gate in the corner. Go through the yard of Clough House Farm and out to the lane at the foot of Cumberland Clough.

Shutlingsloe

To visit Shutlingsloe continue along the tarmac road and follow it up the hill, then turn left beside the wall on the waymarked footpath. The path heads up the grassy hill slope through a couple of stiles, climbing steeply to a rocky

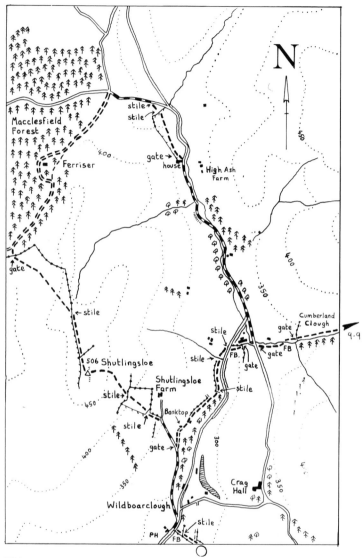

finish on the summit. The flat grassy top with its OS trig point feels higher than its 1659ft. There is a fine view and a topograph beside some ancient graffiti.

Each year around 2700 walkers visit the top and in 1992 with the help of a helicopter which lifted gritstone slabs, the muddy footpath was repaired. Follow the path down to a stile and then keep beside the wall. Another stile leads to a board walk over the moor and the path then descends to the edge of Macclesfield Forest. Joining the forest track turn right to follow it through the forest for nearly a mile past the ruined buildings of Ferriser. At the crossroads on the top of the hill turn right and follow the road downhill then near the bottom a path cuts across the fields to rejoin the road by a farm. Turn right, then after ³/₄ mile fork left along the narrow road just before Clough House and the car park.

Cumberland Cottage

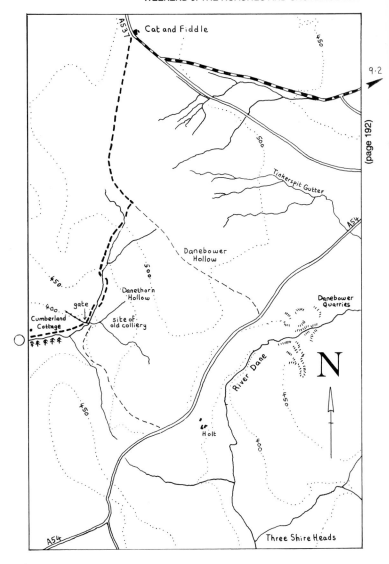

9·2

(page 192)

Cumberland Clough

The track through the field gate opposite the farm is the public footpath to the Cat and Fiddle Inn, our next destination. It follows Cumberland Brook and crossing a footbridge continues beside the stream. Pass below Cumberland Cottage which is now a scout hut and then turn left at the T-junction by the waterfall where above on the moor only faint traces remain of the once busy Dane Thorn Colliery.

The path follows the stream up Danethorn Hollow hopping from side to side and continues up onto the bleak open moorland. Turn left at the bridleway to the Cat and Fiddle Inn which, though it is nearly a mile away, soon appears ahead. The inn was built early in the nineteenth century but no one really knows where the name came from and various theories have been proposed. It may have come from the game "cat", or from Catherine le Fidèle, wife of Tsar Peter the Great, or even from the Duke of Devonshire who is supposed to have practised his fiddle here. Maybe John Ryle, the Macclesfield banker who built it, just liked the name.

Macclesfield Old Road

Turn right along the main road for a few yards and then take the minor road to the left. This follows the line of the old turnpike from Macclesfield to Buxton which was built in 1759 and passed behind the Cat and Fiddle. The old road descends 300ft to Derbyshire Bridge car park where the tarmac bends away down the Goyt Valley.

Keeping straight on past the toilet block and an interesting information board, the rough-surfaced track climbs across the moors with more evidence of coal workings on either hand. Rising to 1559ft in ³/₄ mile, there is an old milestone just before the highest point. Macclesfield Old Road then descends gently towards Buxton.

Before the gate by Burbage-edge Plantation an old tramway leads back towards the stream. Detour a short way along this to see the remains of the former Goyt Colliery which was worked until around 1890. A stripe of coal down the hillside with the remnants of wooden supports marks the position of the incline, two well preserved beehive coke ovens are set into the hillside and a section of the original gritstone plateway can be seen. The tramway led to the entrance of the 1812 Goyt Tunnel of which all traces have disappeared and in the valley below you can make out the route of a siding of the Cromford and High Peak Railway.

Continuing down the old Coach Road cross the disused railway line and follow the road down into Burbage. Halfway down the hill you pass Level Lane which led to the dock at the end of the earlier 1770s Duke's Level. The coal was shipped out of the tunnel in boats though there is little to see now save a coal tip. The road is now metalled and soon arrives in the centre of

John Nuttall

Cat and Fiddle

Burbage by the church where you cross the main road and follow Green Lane to Poole's Cavern.

For Buxton Youth Hostel

Continue along Green Lane to the bend beyond Buxton Community School and take the path through the fields. Meeting Fern Road turn right past the houses then go left to a stile into Sherbrook Wood. After crossing a footbridge keep left along the main path near the stream to the road and the youth hostel.

For Grin Low

From Poole's Cavern take the public footpath on the far side of the car park which climbs through Grin Low Woods. Keep to the main path which emerges onto the open hillside below Solomon's Temple which was built by Solomon Mycock in 1895 to provide labour for unemployed men. The flowers on Grin Low are as fine as anywhere in the Peak District and the grass of Parnassus, the autumn gentian and the tall purple spears of the fragrant orchid can all be found here in abundance. Turning right along the top of the wood the path leads down through a little cutting to the car park in the reclaimed quarry.

Burbage

Excluded from the National Park because of the large limestone quarries nearby, modern Burbage is now merely a suburb of Buxton. Among the regimented rows of houses there is no hint of its unorthodox past reported by Croston.

"The scene here is wild and barren in the extreme, and the effect is rendered more striking by the clouds of smoke which issue from the adjoining kilns and roll in heavy masses about the shattered cliffs and misshapen fragments that lie scattered about. There is not a vestage of green to be seen upon the parched surface, vegetation being entirely precluded by the sulphureous fumes which arise from the smelting furnaces. Havoc and destruction are everywhere apparent, the bowels of the mountain seem literally torn out and the rocky ruin spread before the eye excites in the mind the idea of nature returned again to universal chaos."

Above the houses rises Grinlow whose summit once bore an ancient burial mound. In the eighteenth century this hill was the site of a large number of lime kilns and the spoil from these was hollowed out to form caves in which people lived. However by 1876 things had changed.

"These wretched hovels have been destroyed, and in their stead a number of neat and comfortable dwellings have been erected at Burbage, a hamlet close by, for the poor lime-burners who fomerly located here. A pretty little church in the Norman style has been erected, the seats of which are entirely free, schools have also been established, and every care seems to be taken to improve the condition of the poor and scattered population."

This village with its 1860 church is what we see today and the wooded slopes of Grinlow are now topped by the conspicuous landmark of Solomon's Temple. The "sulphurous quarry" vividly described by Croston was reclaimed by Derbyshire County Council in 1980 and Grin Quarry has been transformed to a place of beauty, a natural rock garden with a wealth of wild flowers. It now encloses a campsite and picnic area adjacent to Buxton Country Park.

WEEKEND 10: THE GOYT VALLEY

DAY 1:
STARTING POINT:

Whaley Bridge to Buxton 10½ miles (011815) Whaley Bridge Railway Station

DAY 2:
STARTING POINT:

Buxton to Whaley Bridge 10 miles (045728) Burbage, 1 mile south-west of Buxton

ROUTE SUMMARY:

Following the Goyt Valley past Errwood Hall the moors are crossed to reach the fringe of Buxton. The return follows an old packhorse trail back into the valley before climbing to the ridge of Shining Tor. Easy walking with a couple of steep climbs each day.

DAY 1: WHALEY BRIDGE TO BUXTON

In spring as you walk up the long drive towards Errwood Hall through woods

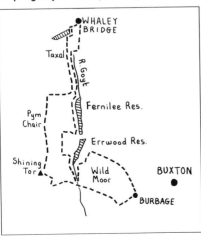

bright with rhododendrons and the air filled with the heavy scent of yellow azaleas, it is easy for a moment to imagine yourself back in the nineteenth century. Beside the path a little stream splashes down towards the River Goyt, the trees cast a cool shade and a blackbird rustles through the dried leaves. Then the trees open out, you turn the corner and there across the grass which was once a lawn, are the three arched windows, all that remains standing of the once lovely hall. The Grimshawes are long gone, the valley has changed, but in quiet moments their ghosts live on.

The River Goyt rises on Axe Edge Moor above Buxton and flows north to join the Mersey at Stockport whose water board have appropriated the valley and its water for their own. Fernilee Reservoir came first in 1938, and the worry of it hastened the end of the Samuel Grimshawe's granddaughter who lived at Errwood Hall. The hall, which was later demolished, was a family home built by the industrialist Samuel Grimshawe as a wedding present for his son in 1830. There was a village community centred around the 300 year old Goyt Bridge, a single arch packhorse bridge that spanned the stream, with cottages, a private school, a watermill, and even a small coal mine which supplied local needs.

But Stockport was not finished with the Goyt. Another reservoir was needed and despite protests, plans were made for a dam higher up the valley. Soon the bulldozers moved in. Rowan trees, whose scarlet berries every year heralded the autumn, lay uprooted and smashed amid a churned up sea of mud. The sparkling stream was now a sluggish brown liquid, a column of blue smoke rose from a pile of brushwood and as for the packhorse bridge, every last stone had gone.

The excavators dug deeper. The foundations of the dam were laid and reinforced deep into the rock. A huge concrete lined shaft appeared and from its mouth great subterranean rumblings could be heard. Beside it a tunnel led into the hillside, deserted but for a line of lights leading into the unknown.

The year passed, the rains came and gradually the barren mud waste slipped from view beneath the growing expanse of the lake that began to fill the valley. On the hillside the bracken again glowed orange in the colours of autumn, the pine woods too were as before and the infant River Goyt still ran beneath the rocks and over gritstone slabs through the unspoilt upper valley. The drive to Errwood Hall, now crossed by a concrete bridge, lay beneath the water, but the ruins looked out still on the thousands of rhododendrons and azaleas and high on the moor, in recompense for their transformation of the valley, the water board had repaired and re-roofed the little shrine built to commemorate Miss Dolores, the much loved Spanish companion of the old Mrs Grimshawe. The valley will never be the same, but it is far from ruined and watching the boats that tack to and fro across the water it is difficult to remember how once it was, while beneath Goytsclough Quarry the packhorse bridge we thought gone forever has been rebuilt, its reassembled stones once again across the River Goyt.

As the valley is left behind and you climb the flanks of Wild Moor you come to a well made track carefully fitted to the slope. The closed off tunnel mouth into which it disappears reveals the purpose of the track, but not its age. One of the earliest railways in the country, it was constructed when Samuel Grimshawe on the other side of the valley was building his mansion

Goyt Bridge

and when canals were the usual mode of long distance transport. The line, which carried passengers from 1855 to 1877, was tunnelled under Burbage Edge and after descending to the side of the reservoir, it continued to Whaley Bridge. The old Bunsall Incline is now the steep straight road down into the valley by Errwood Dam. Although the Cromford and High Peak railway eventually closed in 1967, the Goyt Valley section was abandoned in June 1892 when more powerful engines allowed a new route into Buxton to bypass the inclines. With its floor littered with fallen bricks the walk through the 580 yards tunnel in total blackness was an exciting adventure.

213

Winter brings a new magic to the valley. After the snowploughs have cleared the way to the Cat and Fiddle, cars with skis strapped to their roofs slither across the moor above and on a sunny day it feels like Switzerland. It's cross country ski terrain, but the slopes of Errwood Dam provide a good short run downhill with the added hazard of an ice covered reservoir if you can't stop.

Because of the valley's close proximity to Stockport and Manchester it can be busy at summer weekends, tame sheep beg for food in the car parks, a one way traffic scheme operates and some of the roads are closed to cars. But for walkers this doesn't matter, you are soon away from the crowds. Up on the tops, on the moors, there is still peace and seclusion to be found and the only people you will meet are other walkers.

ROUTE DESCRIPTION
Cromford and High Peak Railway

From Whaley Bridge railway station take the main road towards Buxton. Passing under the 1864 cast-iron railway bridge, turn left up the footpath just after the Cock Inn to join the disused track of the Cromford and High Peak Railway. The line ran under the higher and more recent Midland Railway and this section, like its eastern end, was made into a footpath after the railway closed.

After going through a tunnel fork right by a plaque inscribed "Cromford and High Peak Railway Co" set above a piece of the original fish bellied rail. Pass in front of the new houses to a Scout hut where a path leads uphill following an old colliery incline over a footbridge and up a field. Keep right through a children's playground which has been made on the site of Brickbarn Pit. This big colliery joined up underground with the Shallcross Colliery and mined a thick seam of "Kiln Coal" which was used mainly for lime burning. A few of the earliest houses here were built for the miners but the rest of the estate was constructed in 1920 after the pit had closed.

River Goyt

Mevril Road goes down to the A5002 (now the A5004), then, crossing over the busy road follow the track opposite. Passing a footbridge where the old saltway from Sheffield forded the Goyt on its way to Macclesfield, the path bends left uphill to a stile, then continues above the river. The muddy way leads through the beautiful Shallcross Wood and then entering the fields follows the river to a footbridge by Hillbridge Wood Nature Reserve. Fifty different species of birds have been seen here and in the spring the wood is full of bluebells and wood anemones.

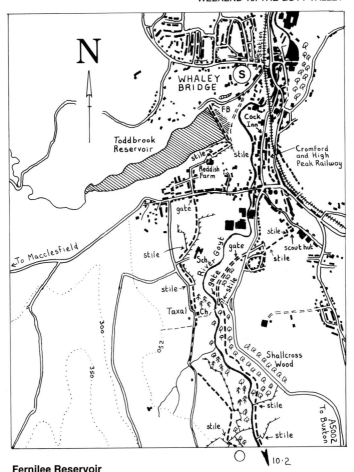

Fernilee Reservoir

Crossing a second bridge the path climbs the hillside and then passes to the left of Knipe Farm on a footpath diversion, going out to a track which leads to Fernilee Reservoir.

From the dam follow the road uphill then in 100 yards go over a stile and take the path through the Forestry Commission woods above the reservoir. After ½ mile of nearly level walking the path rises a little and crosses Deep

10.3

Clough by a footbridge. Continuing through the wood the path descends through tall trees to the water's edge. Just before a gate and stile is reached slant back up the hillside through the trees and then follow the perimeter of the forest up to join the road by a forest track.

Errwood Hall

"The Street", an old Roman road, leads uphill towards the high ridge which is tomorrow's route back to Whaley Bridge. Two hundred and fifty yards past the top of the forest take the path left down a wooded valley. In a short way

Errwood Shrine

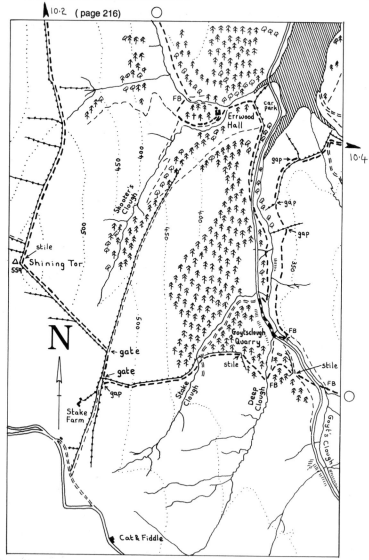

10·2 (page 216)

10·4

N

you pass a flight of steps down to the tiny shrine of St Joseph which was built in 1889 to the memory of the much loved Miss Dolores, a Spanish aristocrat who ran the local school and was the companion of Mrs Grimshawe. Passing the tumbled stones of ruined cottages, the path continues along the hill slope before descending to the valley through the rhododendrons, over 40,000 of

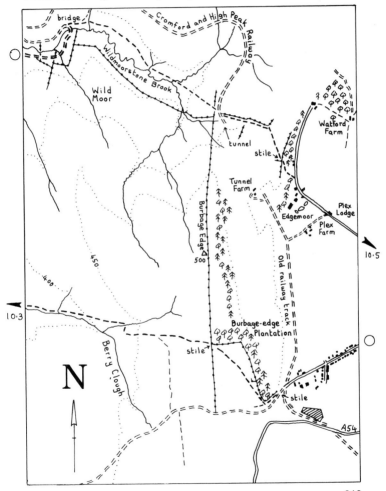

which were brought back by the Grimshawes in their ocean going yacht.

Crossing a footbridge follow the path round a little hill past low walls which are all that remain of the estate cottages. A detour may be made to the top of the hill to visit the private burial ground where members of the Grimshawe family and some of their servants are buried, including the captain of their yacht, Mariquita. Following the track downstream, fork left between a pair of old gate pillars to visit the ruined Errwood Hall.

Goytsclough

The drive in front of the house leads back to the stream. Follow it down and then round to the right above a wall. Crossing the road the old driveway continues beside the River Goyt upstream to a flight of steps where you join the road at Pickfords old gritstone quarry.

Beyond Goytsclough Quarry descend to the river to cross the reconstructed packhorse bridge, then double back on the other side. After crossing the odd boggy section the path swings away round the end of the reservoir following a wall to join a track and this leads down to a girder bridge.

Wild Moor

Turning right, fork right again in a few yards to follow the clough upstream into the lovely empty valley of Wildmoorstone Brook. Keeping near the stream the path crosses a side clough and climbs to the Cromford and High Peak Railway by the entrance to the Burbage Tunnel which was not bricked up until the 1960s. Continue climbing beside the wall and over the ridge where the path leads down to the right of the wood to a ladder stile. The little tower you can see ahead standing above the houses of Burbage is Solomon's Temple.

Slant down across the hillside to the field corner. In summer the slope is scented by the dainty white flowers of the heath bedstraw and coloured by the four petalled tormentil. Follow the road down past Edgemoor, a large private house. Bishop's Lane is long and straight and leads by a golf course to the limestone walled fields of Burbage. Crossing a small brown stream it is difficult to realise this is the infant River Wye, which is usually stained a rusty colour by iron bearing strata as it drains the old coal mines above. The road forks when it reaches the built up area, left towards the centre of Buxton and right along Nursery Lane to join the main road by St John's Church and The Duke of York pub in the centre of Burbage.

For Buxton Youth Hostel

Follow Green Lane past Poole's Cavern to the bend beyond Buxton Community School. Go through the gate and take the path round the building and across the fields to the road. Turn right past the houses then go left to

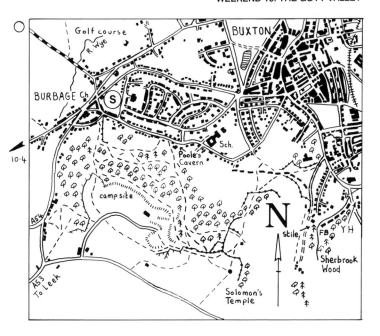

a stile into Sherbrook Wood. After crossing a footbridge keep left along the main path near the stream to the road and the youth hostel.

Buxton

Although surrounded by the Peak District, and ideally placed to be the capital of the National Park, Buxton is excluded. Like a man refused membership of an exclusive club because of his undesirable friends, Buxton is kept out by the quarries strung along a line to the south. The town itself though is far from industrial, with a good shopping centre, some imposing Georgian buildings and, with the revived fortunes of the Opera House, the one time spa attracts many visitors.

Built on the site of a Roman settlement, Buxton competes with Alston for the title of the highest market town in Britain. It is almost certainly the coldest and on a winter Saturday it is hard to imagine a chillier spot than the market at High Town from which to sell your wares.

With their penchant for hot baths, the Roman development of Aquae Arnemetiae with its thermal springs was an obvious choice and while much of the Roman remains were destroyed around 1700, the bath itself was found in 1781 when the Duke of Devonshire, newly wealthy from his copper mines on Ecton Hill, commissioned the architect John Carr to build the Crescent. The town was already famous as a spa and had been for at least the two preceding centuries with many society visitors including Mary Queen of Scots. As well as the warm spring there is also a chalybeate spring and the water was taken as an iron tonic in the Pump Room.

The magnificent Crescent was followed four years later by the Great Stables with its huge central courtyard for exercising horses, and with the Park and many fine houses and churches Buxton was a grand place when the railway arrived in 1863. The Great Stables were converted to the Devonshire Royal Hospital and its exercise yard covered by a dome which was at the time the largest unsupported dome in the world.

Though over the years Buxton as a spa has fallen out of favour for it does not have the grandeur of Bath or Cheltenham, the fine Crescent and the Pavilion Gardens are well worth a visit. The Thermal Baths are now the Cavendish Arcade and the Pump Room, where once society gathered, houses an unusual exhibition called the Micrarium where visitors view nature through microscopes, while the legacy of the copper mining fortune has left Buxton with some very attractive Georgian architecture.

DAY 2: BUXTON TO WHALEY BRIDGE

Following Macclesfield Old Road as it climbs away from Buxton, it is easy to feel sympathy for the horses which once laboured this way with the stage coaches in the middle of the eighteenth century, for having reached the crest of Burbage Edge they descended to the Goyt Valley only to be faced with yet another climb to the moor beyond. The present road with its sinuous curves was built in 1821 and although it adds more than a mile to the route, its easier gradients were much preferred. However an even earlier track is the one chosen for today's walk and eschewing modern easy options we descend an old packhorse way over Wild Moor to cross the River Goyt above Goytsclough Quarry.

The quarry long disused and empty, was once owned by Thomas Pickford, a successful entrepreneur of the eighteenth century. Noting that his packhorse trains returned empty after delivering their flagstones to London he advertised for business and soon had a profitable transport company established. The name sounds familiar and it is, for this was the origin of the modern removal firm.

In contrast to the more open fields and moorland, the western slopes of the valley are extensively wooded and drained by streams that flow in the attractive valleys of Deep Clough, Stake Clough and Shooters Clough, sheltered by silver birch, larch and pine. Above the tree line is the broad moorland ridge that separates the Goyt Valley from the Todd Brook beyond and while a narrow road follows the northern part of the ridge past Windgather Rocks, the southern end is a typical Pennine moor of peat and rough grass. Here is Shining Tor, at 1834ft the highest point where from the rocks of the escarpment edge you look across to Macclesfield Forest and the distant cone of Shutlingsloe.

Midway between Cats Tor and Windgather Rocks the ridge is crossed by a steep narrow road that climbs from Jenkin Chapel before descending to the Goyt Valley. The road is little used nowadays except at weekends, but before the valley became synonymous with reservoirs this was a trade route. Although it can never have been as thronged then as it sometimes becomes on a sunny Sunday, it was still worth a highwayman's time to spy on travellers and Pym Chair was a rock seat at the top of the pass where Pym the highwayman stationed himself.

Northwards the ridge continues to Windgather Rocks, which look out over the valley of the Todd Brook. The rocks are not very extensive and are relatively low, but while they cannot compare with the grand buttresses of the Roaches or the climbing grounds of the Eastern Edges, they are nevertheless very popular especially for training or a quick evening climb after work. At one time after a climb or a walk you could descend to the Chimes of Taxal, but alas the pub has closed and walkers, who with their muddy boots were once served like lepers through a small hatch in the back room of the inn, now have to look further afield to quench their thirst.

With first Fernilee and then Errwood Reservoir the water board surely has enough and yet as you descend to Whaley Bridge another reservoir comes into view. Toddbrook however predates both the other two and was built to supply, not water for drinking, but instead the Peak Forest Canal, one of the highest sections of water navigable by boat in England.

It was late evening as we made our way up the Goyt Valley. In the half light a line of pipes could be seen which followed the hillside down to cross the infant river and then, like a long thin snake, climbed the heather clad hillside beyond until lost to sight in the distance. At the forest edge diesel engines rumbled and beside them stood an office, a box on wheels, grey and official looking. "It's privatisation" said the men. Stockport having built first Fernilee and then Errwood reservoirs, now had a surplus and was selling its valuable asset by the gallon to Severn Trent, while all day and all night these men watched the gauges for the tell tale drop in pressure which would mean a leak.

Errwood Reservoir

ROUTE DESCRIPTION (See map 10. 5 page 221)

Goyt's Clough

Leave Burbage by Macclesfield Old Road which climbs from the limestone fields up into gritstone country. After ½ mile you cross the track of the disused Cromford and High Peak Railway, then take the public footpath signed "Lamaload via Shining Tor". The path climbs by Burbage-edge Plantation and up across the rough grass to a stile onto the moor. Ahead on the skyline is the Cat and Fiddle Inn, the second highest inn in England. Crossing the heather and bilberry, the route drops down into the steep sided Berry Clough which leads to Goyt's Clough and a footbridge over the River Goyt.

Shining Tor

Climbing up to the road the wood above is entered at a stile. After crossing Deep Clough beside a water works sluice the path climbs on through the trees, then leaving the wood follows the edge round to cross a forest track in Stake Clough. Continue beside the forest and then follow the wall uphill to join a track along the ridge at a signpost. The flat topped hill ahead is Shutlingsloe, to the right a BT repeater tower stands on the top of Croker Hill and midway between the two and just below the skyline Mow Cop folly can be made out on a clear day.

A ten-minute detour to the left is the Cat and Fiddle Inn with its attendant radio mast. Turning the other way go over the ladder stile and along to the brow of the hill. Turn left at the step stile and take the repaired path beside the wall which climbs to Shining Tor. This footpath surface is the result of a joint project by the Peak National Park, North West Water and the Forestry Commission. Constructed by the British Trust for Conservation Volunteers, the path's artificial appearance will hopefully mellow with time and it will not have sunk without trace in a few years.

Access to the summit trig point is permitted via a ladderstile and there is a grand view. Nearly 50 miles away, between Shutlingsloe and the BT tower and above Macclesfield Forest, lies the blue-grey point of the Wrekin, Jodrell Bank can be picked out on the Cheshire Plain and the far Welsh hills, while northwards beyond the industrial conurbation of Manchester is Winter Hill. Kinder and the little cone of Win Hill can be identified to the north-east while closer and to the south-east are the bare slopes of Axe Edge Moor.

Pym Chair

Return over the stile and follow the wall along the ridge for a couple of miles. Apart from a bit of bog hopping, as on our last visit the path had not yet been "improved", the going is easy. After climbing to Cats Tor you pass the outcrops at Oldgate Nick where model aircraft often swoop and dive realistically. The road is reached where it crosses the ridge. A broken rock

Shutlingsloe from Shining Tor

by the roadside bearing an OS bench mark and the letters "PC" is all that remains of Pym Chair.

Windgather Rocks

Turn right down The Street for a few yards to a ladder stile. A concession path goes over the moor and continues beside the wall with Windgather Rocks in profile ahead. The path passes above the rocks and turns down over a stile beside the field. After continuing along the edge of the forest to another stile, go right to dip down through the trees and then climb to a stile and the crest of the ridge beyond. Ahead is the Goyt Valley and to the north-east the high ground on the skyline is the vast expanse of the Kinder Plateau.

Taxal

Descending to the left of the forest continue straight on past Overton Hall Farm down the lane which is "Unsuitable for Motors". Where the road hairpins back carry on over a stile and along the hillside. On the far side of the River Goyt is the little village of Fernilee after which the lower reservoir is named. The path crosses a small stream then continues over the fields to join a metalled lane into the tiny village of Taxal. An exploration of the church will reveal not only the grave of Samuel Grimshawe, builder of Errwood Hall, but also an unusual memorial to the "Gentleman of the Pantry & Yeoman of the Mouth to his late majesty King GEORGE the second, who died June the 22nd 1768 aged 75 years". Michael Heathcote had the unenviable job of tasting all the king's food in order that he should not be poisoned.

Passing below the houses to enter the trees, keep to the uphill path over a stile and skirt the boundary of Taxal Lodge, a special school. Crossing the driveway, slant down over the fields, with to the right the tall chimney of Goyt Mills. At the road keep straight on and follow Reddish Lane past an incongruous mock tudor "select development of 4 and 5 bedroom detached homes". Round the corner the lane becomes a footpath by Toddbrook Reservoir then, high above Whaley Bridge, turn across the reservoir dam where the wide spillway sweeps down into the Memorial Park. Joining Reservoir Road follow it down into Whaley Bridge to emerge in the centre of the town by the railway station.

Whaley Bridge

Brightly painted barges line the canal basin, streets of old dark gritstone houses straggle up the valley sides and while the estate agents' windows entice with coloured photographs of terraced cottages and superior country mansions, up the hill is a modern housing estate.

The Romans were here first and their road can be traced over the hills to Buxton. In 1724 the way was turnpiked and around 1780 the present A5002 (now A5004) was laid out by Blind Jack of Knaresborough.

227

Whaley Bridge is the terminus of the Peak Forest Canal which was completed in 1800 and joined the Manchester, Ashton and Oldham Canal. To south and east the land rises into the high dome of the Peak District and this was as far as the canal system could reach, for the mountainous inner region could not be overcome by locks. The solution was a railway, but no ordinary railway could climb the 700ft to the plateau top and so in 1831 the Peak Forest Canal was connected with the Cromford Canal near Matlock by a system of levels and inclined planes.

Trucks were hauled by steel cables up the inclines powered by stationary engines and on the level sections a locomotive was used. It was a remarkable engineering achievement, a milestone in railway development and one of the first public railways in the world. The warehouse into which the trucks ran still stands at the end of the canal and on the final incline, which is now a public footpath, there was no steam engine, but instead a capstan powered by horses. Amazingly this horse gin remained in use until 1952.

WEEKEND 11: THE KINDER ROUND

DAY 1:   Hayfield to Edale 14 miles
                         (Short Route 11½ miles)
STARTING POINT: (049869) Bowden Bridge car park,
                         1 mile east of Hayfield

DAY 2:   Edale to Hayfield 8½ miles
STARTING POINT: (123860) The Old Nags Head, Edale

ROUTE SUMMARY: This classic route follows the plateau
                         rim which acts as a guide to the
                         navigation, but it is a tough walk in an
                         exposed situation and can be hard
                         going in wet conditions. The first day
                         follows the northern edges while the
                         return keeps to the southern side.

NOTE: Kinder may be closed for grouse shooting for a few days
between 12 August and 10 December. Check locally.

DAY 1: HAYFIELD TO EDALE

From many a city bound desk in Manchester's high rise office buildings
longing eyes scan the blue line of the eastern horizon for the white plume of
spray that is Kinder Downfall. Just 15 miles from the city centre are the wild
hills and moors where the Kinder River after gathering its water in a thousand
rivulets, reaches the rim of the plateau and throws itself into space. As the

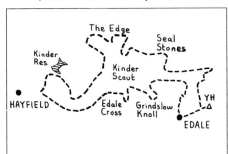

falling water meets the
west wind funnelling up
the valley from Hayfield,
the spray is caught and
hurled skywards, arch-
ing back over the edge,
an upside down water-
fall. This is the land of
heather, bilberry, and
crowberry, of white
feathery cotton grass
and silver gold mat

grass, the land of the grouse and curlew, and of gaunt black gritstone rocks and peat. Here is escape, when at weekends eager feet turn to the hills and climb the steep sides of England's most popular wilderness.

Kinder Scout, whose name means "Water over the Edge", reaches to just over 2000ft and is the highest summit in the Peak. But there is no peak. The flat almost featureless plateau is overlaid with peat, the long dead remains of plants that flourished after the last Ice Age. Dissecting the plateau streams wriggle and meander, eroding channels as they slowly drain the sponge like mass and, as they cut down, the underlying grit is exposed, glinting silver grains in the sun. The edges however are Kinder's finest scenery, with the gritstone revealed in crags and boulders, carved and rounded by the weather into enigmatic forms.

Kinder is not vast, a little over a mile north to south on the western side and no more than 4 miles in width, but to attempt a crossing is a challenge. Groughs, the natural drainage channels in the peat, intersect in a complex dendritic pattern that defies map reading skills and one is reduced to setting a compass course and heading resolutely in a straight line over the moor. A straight line is the intention, but it is impossible to achieve with the steep crumbling peaty sides of the groughs repelling attempts to climb out of their depths. Progress depends on constant checking of distant landmarks or, if the mist is down, waiting for hands to steady so that a compass reading can be taken.

Most walkers stay by the edge where the walking is easy and crossing the centre of Kinder is something to be avoided unless you like getting wet and dirty and you like your walks tough, or you just like getting away from other people. But if the challenge of the groughs cannot be ignored, then pick a dry spell when the peat turns from black to brown, or the perfection of a sub-zero day in mid winter when Kinder is transformed by blue ice and snow and the miles pass more easily across an iron hard arctic wilderness.

Although a clear path follows the rim all the way, a complete circuit of Kinder in one day is a long hard walk, for the edges are far from straight and their convoluted meanderings sweep round great valleys that cut into the plateau adding many miles to the journey. Better to explore first the northern edge and then after a night spent at the little village of Edale, tackle the easier southern side.

The northern edge swings round the great promontories of Fairbrook Naze and Seal Stones and on a grey day it can at times seem endless, but when the cloud lifts and the sun breaks through it is a magnificent walk high above Ashop Clough and the Woodlands Valley. The western end, simply and confidently called "The Edge" as if there were no other, links to Seal Edge looking down on the great valley of Fair Brook while at the eastern end is Blackden Edge, where the rocks give way to gentler heather moor. Madwoman's Stones would hardly merit a name were it not so isolated, and

Crookstone Knoll has just enough rock to provide a comfortable seat, but what a view! Nearly a full circle of hills can be seen from this eastern extremity of Kinder. Northwards is Bleaklow and the Howden Moors, to the east the distinctive silhouette of The Coach and Horses marks Derwent Edge, Ladybower Reservoir gleams blue or silver grey and beyond is Stanage Edge. To the south-east rises the cone of Win Hill, while southwards is Lose Hill and the Great Ridge which links it to Mam Tor.

"We've got nothing like this back home!" The speaker was an American who had taken a day off from an international conference in Cambridge to walk the Kinder Round with his wife. It was a grey day with clouds chasing each other across the sky, but as the sunlight drew swiftly across the moor it painted in the colours, the brilliant yellow gold of the grass against the purple of the heather.

Until around 1830 this was King's land where all might wander freely, but the Enclosure Act allocated the land as grouse moor, preserved and protected and only walkers "in possession of an order" were permitted an occasional visit. Frustration eventually erupted in the famous Mass Trespass of 1932 and the subsequent iniquitous prison sentences, but with the designation of the National Park in 1951 Access Agreements were signed which opened up the moor and then in 1982 Kinder at last came into the ownership of the National Trust.

Now every weekend they come, thronging Edale and Hayfield like alpine villages at the height of the season, the enthusiasts for whom there is nothing better than Kinder, the wildness and the wet.

ROUTE DESCRIPTION
Kinder Reservoir

From Bowden Bridge car park follow the tarmac Kinder Road on the left of the stream for $\frac{1}{3}$ mile to the gate of the Water Treatment Works. Crossing the Kinder River take the footpath to the left and follow the river upstream through the trees to the dam of the Kinder Reservoir, which was built around 1900 by Stockport Corporation.

Short Cut to The Edge

By climbing straight to the western end of the plateau, Cluther Rocks and Kinder Downfall are omitted. Turn left across the footbridge and passing in front of the Waterworks buildings take the cobbled way uphill. The path keeps above the reservoir then follows William Clough, hopping from side to side of the stream before climbing steeply out to the signpost on the boggy col. Turning right up onto the Kinder plateau the Main Route is joined at the large cairn near Mill Hill Rocks.

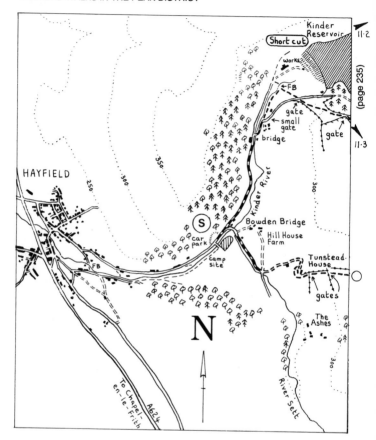

Cluther Rocks

Turning right at the footbridge below the dam the route climbs and crosses a lane. A rough track ascends the hillside with the reservoir soon coming into view. At a gate by the wood turn right and follow the fence uphill. Veer left beside a ruined wall then keep straight on across the fields on the line of an old trackway to a gate at the Boundary of Open Country.

Follow the old lane uphill to the wall corner then climb to join the path which slants up the hillside. After an initially steep section below Kinderlow End the path continues easily across the hillslope climbing gently by the

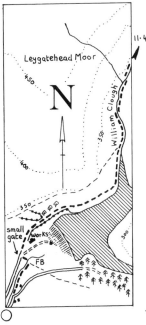

Three Knolls and the jumble of Cluther Rocks. This was the site of a millstone quarry where there was once a smithy and an occasional millstone can still be found. Choosing the higher path a steady climb then gains the plateau by Red Brook where the Pennine Way is joined. From now on the navigation is easy, just keep on following the edge.

Kinder Downfall

After nearly a mile Kinder Downfall is reached. Although the Kinder River which spills over the edge may be only a disappointing trickle, after prolonged rain the waterfall is often blown back by a strong westerly wind, making a great fountain. The rock scenery is very fine and there may be the added entertainment of rock climbers to watch on the face below. This is a popular spot and pestering sheep push their noses into unattended rucksacks, for the Pennine Way arrives with the Kinder River from the peat hags and the next couple of miles is often busy as all walkers follow the same route.

After circling the huge rocky amphitheatre the path continues along the edge past a ruined wall by a new fence which is part of a National Trust scheme to protect the vegetation from over grazing. The plateau now juts out into a large prow of rocks known as the Armchair where there is a natural stone water trough and on the far side, on the edge of the drop, white painted symbols mark the sacred place of the Etherios Society. The initials GK are those of their leader George King. On a good seeing day the industrial conurbation of Greater Manchester spread out beneath the foothills of the Pennine Chain looks surprisingly close. Below on the moor is the Mermaid's Pool, an enchanted spot where if you glimpse the mermaid on Easter Sunday you will be granted a wish of everlasting life. The sandy path now leads above an area of jumbled boulders and landslips then continues through a broken wall past Mill Hill Rocks to a large cairn where the Pennine Way departs soggily to Crowden.

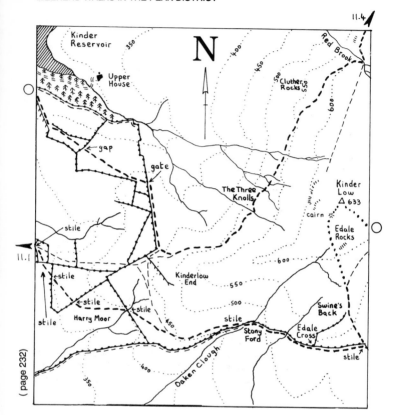

The Edge

The route now sets off along the north edge of Kinder. There is at first no sign of a path, but after climbing eastwards to the rocks above, one soon materialises again and heads purposefully along The Edge with splendid views down into Ashop Clough and towards the summit of the Snake Pass where cars are parked at the crossing point of the Pennine Way onto Bleaklow.

After about a mile the Boxing Gloves are reached, a gritstone tor which approaching from this direction really does resembles its name. The path crosses Upper Red Brook and passes above gritstone buttresses and more weirdly shaped rocks to the indentation of Nether Red Brook. Continue

234

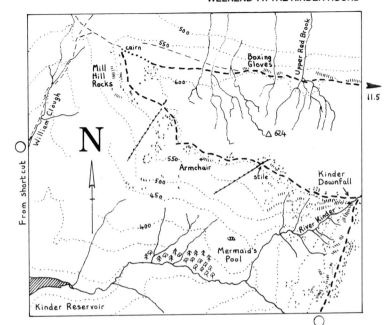

climbing gently past huge rocky cliffs to the highest point on the northern edge then round the tip of Fairbrook Naze past a diminutive Anvil stone. Ahead, somewhat dauntingly, appears the huge scooped out bowl of Fair Brook and the rest of the northern edge is revealed, stretching away into the distance.

Seal Edge

Making what feels like a massive detour to contour round the rim of the escarpment one or two short cuts are tempting but purists will head resolutely inland without loss of height. The path wanders on past the prominent outcrop of the Chinese Wall and then along Seal Edge where it slips a little down the hillside. Down below is the Snake Inn in the Woodlands Valley. Built in 1821 on the new Manchester to Sheffield turnpike this is not named after the sinuousness of the pass but after the family crest of the Duke of Devonshire.

Kinder North Edge

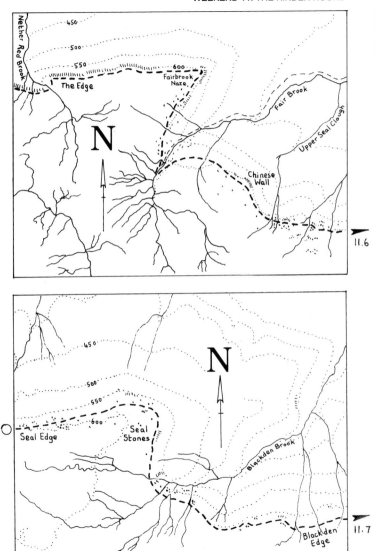

11.6

11.7

237

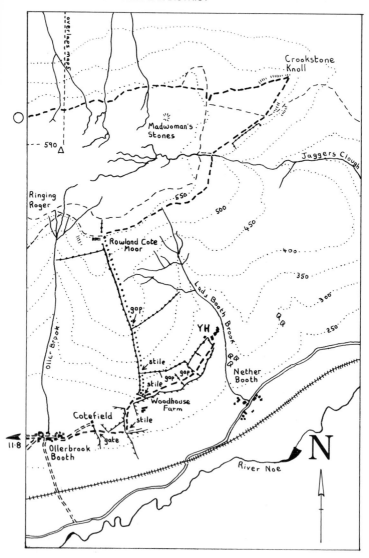

Blackden Edge

The path rounds Seal Stones past a group of rocks resembling Gruyère cheese and then sticks to the rim of another big scoop in the hillside above Blackden Brook. There are still plenty of rock features of interest on either side of the path though the escarpment is less dramatic here. The gritstone outcrops now give way to gentler slopes of heather and bilberry then at a low gritstone slab keep straight on to cut off a large loop of path. At a T-junction turn right then left onto the edge path again.

Crookstone Knoll

Crookstone Knoll is the easternmost point of the plateau and is a fine viewpoint with an almost 360 degree panorama. To the north lies Alport Dale and the landslip of Alport Castles with on the skyline above, the moors of Bleaklow and Howden. To the east the Coach and Horses rocks are silhouetted on Derwent Edge and beyond Ladybower Reservoir is Stanage Edge, while flanking the Hope Valley to the south-east are the tops of Win Hill and Lose Hill with the Great Ridge continuing over Back Tor and Mam Tor.

The plateau terminates abruptly here and the path loops back. Continuing southwards round the edge climb a little to cross first Jaggers Clough and then pass above Lady Booth Brook, where at the bottom of the steep sided clough you can glimpse the buildings of the youth hostel. At the next rocky high point on Rowland Cote Moor the ridge of Ringing Roger comes into view ahead with the huge bowl of Grindsbrook Clough beyond.

Vale of Edale

Leaving the plateau follow the wall down into the valley. The first section is a little awkward, scrambling down the rocky escarpment, then it is an easy walk over springy turf down into the Vale of Edale where little trains busy to and fro on the only line that now connects Sheffield with Manchester. Joining the track, hostellers turn left to Rowland Cote Youth Hostel, formerly a private house, which is only ten minutes walk away.

For Edale village, turn right on the track then the path goes down across the field to a stile in the opposite corner and follows the waymarks to pass in front of Cotefield Farm which has a Camping Barn. Following the farm track go straight on through the buildings of Ollerbrook Booth. After the last house keep straight on through the fields and cross the little packhorse bridge to arrive in Edale by the Old Nags Head.

Edale

The little alpine-style village of Edale which sits huddled in a hollow under the southern slopes of Kinder Scout must once have been an important place as five packhorse routes meet here. It has been a settlement since Anglo-

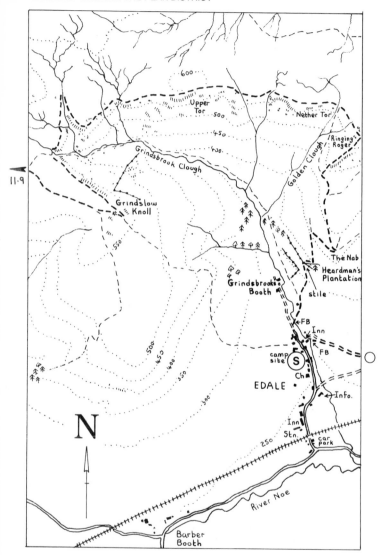

Edale

Saxon times and is mentioned in the Domesday Book, while the temporary shepherd's huts of the Tudor period are now the hamlets of Barber Booth, Nether Booth and Upper Booth.

For centuries Edale remained isolated in its narrow valley, then in 1894 the railway arrived, emerging from the Cowburn Tunnel. The station is still open with frequent trains joining Sheffield and Manchester, but Edale's days of anonymity are over, since in 1935 Tom Stephenson proposed the Pennine Way. It took thirty years before the 270 miles from Edale to Kirk Yetholm were officially open and this long distance footpath was the first National Trail to be created. While researchers claim that around 10,000 walkers set out each year, many fail even before they reach Crowden, the first night's halt.

Edale is little spoiled by all the attention with the majority of visitor's cars excluded from the village. The Nags Head and the Rambler Inn, a few B&Bs, a campsite, a splendid Information Centre and a little shop supply one's needs, while the very basic walkers' café, which serves huge mugs of tea and substantial portions of cake, is constructed from two old railway waggons and has been here since 1930.

Because of severe frosts in the valley bottom caused by temperature inversions, the farms are mostly situated on the warmer southern facing slopes. The great ridge of Mam Tor to Lose Hill casts a huge shadow over the valley and any snow that falls lingers a long time. Following the hard winters of the 1960s Edale attained popularity as a ski centre and the youth hostel ran skiing courses. Enthusiastically we bought cross country skis and that was the end of the hard winters. There haven't been any since although on our first outing we made the front page. We had gone to Rushup Edge to practise, but as soon as we had put on our skis and before even moving a yard, a photographer from the *Derbyshire Times* appeared and asked us to pose. "Don't worry," he replied to our protestations that we were beginners, "I only want you as foreground."

DAY 2: EDALE TO HAYFIELD

As you watch the groups of walkers standing about in front of the Nags Head, or finishing their breakfast in the railway carriage café before setting off purposefully north towards Grindsbrook, it is often impossible to distinguish those who will return at day's end from those who at nightfall will be descending to Crowden, the first stop on the Pennine Way. Rucksack size has nothing to do with it. A huge knee groaning sackful may conceal ropes and assorted climbing gear or just indicate excessive caution in the wilderness, while a diddy day sack, or no sack at all may simply mean the owner is taking full advantage of a daily transport service which for a fee will carry your gear all the way to the Scottish border.

Down the steps to the wooden bridge over Grinds Brook it is easy enough, though one winter with the steps sheathed in ice we put our crampons on in the village street. Tales of dreadful Pennine Way erosion are forgotten as you tread the neatly paved path, but you must forsake the plod up Grindsbrook Clough, for that would be to miss some of the edge, and turn aside for the infinitely preferable ascent of Ringing Roger. The Pennine Way is for another time.

Grindsbrook Clough cuts north, taking a great chunk out of Kinder, and on either hand steep slopes rise to the plateau edge over 1000ft above. Facing each other across the valley are Grindslow Knoll and Ringing Roger, the echoing rocks, and on the plateau rim the rocks of Nether Tor and Upper Tor stand guard.

While the valley floor is grass the upper slopes are heather, a sea of purple in August. As the edge is reached the heather gives way first to bilberry and then to crowberry, peat and stones, while the wetter land beyond is cotton grass moor. The cotton grass, which is not really a grass at all but a sedge, is one of the very few plants which can grow in waterlogged peat as its roots have aeration canals, but the sphagnum, whose remains make up the peat, has all but disappeared from the moors. This lovely green moss, which likes nothing better than being thoroughly saturated, is sensitive to pollution and the smoke of the Industrial Revolution, which so changed the face of Britain, has killed it off. However botanists have observed that lichens are a good indicator of air quality and it is encouraging to see in recent years on some rocks a crumpled leafy growth showing an improving purity of air.

Peat, acid and airless, is a preservative and buried in its depths can be found the roots of trees which covered Kinder thousands of years ago. As the climate changed to cooler and wetter conditions, peat growth accelerated while the tree line retreated, helped by the forest clearance of primitive man, but the history of those times is also locked up in the peat, for preserved along with the tree roots are minute pollen grains trapped as the successive layers of peat were built up. Every plant has a characteristic pollen grain and by identifying and painstakingly counting them at various depths in the peat it is possible to get a picture of the vegetation which once covered the land.

Although some of the rocks of the plateau edges are angular, indicating nineteenth-century quarrying, many of the rock formations of Kinder are rounded into beautifully shaped sculptures, with the Woolpacks beyond Crowden Tower the most fantastic. While erosion continues and the rocks crumble into the silver sand from which they came, it can be seen from half buried rounded boulders that much of the weathering must have occurred long before the peat was formed. In the freeze thaw conditions following the last Ice Age the land was bare and in the harsh conditions the rocks were shaped while streams swollen to rivers carved valleys into the moor.

Kinder Low, with its trig point perched atop a massive boulder, is a detour away from the edge, but it is worth it just to see the extensive areas of naked peat. Don't let the over zealous ecologists tell you that only human erosion is to blame. It isn't feet that have worn away the vegetation, but where the voracious sheep, the climate and polluted air have left the surface bare, Sheffield University is attempting to revegetate the area with cotton grass.

At Edale Cross you finally leave the wilderness of Kinder behind. By then you will be either converted, a devotee eager to return or perhaps, if it has been a sodden wet weekend, you will vow never again, but whichever your response, Kinder will not be forgotten.

ROUTE DESCRIPTION (See map 11.8 page 240)
Ringing Roger

Take the road to the left of the Old Nags Head, the "Official" start of the Pennine Way, then fork right down the steps to cross Grinds Brook by the footbridge. Passing a notice which in four languages forbids camping on the moor, leave the eroded path by a small barn and climb up the field to a stile and the Boundary to Open Country. The plantation is named after Fred Heardman "Bill the Bogtrotter" who was the landlord of both the Edale inns. A member of the National Park board and a rural district councillor he fought to preserve the valley and the Nag's Head became the first information centre and mountain rescue post in the newly formed National Park. The stepped path zigzags up to the grassy prow of the Nab where from its edge there is a bird's-eye view of Edale village and across the grassy bowl of the head of the Vale of Edale lies Mam Tor and the Great Ridge.

Continuing up the main path you can see the orange ribbon of the original Pennine Way path snaking up Grindsbrook Clough. Ahead is a rocky ridge leading to the skyline, one of the best ways up onto Kinder and this brings you to the bare silvery top of Ringing Roger.

Grindslow Knoll

From the large cairn just beyond the rocks turn left along the edge path to follow the rim of the escarpment westwards crossing Golden Clough to Nether Tor, whose quarry supplied the stone for Edale Church in 1885. The path then dips to the narrowest part of the plateau, the "Seven Minute Crossing" before climbing to Upper Tor where you can look across to the northern edge of Kinder with Bleaklow and the Howden moors beyond. The eroded rocks by the edge form interesting shapes and the cliffs below attract rock climbers, while on the other side of Grinds Brook rises the dome-shaped hill of Grindslow Knoll. The path then continues past Far Upper Tor and crosses a deep nick in the hillside to reach the head of Grindsbrook Clough.

Follow the edge round past the Anvil Stone, which is hard to climb onto and even harder to get off, to reach the tumbled cairn on the summit of Grindslow Knoll. From this windy spot where the plateau declines to the

Grindslow Knoll

south in a grassy shelf, double back heading north-westwards on a narrow path which rejoins the edge.

The Woolpacks

After a generous mile you reach the head of Crowden Brook and climb to pass above the cliffs of Crowden Tower. Next are the finest of all the Kinder rock formations, the Wool Packs. These weirdly sculpted gritstone tors are fascinating, resembling a bizarre collection of strange creatures fashioned in the style of Henry Moore. Reaching the rocks on the skyline known as the Pagoda, the rightmost outcrop is the twin topped Pym Chair, named after a seventeenth-century minister who preached here. It is an easy scramble to the top to sit between the arms. The highest point in the Peak District is marked by the stake on the skyline 500 yards to the north-west. Recognised as a separate 2000ft mountain this top has moved about over the years finally coming to rest at point 636 metres.

Noe Stool

Continuing along the edge to the solitary Noe Stool, named after the River Noe which rises here, there are good retrospective views of the Pagoda and Pym Chair. In fine dry weather only, the route heads just north of west to visit the OS trig point at Kinder Low which stands on a large gritstone boulder, one of our favourite spots, then heading south, passes to the right of the prominent Edale Rocks to rejoin the path.

Edale Cross

Heading towards the hump of Swine's Back join the Pennine Way which, newly repaired by the National Trust, descends to an ancient track where you turn right to Edale Cross. Now enclosed by a wall this medieval boundary marker stood at the junction of four of the wards of the Peak Forest, Longdendale, Ashop, Edale and Champayne, but the initials and date were scratched on in 1810 by Thomas Gee of nearby Ashes Farm when he restored the cross to its upright position.

Harry Moor

After continuing down the rough track for ½ mile, take the footpath to Hayfield just after a stream crosses the path at Stony Ford. The stone walls in this area were all repaired by the National Trust in 1985. The narrow path contours along the hillside with views across the valley of the River Sett to the sharply pointed South Head and the adjacent ridge of Mount Famine. Forking left take the path down to a ladder stile leaving the Open Country for the fields of Harry Moor which conceal a huge underground water storage tank supplying all the surrounding district. This was the work of a Thomas John

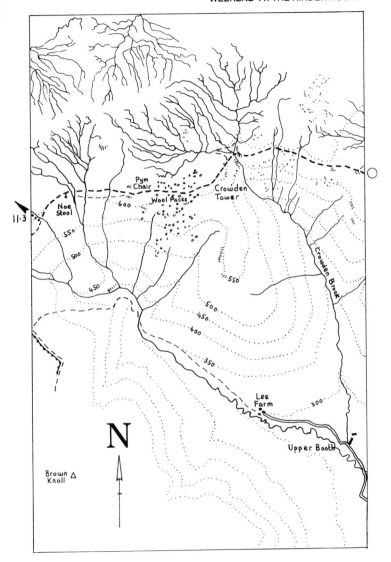

Gee of Ashes, presumably a descendant of the cross restorer.

Crossing a series of stiles descend to the seventeenth-century Tunstead House and Farm and go round to the left of the buildings to join a track down to the road. These isolated houses soon become cut off by the winter snows and one February we passed the owners hauling bags of coal up the hill on a sledge. Turning right at the bottom along the road, follow the River Sett back to Bowden Bridge.

Hayfield

The little village of Hayfield nestles in a grassy hollow under the western slopes of Kinder Scout, some 500ft above sea level. Once its narrow streets jammed with traffic, but now bypassed by the busy A624, it has regained its charm. Solid gritstone houses and shops line the street and Hayfield has reverted to the pace of former times. However with only one narrow road into the village it is all too easy to miss Hayfield altogether, a momentary lapse of concentration on the main road and it is too late.

Hayfield was in the medieval parish of Glossop and a chapel was built here in 1386. An important packhorse route led eastwards over the moors by Edale Cross to Edale. There were several woollen and cotton mills powered by the River Sett, the corn was ground in a common mill, and by the mid nineteenth century there were three print works and two paper mills. Bowden Bridge at the confluence of the River Sett and the River Kinder is very old, probably sixteenth century, and it is thought that the original medieval church was near here. The large adjacent campsite is on the site of the old Kinder Print Works, a calico print factory, but before 1830 this was common land known as Cutlers' Green or Cutlers' Wheel.

A guide to Kinder Scout published in 1880 spoke of the village's past when "Hunting, bull and bear baiting, were the favourite sports of the ancient inhabitants of Hayfield, but on the introduction of commerce they earned high wages, and, indulging in luxury, became effeminate, and their rude sports began to decline".

From the village many paths lead up into the hills and though set on the edge of wild country, its relatively low altitude means that it can be reached by bus and car when many of the higher villages are cut off by snow. Thirty years ago ramblers packed the trains from Manchester, but the line closed in the 1960s and is now the Sett Valley Trail.

The car park in a disused quarry opposite the camp site was the site of the rally for the Kinder Mass Trespass in 1932. About 400 ramblers gathered in the quarry which now bears a commemorative bronze plaque and Benny Rothman addressed them from a natural pulpit of rock. The walkers then marched off up the Kinder Road onto the plateau, the rest is history.

LONG WEEKEND 12: THE DERWENT WATERSHED

DAY 1:	Glossop to Langsett 16½ miles
STARTING POINT:	(035941) The crossroads in the centre of Glossop
DAY 2:	Langsett to Castleton 17½ miles
STARTING POINT:	(211005) Langsett car park
DAY 3:	Castleton to Glossop 15½ miles
STARTING POINT:	(150828) The centre of Castleton by the youth hostel
ROUTE SUMMARY:	A long tough walk round the headwaters of the River Derwent. The high moors of Bleaklow and Howden are followed by the summits of Win Hill and Lose Hill, then the Great Ridge leads to Rushup Edge with a finish over Kinder. An ability to navigate by map and compass is essential.

NOTE: The moors may be closed for grouse shooting for a few days between 12 August and 10 December. Check locally.

DAY 1: GLOSSOP TO LANGSETT

Above is the song of the lark and the plaintive call of the curlew, beneath is a carpet of honey scented heather, of black berried crowberry and bilberry, of yellows, browns, greens and purples, of sedge and tough Nardus stricta. Eroded gritstone rocks sculpted by wind and rain into fantastic shapes shimmer in the haze, the peat is brown and dust dry and into the distance the moor stretches away to the far horizon. A grouse starts up from beneath one's feet and with staccato calls of complaint skims low over the moor. A lizard darts and then freezes still, motionless, watching with an unblinking eye. It is summer and contentment is to lie on your back in the heather listening to the hum of insects and watching the sky.

Then comes the rain, sweeping in across the open moors, a steady relentless rain that soaks into the earth until it can take no more. Great

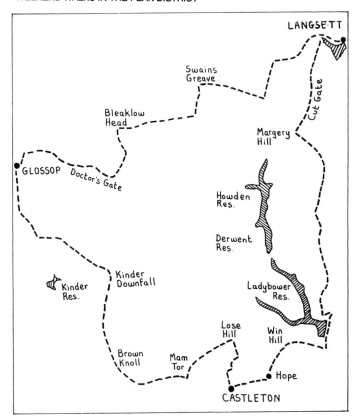

torrents of foaming dark brown, peat stained water fill the groughs, the sheep huddle in the lee of the rocks, nothing can be seen in the grey mist and a clinging black ooze sucks at your feet as you stumble across the moor.

Winter approaches and now the peat freezes to an iron hard surface, the snow piles into huge drifts against the gaunt black rocks, blue shadows reach out across the crystal surface, an ice wind numbs your face, skiers carve tracks across the moor and icicles rim the glistening frozen streams.

Then once again it is spring. The ground steams in the sunshine, the bare twigs of bilberry come alive, first with the early flush of pink new leaves and then with tiny red bell-like flowers, the arctic hares, camouflaged against winter in their white coats, now stand out conspicuously, lambs nuzzle close

250

to their mothers, the lark soars once again and the grouse redoubles its gruff complaints.

This is Bleaklow, the moors between the flanking cities of Manchester and Sheffield, a wilderness but not a waste, desolate but not abandoned, a magnificent wild upland country of hill and moor.

But the wilderness isn't natural. These vast open spaces stretching away emptily to the horizon are managed, the heather carefully controlled and until the late fifties this was forbidden territory, jealously guarded by its owners and preserved for grouse. "In those days," said Jack, one of the National Park Rangers, "we were chased and beaten by keepers with sticks. Sometimes they would even fire a shotgun over our heads."

Yet the moors are what they are because of the grouse. Heather left to itself becomes lank and straggly and the fresh shoots on which the grouse depend for much of their food too tough. The red grouse, a native bird only found in Northern England, Scotland and Ireland is, unlike the cossetted pheasant and partridge, a wild bird. Were the grouse not of value for sport, were the moors not managed, burnt in rotation to provide young new shoots for food with older areas providing cover, then the ground would quickly revert to its far less attractive natural state.

The "Glorious Twelfth" is still a notable date in the calendar, but now the moors are open to walkers to roam freely, to find the secret source of the River Derwent at Swains Greave, to climb on the gritstone edges, to test themselves with long walks or simply to watch the day unfold.

While the cities come to the very foot of the hills, there are few roads that intrude upon the wilderness and it is 16 miles from Glossop at the foot of the western slopes of Bleaklow to the tentacles of Sheffield reaching out from the east.

Bleaklow, the largest and most remote of the moors, is bounded on the north by the Woodhead Pass, whose long chain of reservoirs lie beneath Black Hill. When constructed in the nineteenth century these were the largest stretch of man-made water in the world, while the twin tunnels of the railway which march in tandem up the narrow Longdendale valley, once the main link between Manchester and Sheffield, were the longest tunnels anywhere.

The main A628 is hidden in the trough of the Woodhead Pass, and so the eye travels on northward to Black Hill and beyond. After a 5-mile walk from the road to the south, Bleaklow Head feels a very remote spot indeed. The Pennine Way, although it crosses some rough terrain, stays on the western edge passing Hern Stones and Wain Stones to reach Bleaklow Head before descending to Crowden.

The rocks are like islands in the sea of peat, where one may rest and recuperate before plunging on again, up and down over the black groughs. Wain Stones is the most famous and is known as "The Kiss" because of its uncanny resemblance to two heads whose lips are about to meet. At

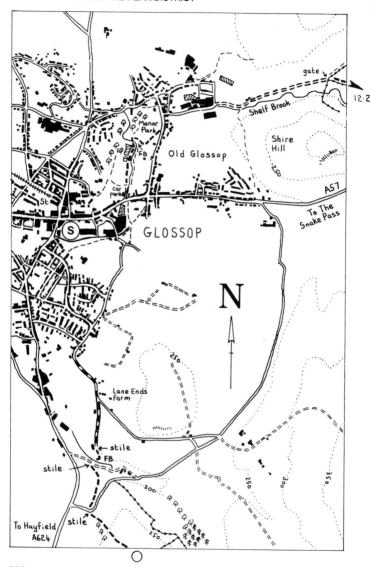

Bleaklow Head there is also a cairn marking the highest point of the plateau, but just over a mile to the east and a few feet lower is the heart of Bleaklow at Bleaklow Stones. The Anvil Stone which predates Henry Moore sculptures by several thousand years is our favourite pilgrimage, either in August with the heather at its best, or in February under a covering of snow with a return in fast gathering darkness to finish over a moonlit moor.

ROUTE DESCRIPTION
Doctor's Gate

From the centre of Glossop take the A57 towards Sheffield for ¼ mile. King Edward Avenue leads to Corn Street and the attractive Manor Park where you keep beside the river past an ornamental pond, busy with ducks. The park, the former estate of Lord Howard of Glossop, was sold to the town council in 1924 and the hall demolished. Crossing the stream turn right through a formal garden and past the miniature railway and obstacle golf to Manor Park Road. Turning left over Shelf Brook walk in front of the Queens public house up Shepley Street, past the factories and out into the country along the track by the brook. After passing Charlesworth Shooting School and Mossy Lea Farm the way, signed "via Doctor's Gate Roman Road to the Snake Inn", ascends the valley gently to a barn by the Boundary of Open Country.

Forking right stay by the stream for another mile. The valley sides steepen and a memorial footbridge, erected in 1965 by the Manchester Rambling Club, is crossed. The path now climbs purposefully, flattening out opposite the obvious buttress of Lower Shelf Stones, then climbing on again. After crossing Urchin Clough high above the valley, the path zigzags up to the valley rim where there is a good view back along Shelf Brook.

The way now continues as a broad track to the highest point of Doctor's Gate where the original paving stones of the old packhorse way are set on edge between kerbstones. The Roman road linked the fort of Navio at Brough with Melandra at Glossop, but it has been known as Dr Talbotes Gate since 1627 after a vicar of Glossop who often travelled this way.

Bleaklow Head

At the crossroads turn left along the repaired highroad of the Pennine Way where it sweeps across the open moor with views across to Higher and Lower Shelf Stones. This section makes for easy walking and even in the stickiest of conditions can be followed in a pair of open-toed sandals. Glancing back it is a surprise to see how close the cars are on the summit of the Snake Pass. Already you feel miles away from anywhere.

The last of the board walks deposits you on the sandy bottom of Devil's Dike, which was probably an old boundary ditch. The Pennine Way has been realigned to follow a natural route along the cloughs and it is easy going in dry weather along the stony bed. Follow the waymarked route along to Hern Clough whose little falls and pools flow down into the remote grassy bowl of Grains in the Water. The "floating" path was made during 1991 by laying stone slabs on top of a fabric membrane.

The neat path leads up the clough, crossing and recrossing the stream by stepping stones, then after passing a useful spring of clear, cold water, the waymarked route bends away before Hern Stones and Wain Stones are reached. Continue through the peat hags to Bleaklow Head, the summit of

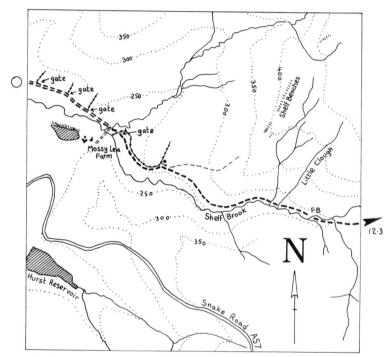

Bleaklow, a huge pile of stones in the middle of a silver sandy sea. To the north, on the far side of the Woodhead Pass is the long curving tier of Laddow Rocks and the winking 750ft mast on Black Hill. From here the Pennine Way departs down Torside Clough to Crowden, the first night's stop, so now you're on your own!

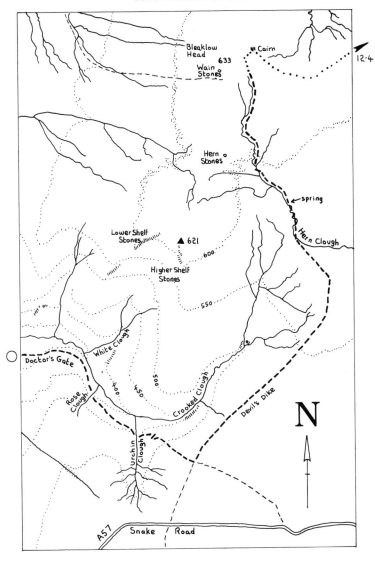

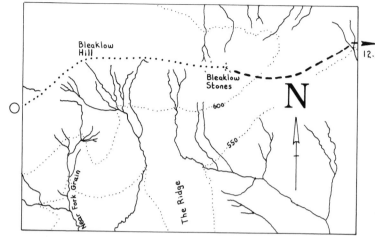

Bleaklow Stones

Heading south-east pick up a somewhat intermittent line of stakes that heads eastwards across Bleaklow Hill along the ridge. Following ribbons of silver sand and trudging over black peat hags it can be tough going, but it is easy enough in dry weather and after an uncharted couple of miles, the Anvil Rock is reached at Bleaklow Stones, the very heart of Bleaklow.

Barrow Stones

A narrow path sets off south-east and contours round half way down the hill slope to Grinah Stones where the rocks are piled into a huge, rocky nose. Cutting across the corner continue round the edge to the massive Crown Stone, the largest of the scattered, weirdly shaped Barrow Stones. It is tempting to linger here among these strangely weathered boulders, but there is still a fair way to go, so head just west of north towards the Black Hill mast. You soon pick up the end of a clough and though there is little sign of a path, follow it down to the rather boggy basin of Swains Greave. This is the source of the River Derwent and the name means Swine's Grove, though the trees and pigs are long gone.

Swains Head

Following the infant River Derwent keep to the left of this quiet and secluded valley. A little trod develops as the valley sides steepen and this contours along towards the distant outcrops of the Shepherd's Meeting Stones, a central point where once the sheep were gathered and sorted. Just before
256

Bleaklow Stones

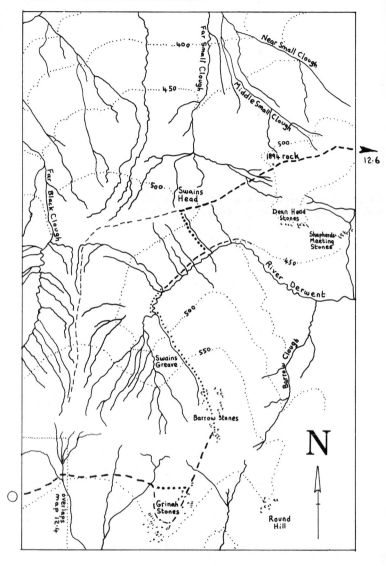

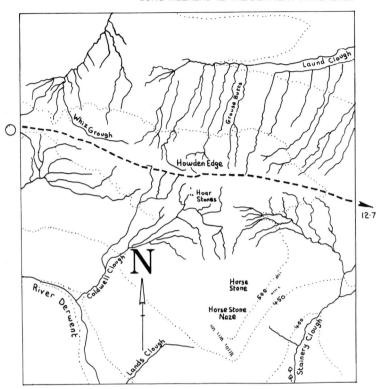

the river bend leave the path and turn up the clough to the left to join the well trampled way along the ridge near Swains Head.

Howden Edge

With views across to the moors below Black Hill, follow the ridge along Featherbed Moss past a mushroom shaped rock set in a little pool and inscribed 1894. After crossing a few shallow, heathery groughs the path then wanders on over Howden Edge, featureless grassy moorland bright in summer with occasional purple patches of cross-leaved heath and the rarer yellow bog asphodel. Passing to the left of the Hoar Stones, which disappear from view as you get near, continue along the ridge. A modern windmill which appears away to the north-east powers a plastics factory and then the Rocking Stones come into view.

259

Cat Clough

After following the watershed for 3 miles you reach the groughs of Cat Cloughs Head above the deep indentation of Stainery Clough. A stake marks the top of Near Cat Clough, the third water channel and the lowest point on the ridge. The clough runs straight up to the ridge path and a faint trod follows its steep black sides down across the moor. Ahead you can see the long valley of Hordron Clough and on the hillside opposite a track leads up to a barn where the hillside has been cleared and at one time was cultivated. Further down are the buildings of Hordron Farm. Now derelict and only used by the local farmers for shearing, it was once the home of a couple who brought up seven children in this isolated spot. An occasional stake marks the path which becomes more obvious as you pass a series of superior grouse butts, each with a neat gritstone wall banked with the heather and bilberry that grows on these drier flanks of the moor. Many old root-stocks lie half buried in the peat and the heather has been managed and burnt so the walking is easy.

Little Don River

A footbridge at the bottom of the clough crosses the Little Don River then crossing and recrossing the stream follow it on the left bank. You can avoid the river crossing by taking the track up the hill for a short way to get round the steep bank. The five star sheepfold below Hordron Farm has a piped water supply to its sheep dip. The sheepfold, which resembles a miniature fort, was built by the man who constructed Langsett Reservoir and the castellated top is in his characteristic style. The path continues by the stream which has cut down through the hillside exposing bedding planes of alternate rock and shale. The course has altered over the years for it used to flow by the little cliff to the left and the OS map shows the District Boundary following the original meander.

At the end of the grassy field the path slants up the hillside, a green strip through the bracken and a little trod keeps below the field boundary. Joining a grassy track descend to cross the foot of Long Moor Clough where the beautiful Scots Pines are reminiscent of the lower slopes of the Cairngorms. The track rises again through Swinden Plantation then descends and swings away up Fox Clough. Keep straight on, climbing above the river to follow the edge of Crookland Wood where there are lovely views back up Hordron Clough towards Bleaklow. The path dips to the river again for a final time and cuts across the end of the trees to a stile. After climbing a flight of gritstone steps by Hagg Brook cross the stream and continue to the track ahead.

The Flouch Inn is to the left but keep straight on through the plantation high above Langsett Reservoir which is only glimpsed through the trees. After passing a large derelict gritstone quarry the path arrives at Langsett where the youth hostel is on the far side of the main road.

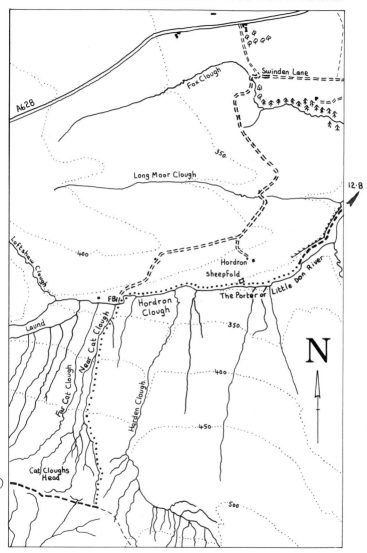

Swinden Lane

A628

Fox Clough

350

Long Moor Clough

12·8

Loftshaw Clough

400

Hordron
sheepfold

The Porter or Little Don River

Laund

FBr

Hordron
Clough

350

Far Cat Clough

Near Cat Clough

Hadden Clough

400

450

N

Cat Cloughs
Head

500

Ice on the Little Don River at Langsett

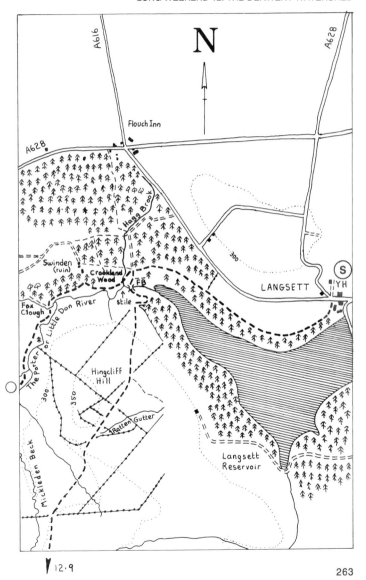

N

A616

A628

Flouch Inn

A628

Hagg Brook

300

S

YH

LANGSETT

Swinden
(ruin)

Crookland
Wood

FB

Fox
Clough

stile

The Porter or Little Don River

300

350

Hingcliff
Hill

Rotten Gutter

Mickleden Beck

Langsett
Reservoir

12.9

Langsett

A few houses crowd together for company on the edge of the moor, watching over the reservoir like sentries beside the Gothic valve tower, a copy of a turret at Lancaster Castle. The hamlet is usually mentioned, if at all, as the destination of a long walk, with little to commend its history, its architecture or its famous sons. But with newly built expensive cottages and a beautiful old barn converted to a visitor centre, Langsett is rapidly becoming a desirable place in which to live. It is also one place in the Peak District that actually encourages visitors. "Our aim is one hundred cars a day, that's one hundred less travelling up the motorway to the Lake District." So said an enthusiastic outdoors instructor as we warmed ourselves beside a blaze of brushwood while watching trees being felled to enlarge the car park.

There are many more trees than people in Langsett and certainly far more grouse on its 3,500 acre moor which belongs to Sir Thomas Pilkington. Although the Langsett Moor is managed for game, most of it is Access Land and it is only closed a few days a year for shooting.

Langsett Reservoir which was completed in 1905 now belongs to Yorkshire Water. It supplies Rotherham and Doncaster and though access to the water's edge is still forbidden, the lake adds to the beauty of the scene. The stream which feeds the reservoir has two names on the OS map. The Little Don River rises high on the Howden Moors then flows down the valley to become the Porter or Little Don, before joining the Don at Stocksbridge.

On the very edge of the Peak District and with the National Park boundary running right through it, there may not be much to Langsett, but it is well supplied with facilities and, with a pub, youth hostel, shop and café, it makes a good stopping place for the night.

DAY 2 LANGSETT TO CASTLETON

After the peat wastes of Bleaklow comes the contrast of the Howden Moors and Derwent Edge, a long high broad ridge that sweeps east and then south from Swains Head until after nine almost level miles it descends to the A57 and the foot of Ladybower Reservoir. A tiny speck in the distance is perhaps another walker, but for mile upon mile the moor stretches away ahead with underfoot crowberry, cotton grass and the yellow mat grass.

In spring there are the pink flowers of the bilberry and the much rarer cranberry, in summer the cotton grass nods its delicate white downy head and in late summer the flanks of the moor glow purple with the heather.

On the flat surface of the moor small pools glint silver and the path meanders this way and that in a vain attempt to avoid them. At first only an occasional rock formation breaks the smooth profile of the horizon, but as Back Tor is reached more scattered outcrops appear with Dovestone Tor, the Salt Cellar, White Tor and the magnificent Wheel Stones, commonly known as the Coach and Horses, a distinctive silhouette in many a distant view. To the east the moor dips gradually, the crowberry giving way to heather and bilberry on the drier slopes, but the western edge is closer at hand with slopes which fall steeply to the valley of the River Derwent.

Rising among the reeds and moss at Swains Greave the River Derwent flows momentarily northwards before turning east in its quiet deserted valley. Splashing down over little waterfalls and growing as it is joined by the waters of Barrow Clough and Coldwell Clough, it curves gradually round the flanks of Ronksley Moor and heads south.

Margery Hill is little more than a grassy mound marked by a trig point where the ridge is reached after the long ascent from Langsett up the Cut Gate path. This route was in regular use by farmers as late as the early decades of this century when they made the journey from the Woodlands Valley to Penistone Market. The trig point at Back Tor however is in a grand position, perched atop a massive gritstone outcrop and looking across at the outpost of Lost Lad.

Like much of Bleaklow the western flank of Howden Moor is owned by the National Trust. Gritstone outcrops line the edge and attractive cloughs descend to the Derwent Valley. Abbey Clough gets its name from the twelfth century when it was part of an estate belonging to the monks of Welbeck Abbey.

The Derwent has been tamed and its waters impounded in the long reservoirs of Howden, Derwent and Ladybower. The construction of Howden and Derwent took fifteen years and started in 1901 while Ladybower, begun in 1935, destroyed the hamlet of Ashopton and the village of Derwent. In dry weather the ruins of the houses appear again on the mud flats as the water recedes. Photographs from the 1930s show the excavations and a strangely unfamiliar bridge towering above the deserted cottages. This now carries the A57, the Snake Pass from Sheffield to Manchester, its low arches barely rising above the water. The stone for the dams was not obtained locally, but came from Bole Hill Quarries above Padley Chapel near Hathersage. A temporary railway was built which ran up the valley to carry the stone, but now only an occasional stone pier at the water's edge remains to show its course. At the height of the construction work of the Derwent and Howden dams, over 1000 men were employed and a temporary village, nicknamed "Tin Town" from its corrugated iron huts, was built to house the workers and their families. There was even a chapel and a school.

In 1990 a lone Lancaster bomber droned its way down the Derwent Valley, the sound of its engines reverberating back from the valley sides. This was a re-enactment, an anniversary celebration of the Dambuster squadron who practiced here before they set out on their mission to destroy German dams nearly fifty years ago.

Below the final reservoir is Yorkshire Bridge where you cross the River Derwent to return from Yorkshire into Derbyshire. It is possible to walk round Win Hill, but the final ascent of the day, up one of the steepest slopes in the whole of the Peak District brings you to the very distinctive summit. The twin of Lose Hill across the Hope valley, Win Hill is an isolated outpost of the Kinder plateau and a superb viewpoint. Then it is down again, but much more gradually, towards Hope and beside Peakshole Water for the final gentle mile into Castleton.

ROUTE DESCRIPTION (See map 12.8 page 263)
Cut Gate

Take the public footpath through the car park in Langsett which leads above the reservoir, retracing yesterday's route for a mile. At the junction with the track from the Flouch Inn and the main road, turn left to Brook House Bridge over the Porter or Little Don River and the Boundary to Open Country. The bridleway zigzags up the hill onto the open moor then it is fairly easy going over Hingcliff Common which gives fine views of Langsett Reservoir and its surrounding conifer plantations. The path then dips and leaves the Access Land. The path that joins from Langsett and Penistone is the old Cut Gate track whose end is now blocked by Langsett Reservoir. The track climbs steadily along Mickleden Edge high above Mickleden Beck where lush vegetation, dense bracken and trees grow in the shelter of the clough. Climbing on across the moor with views to the left of Pike Low which is topped with an ancient cairn, follow a wide grassy ditch known as Black Dike to a big cairn which marks the highest point of the path at Cut Gate End. To the right is the rocky outcrop of Bull Stones and a long view up the River Derwent.

Howden Edge

Turning south along Howden Edge the path follows the lip of the moor with the trig point on Margery Hill a little off route to the left. Continuing along Wilfrey Edge, past Wilfrey Neild or Needle, the green velvety moor of Upper Hey lies spread out below. The path goes above rocky buttresses to High Stones where from the small cairn on the summit there are good views of the Howden Reservoir and down into Cranberry Clough.

The path then runs beside a ditch but leaves it after 200 yards to climb to Wet Stones. From the stones contour the slope then go south down the grassy spur which heads straight for Back Tor, the rocks on the skyline. At the end of the spur there is a grouse butt and a little lower a path is joined which crosses Foul Clough and passes behind Berristers Tor before descending steeply to ford the dramatic gorge of Abbey Brook. The strange hummocks were probably caused when the brook changed its course as it cut down through the rock.

266

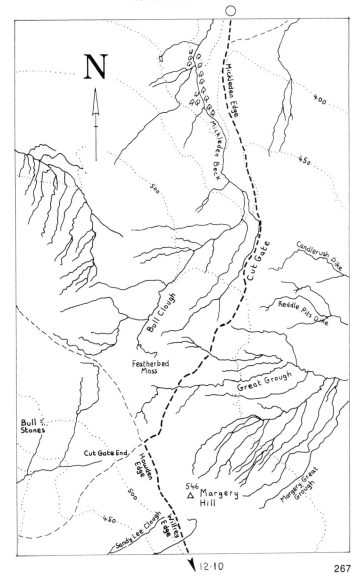

N

Mickleden Edge

400

450

Mickleden Beck

Cut Gate

Candlerush Dike

Reddle Pits Dike

Bull Clough

500

Featherbed Moss

Great Grough

Bull Stones

Cut Gate End

Howden Edge

500

450

Margery Great Grough

546
△ Margery Hill

Wilfrey Edge

Sandy Lee Clough

12·10

Wilfrey Neild

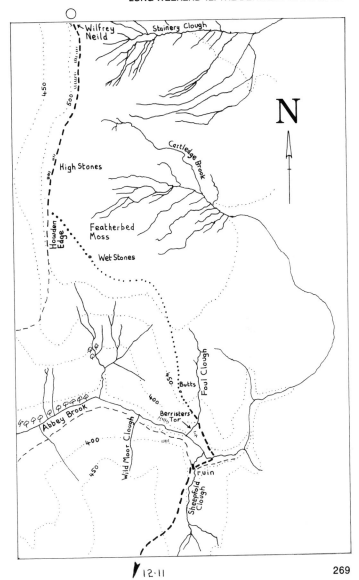

Wilfrey Neild

Stainery Clough

450

500

High Stones

Cartledge Brook

N

Howden Edge

Featherbed Moss

Wet Stones

450

Butts

Foul Clough

400

Abbey Brook

Berristers Tor

Wild Moor Clough

400

400

450

ruin

Sheepfold Clough

12·11

Lost Lad

Slant up the hillside opposite on a matching path to the nearly vanished remains of two shooting cabins, then cross Sheepfold Clough and follow the path up on the far side of the stream. This soon veers away from the clough and is an easy route up through the tussocky grass climbing to join the ridge where you go left to the cairn on Lost Lad. There are several hills called Lost Lad in the area and this acquired its name when a shepherd's boy, lost in a blizzard in the sixteenth century, scratched the words "Lost Lad" on the rocks by the spot where his body was found.

With the help of the topograph you can trace most of the line of the walk. First over the Mam Tor ridge to Lord's Seat, then the route is hidden from view round the back of Kinder to Mill Hill, next over Bleaklow Stones and Barrow Stones and past the Horse Stone to Featherbed Moss then on to Abbey Brook. The direction indicator was erected in memory of W.H.Baxby of the Sheffield Clarion Ramblers, whose son runs the club today.

Derwent Edge

Climbing on towards Back Tor the rocks are soon reached and what must surely be the most difficult trig point to attain in the whole of the Peak District. A good path heads southwards along Derwent Edge to cross the Abbey Grange to Strines path past the squat rocky tors known as the Cakes of Bread. From the cliffs at Dovestone Tor, Ladybower Reservoir comes into view and the next group of rocks is easily identified by the Salt Cellar, which is very obvious coming from this direction. White Tor, with its 1830 graffiti, is followed by the pièce de résistance, the Wheel Stones, which dominate the moor. Keep straight on where the Moscar to Derwent path crosses, wending on down the edge past the Hurkling Stones for another ½ mile to a cross roads where you turn right down a gully.

Ladybower Reservoir

The path descends through the bracken and goes along the edge of the plantation before following the power line through the trees to join a bridleway. Turn right along the track to Ashopton Viaduct then go left along the main road. After passing the solitary house to the right which was spared when Ashopton village was drowned, cross over the Ladybower Viaduct. To the right you can see the summit of Win Hill peeping up above the trees and disconcertingly looking a very long way up. After walking along the road beside the reservoir take the footpath to the right immediately after the dam which goes down to join a track along the bottom of the valley. This passes below houses built to accommodate the inhabitants of the flooded villages of Derwent and Ashopton. Cutting across the corner to Yorkshire Bridge follow the tarmac upstream to a stile and then turn immediately uphill.

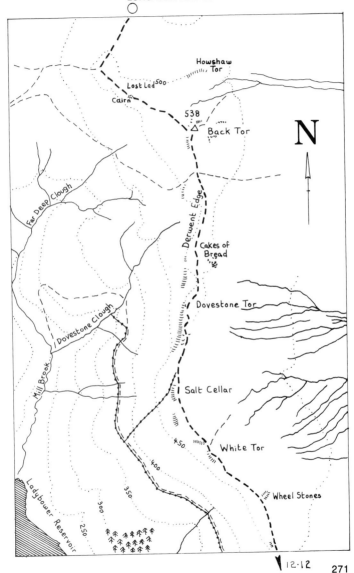

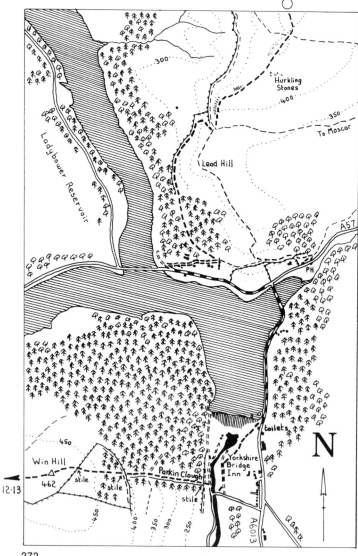

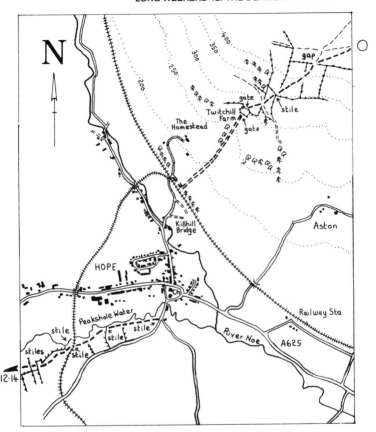

Win Hill

Starting up a helpful flight of steps and soon crossing a disused railway line which was built to carry the stone for the dams of the Derwent and Howden reservoirs, the path climbs with unremitting steepness beside Parkin Clough. After a forest road, it is not much further to a stile and the edge of the trees. Continue climbing to the open moor and the summit appears on the other side of a wall which is crossed by twin ladder stiles. Win Hill is a landmark for miles around and is a very good viewpoint with a wide panorama to all points of the compass. Looking south-east from the Ordnance Survey trig point, past Bamford lies the Derwent valley with to the right Offerton Moor and

273

Castleton, while in the opposite direction is the forked Ladybower Reservoir with the Howden Moors and Derwent Edge beyond.

Hope

Follow the ridge for 200 yards then descend the hillside quite steeply leftwards to a stile and on down, crossing a bridleway, to the left of Twitchill Farm. Continuing along the farm track, bend right to go under the railway line and down the lane to the River Noe. Turn left along Edale Road into the centre of Hope then go to the right of the church down Pindale Road. Take the next right fork and in a few yards turn right over a stile into the fields. The footpath follows Peakshole Water then crosses a railway line before veering away from the river to join a lane which leads to the main road into Castleton.

Castleton

Castleton, the town of the castle, with its four show caves is on a summer weekend almost full to capacity, but as the afternoon shadows lengthen, the crowds depart. Neat limestone walled houses, many of them seventeenth century, line the streets, cottages squeeze into the narrow approach to Peak Cavern and high above is the dominant castle of William Peveril.

While some of Castleton's caves have yielded relics of early man, others contain stalactites, stalagmites and subterranean streams. Peak Cavern has been visited by tourists since the twelfth century and with its huge gaping entrance beneath Peveril Castle used to be called the Devil's Arse, though the name was not approved of by the Victorians. There was a rope-walk within the cave mouth and at one time cottages were built for the ropemakers inside the entrance which is claimed to be the largest cave entrance in Europe.

In Speedwell Cavern, an old lead mine of 1771, visitors travel along a flooded tunnel by boat to see the Bottomless Pit. The mine was designed in this way with an underground canal to ship out the lead, but it proved to be uneconomical and soon had to close.

The Blue John Mine has been worked since the eighteenth century for the decorative stone and the nearby Treak Cliff Cavern is a natural cave with stalactite and stalagmite formations that were discovered by the miners. There is much evidence of lead mining in the Castleton district and the Odin Mine is the Peak District's oldest recorded lead mine.

Castleton is understandably very popular with tourists. There is a small museum, an information centre and numerous pubs and cafés. At Christmas time the town is decorated with fir trees and fairy lights and on Oak Apple Day, May 29th, there is the Garlanding Ceremony and a procession to the church. We stayed one weekend with the daughter of a man who for many years was Garland King. Wearing the heavy frame decorated with flowers which completely enveloped him was hard work and as he sat astride his

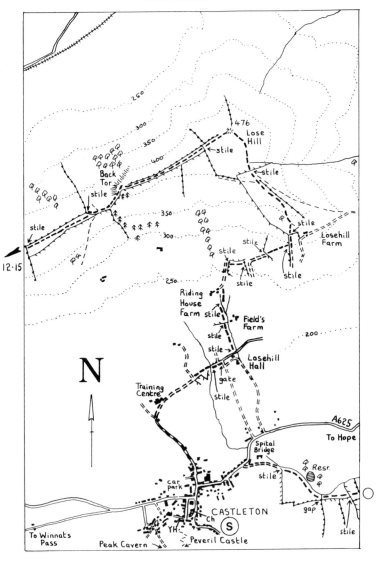

horse, pints were passed up to him beneath the garland and a curl of tobacco smoke hinted at the contented pipe smoker within.

DAY 3: CASTLETON TO GLOSSOP

Kinder Scout, with its small cairn at 2088ft surrounded by a sea of peat, is the highest summit in the Peak District. Much smaller in extent than Bleaklow or the Howden Moors it is little more than five square miles in extent, but it is rough. The streams that slowly drain the sponge like mass here cut channels in the peat up to 10ft deep in places. While walking in their depths and following their meandering course is to be preferred to the almost impossible task of crossing them on a straight line route, the edge is not only much easier, but has the finer scenery, for gritstone cliffs and boulders rim the plateau.

The southern side of Kinder throws out an enfolding arm round Edale with Rushup Edge and its continuation along the Great Ridge linking Mam Tor to Lose Hill. This is the final outpost, where the solid gritstone now gives way to layers of grit and shale, exposed in the crumbling sliding faces of Mam Tor and Back Tor.

The Great Ridge is the division between the gentler limestone hills of the central Peak District and the wild moorland of the north. From Lose Hill to Mam Tor is but a couple of miles of easy going, switchbacking up to Back Tor and down to Hollin's Cross before the steady ascent to Mam Tor. It is a fine airy walk with far below the Vale of Edale, and on the other hand Castleton and the pastoral fields of the Hope Valley.

Lose Hill, from which you look across the valley of the River Noe to Win Hill, may have been the encampment of the losing army of Cuicholme when the victors occupied Win Hill, but more prosaically probably refers to pigs. Hollins Cross, the lowest point on the ridge, marks the path by which the eighteenth-century mill girls made their daily journey on foot from Castleton to Edale spinning mill.

Until 1976 the main A625 crossed the slopes of Mam Tor, but in that year the constant battle to stop the road sliding downhill was finally abandoned and now the traffic follows the steep gradients of Winnats Pass down into Castleton. Encircling the summit of Mam Tor are the ramparts of an Iron Age hill fort, though much of the eastern side has now disappeared, vanished over the edge which like a sea cliff is gradually eating into the hill. Perhaps because of the smoothly rounded shape which it presents to the west Mam Tor seems peculiarly prone to strong winds. On several occasions we have fought our way to the top against gusts which reduced progress to the staggerings of a drunken man.

Beyond Mam Nick, where the narrow road crosses the ridge before winding its way down to Edale, is Rushup Edge. Looking across from Mam

Tor at the steep slopes where hang gliders circle and soar in the upcurrents above the edge, the hillside is littered with mounds as though it had melted and was gradually slipping downhill. This is exactly what has happened but the thaw was several thousand years ago, when the Ice Age came to an end the surface layers began to slide on the still frozen subsoil.

Rushup Edge, a continuation of the Great Ridge, rises to Lord's Seat where there are traces of an ancient tumulus and then joins the gently rising slope of Brown Knoll. In winter with many of the roads into the Peak blocked by heavy snowfalls, Brown Knoll presents us with a convenient objective for a cross country ski trip with an easy approach from Chapel-en-le-Frith, the gentle run downhill afterwards suiting our very modest abilities. Stepping off the skis we once sank almost to our waists in the soft snow, conditions in which skiing is the best or perhaps the only way to cross these moors.

On the flanks of Brown Knoll is a large squat circular chimney which can sometimes be seen steaming in the distance. This is the air shaft of the Cowburn railway tunnel which was bored under the hill to link Sheffield and Manchester, providing the Midland Railway with a through route independent of its rivals. Unlike the Woodhead tunnels, the Cowburn is still in daily use with a regular shuttle service of trains. As they stop at Edale, it is a convenient alternative for the walker to the ubiquitous car.

On the western edge of Kinder is Kinder Low but this is not the highest point on the plateau, that distinction belongs to a bleak, inhospitable and frankly rather boring spot marked by a stake. It is so undistinguished in fact that even the stones for the small cairn have had to be carried there. Kinder Low would be a much better summit with its huge gritstone monolith surmounted by the white column of the Ordnance Survey trig point.

It is the edge of the plateau though which holds the greatest interest. From the western gritstone rim you look down to Kinder Reservoir with above it the tiny Mermaid's Pool. Gaunt black rocks carved by the wind and rain of thousands of years into strange sculptures crumble gradually to silver sand, each grain refracting the sunlight in a million diamond glints. The rocks are at their most magnificent at the Downfall where the Kinder River, after meandering across the peat wastes of the plateau finally reaches the vertical wall of the plateau and throws itself over the edge. In winter the fall freezes to a vast perpendicular sheet of ice while, when there is a westerly wind blowing, the water fails to fall at all and instead curves upwards arching back over the edge.

ROUTE DESCRIPTION (See map 12.14 page 275)
Lose Hill

From the square in the centre of Castleton walk past the church to the main road, then at the bend keep straight on along a lane that leads out into the

Back Tor

countryside. Fork right past Hollowford Training Centre and then cross the fields and ford the stream to join the lane round the back of Losehill Hall. This, the first National Park residential study centre in Britain, was opened by Princess Anne in 1972. Turn off the lane behind the hall and follow the footpath signed to Lose Hill, crossing the stream before you reach Riding House Farm. Joining a ridged concrete path turn right over a stile, and then after crossing three more fields turn left steeply uphill. After a ladderstile join the footpath from Hope above Losehill Farm at a signpost and bend back on a grassy path which climbs up the hillside with lovely expanding views of Castleton and the Hope Valley.

Crossing a track, which bypasses the top of Lose Hill, twin stiles lead to a broad sandy path with a final stiff pull up to the topograph on the summit. This helps to pick out the route of the walk. First past Mam Tor and over Brown Knoll to Edale Rocks, then round the back of Kinder to the Howden

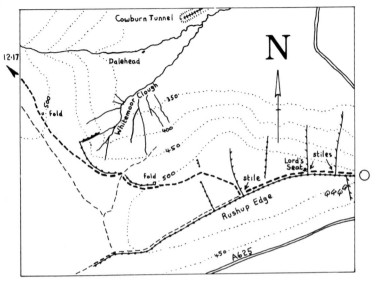

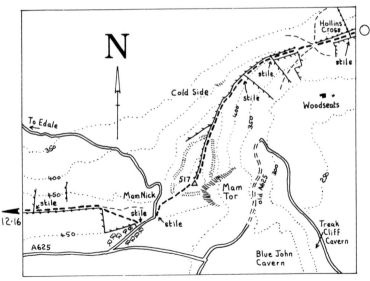

Rushup Edge from Mam Tor

Moors 7 miles away, past Lost Lad where there is another of these topographs, on to Back Tor and the Wheel Stones, which stand up very plainly and lastly over Win Hill. An alternative name for Lose Hill is Ward's Piece and a plaque below the summit explains how this hill was purchased by the Sheffield Clarion Ramblers. It was given to Bert Ward who immediately handed the deeds to the National Trust at the presentation ceremony. G.B.H.Ward, who came from a working class background, was the first chairman of the Ramblers' Association in 1931 and was known as "The King of the Ramblers".

Mam Tor

Heading westwards follow the grassy path down, climbing a little to Back Tor whose flat, grassy top hides an unexpectedly sheer face. To the right is the fertile Vale of Edale and to the left Castleton. Following the fence, cross to the other side at Backtor Nook, then after another bump on the ridge the path descends to the lowest point at Hollins Cross with its circular stone memorial.

280

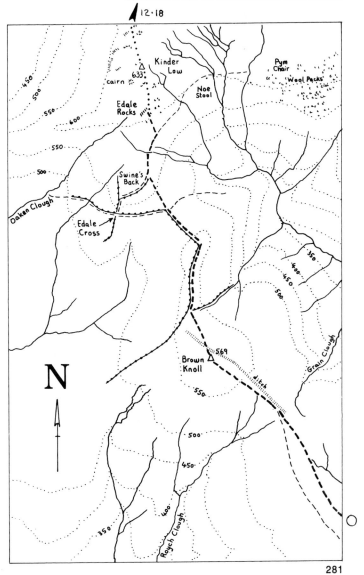

12·18

Kinder Low

Pym Chair

Wool Packs

633

cairn

Noe Stool

Edale Rocks

450

500

550

600

550

500

Oaken Clough

Swine's Back

Edale Cross

350

400

450

500

N

Brown Knoll

569

ditch

Grain Clough

550

500

450

400

350

Rough Clough

281

Joe on Brown Knoll

The old packhorse way from Castleton to Edale crossed the ridge here. In the valley below to the right is Edale Mill and looking the other way you have a good view of the A625 where it slid down the hill. Although uphill, the gradient is easy all the way to the top of Mam Tor where the defensive ramparts of the Iron Age hill fort can clearly be seen and the gritstone trig point is a fine viewpoint.

Rushup Edge

Descending the smart new steps which lead all the way down to the road at Mam Nick, bear left then over a stile to climb back up to the ridge, where an ancient trackway runs to the south of Rushup Edge sheltered from the cold northerly winds. Continue along the ridge to the highest point of Lord's Seat where just after a fence there is a Bronze Age burial mound in a very commanding position. From here you can look along the full length of the Great Ridge, down the Vale of Edale and also into the Hope Valley to the nick of the Winnats Pass. Below the railway disappears into the 2 mile long Cowburn Tunnel while opposite, on the Kinder plateau, is the hump of

Grindslow Knoll with to the left the rocks of the Pagoda, the Woolpacks and Pym Chair, the tiny thimble on the skyline.

Brown Knoll

After the next stile turn right and follow the fence. Though this section is neither on Access Land nor on a right of way, no one objects to walkers providing they keep to the footpath. Ahead is the 900ft ventilation shaft of the railway tunnel. Excavation of the tunnel started from the bottom of this shaft in 1888, working in opposite directions, but it was not opened by Queen Victoria until 5 years later. Beyond the shaft are the more distant hills of South Head and Chinley Churn. The path now leads round the edge following the course of an old wall to cross the Chapel Gate packhorse way which led to Chapel-en-le-Frith. After continuing beside the ruined wall for only a short way climb gently up the hillside along the edge where the path then follows a broad, grassy ditch to a sheepfold and is easy going. Becoming rather indistinct it climbs on over the featureless moor, though a little to the left a more obvious parallel route follows a similar course.

The paths merge below a boundary ditch then, veering away from the dyke, climb to the summit of Brown Knoll. The Ordnance Survey trig point which is hidden from sight until the last few yards, is situated in the middle of a sea of black mud and is often almost impossible to reach. Appearing precariously balanced, the base of the gritstone plinth is rising up out of the peat and eroding away. Ahead beckons the far more interesting Kinder plateau with its strange rock formations.

Kinder Low

The path now heads straight for the distant outcrop of Edale Rocks. After crossing Brown Knoll Dyke, with difficulty, and possibly wet feet, the going becomes easy, heading gently downhill to a new wall, rebuilt by the National Trust to reduce sheep grazing pressure. Edale Rocks, the Pagoda and the Woolpacks stand silhouetted against the sky as you follow the wall down to cross an old medieval way and meet up with the Pennine Way. Climbing on the newly repaired path around the foot of Swine's Back, leave it at the dip to struggle up to Edale Rocks, which though unassailable from the front are level with the moor at the rear.

Continuing in the same direction to the highest ground, through gritstone boulders and over silver sand, you soon arrive at the trig point on Kinder Low. By sharing the top of a gritstone boulder with the Ordnance Survey column there are extensive views over Kinder's rocky tors to Win Hill and the Great Ridge, back to Brown Knoll and on to Mill Hill Rocks on the plateau's north-eastern tip.

A few yards to the south-west is a large ancient cairn. An attempt has also been made at modern cairn building and these point the way northwards

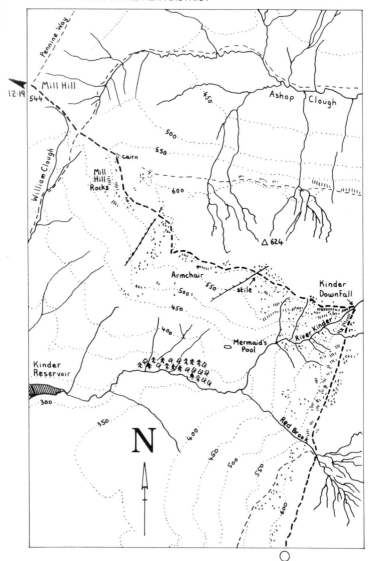

to the plateau's edge. Passing below a fenced in enclosure erected by Sheffield University for studies on the vegetation, stay along the edge with good views of the Kinder Reservoir. After crossing the often dry bed of Red Brook, the huge rocky amphitheatre of the Kinder River comes into view.

Kinder Downfall

Circumnavigating the massive ravine takes longer than you think and it is a popular picnic spot with walkers arriving from Edale on the Pennine Way. After teetering on the brink for a good view of the Downfall, it is easy walking round the edge where below on a grassy shelf is the legendary Mermaid's Pool. The path now crosses a new fence by a ruined wall, erected by the National Trust to control the sheep, then climbs to the Armchair or the Upper Western Buttress which has mysterious properties, being a charmed rock of the Etherios Society. The sandy path now passes above an area of jumbled rocks and landslips, then wanders on round the edge crossing a broken wall to reach a large cairn beyond Mill Hill Rocks, the most westerly point of the plateau.

Mill Hill

Turning downhill and still keeping company with the Pennine Way, cross the soggy bridge of land which separates William Clough from Ashop Clough. Climbing past a signpost at the cross roads continue to a post set in a small cairn on the summit of Mill Hill from which there are fine retrospective views of Kinder's northern edge. The Pennine Way is now abandoned and you head westwards along the broad grassy ridge of Leygatehead Moor.

Harry Hut

There is at first little sign of a path, but a broad and boggy way through the tussocky grass soon develops which passes the strewn wreckage of a Liberator that crashed when the damaged bomber was returning from a raid over Germany. Quite a lot of the aircraft remains, including the engines and there are more pieces over to the north-east. Shortly after the vegetation changes to heather and bilberry leave the main path and take a smaller one to the right which veers away towards the trig point of Harry Hut.

The concrete trig point stands on Chunal Moor at the flat end of a subsidiary ridge and the path continues northwards down the ridge heading towards Glossop far below. After passing the Worm Stones cross a ladder stile and go down to join the road. The footpath opposite leads to a track where you turn right for a very short way and then left over a footbridge. Zigzag up the hillside towards the houses and follow the lane out to a minor road where you go left into Glossop.

Kinder Downfall in January

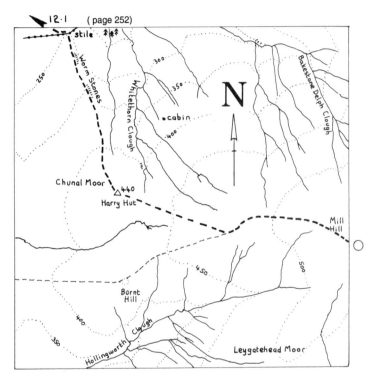

12·1   (page 252)

Glossop

Sited in the valley of Glossop Brook which drains the high surrounding moorland this busy little town has an ancient history. The Romans were here first and built their fort Melandra to the west of the town, connecting it by Doctor's Gate to the fort at Brough. They were followed by the Saxons and the Normans who developed a vast medieval parish, but Old Glossop remains a little apart from the community created in the Industrial Revolution.

The architectural heritage of Old Glossop sounds most interesting in the town's History Trail leaflet. "The Post Office was at one time a public house, the buildings down by the river were once three cottages, the village bakery used to be the Lock-up." We were only half way down the second paragraph but realising we had left our visit a few centuries too late we set out hurriedly to see if any of it was still standing.

287

Old Glossop now has a neat suburban air. The medieval market cross stands in front of a lovely old stone manor house with mullioned windows and the tiny Market Square is flanked by weaver's cottages which date back to the seventeenth century. Nearby is the Norman church which was modernised by the Victorians and there are still some beautiful old houses, but of the butchers shops and grocers shops, clog shops and coffin maker's shops, no trace remains.

The new cotton-town, which we know today as Glossop, was initially called Howard Town after the chief landowner the Duke of Norfolk, Lord Howard, MP and Vice Chamberlain to Queen Victoria. It was born early in the nineteenth century and by 1809 there were fifty-four cotton-spinning mills, nearly half of the total of all Derbyshire. Growing into a planned town it was connected to the main railway line by a one mile branch and the 1845 railway station is still open.

"Gateway to the Peak" the town guide proudly proclaims, and indeed it is. Standing on the edge of Bleaklow and Kinder it makes a fine start for a walk and as soon as the houses are left behind you are in wild country, heading for the open gritstone moors.

Millstones below Stanage Edge

GENERAL INFORMATION

This table can only be taken as a guide as although up to date in 1993, things are always changing

	YOUTH HOSTEL	PUB OR HOTEL	B&B	CAMP SITE	CAMPING BARN	FOOD SHOP	TRAIN	BUS	INFO CENTRE
Ambergate	-	★	★	-	-	-	★	★	-
Bakewell	★	★	★	★	★	★	-	★	★
Baslow	-	★	★	-	-	★	-	★	-
Buxton	★	★	★	★	-	★	★	★	★
Castleton	★	★	★	★	★	★	-	★	★
Edale	★	★	★	-	★	-	★	★	★
Elton	★	★	★	-	-	-	-	★	-
Eyam	-	★	★	-	★	★	★	★	-
Glossop	★	★	-	-	-	★	-	-	★
Gradbach	★	-	★	-	-	-	-	★	-
Hartington	★	★	★	-	-	★	★	★	-
Hathersage	-	★	★	★	-	★	-	★	★
Hayfield	★	★	★	-	-	-	-	★	★
Ilam	★	★	★	-	-	★	-	★	★
Langsett	-	★	★	-	-	★	-	★	-
Longnor	-	★	★	-	-	★	★	★	★
Matlock	★	★	★	-	-	★	-	★	★
Miller's Dale	★	★	★	-	-	-	★	★	-
Whaley Bridge	-	★	★	-	-	★	-	★	-
Youlgreave	★	★	★	-	-	★	-	★	-

DISTANCES AND ASCENTS

WEEKEND	DAY 1 miles & ascent	DAY 2 miles & ascent	DAY 3 miles & ascent	PATHS
1	8.5 easy	11.5 moderate		Good
2	9 moderate	9.5 moderate		Good
3	12.5 easy (S)	13 easy		Good
4	12 moderate (S)	11 moderate (S)		Good
5	9 .5 easy	11.5 moderate		Good, but with a short rough section
6	8.5 easy	12.5 moderate		Good, but Monk's Dale is awkward
7	8.5 easy	9.0 moderate	7.5 easy	Good
8	12.5 moderate (S)	13.5 moderate		Good
9	12.5 moderate (S)	11.5 strenuous (S)		Good
10	10.5 moderate	10 moderate		Fair
11	14 moderate (S)	8.5 moderate		Rough moorland
12	16.5 strenuous	17.5 strenuous	15.5 strenuous	Rough and pathless moorland

(S) Indicates the route may be shortened

Ascents	Easy	up to 1000ft
	Moderate	1000-1800ft
	Strenuous	1800-2600ft

NOTES

NOTES

CICERONE GUIDES

Cicerone publish a wide range of reliable guides to walking and climbing in Britain, and other general interest books.

LAKE DISTRICT - General Books
A DREAM OF EDEN
LAKELAND VILLAGES
LAKELAND TOWNS
REFLECTIONS ON THE LAKES
OUR CUMBRIA
THE HIGH FELLS OF LAKELAND
CONISTON COPPER A History
LAKELAND - A taste to remember (Recipes)
THE LOST RESORT?
CHRONICLES OF MILNTHORPE
LOST LANCASHIRE
THE PRIORY OF CARTMEL

LAKE DISTRICT - Guide Books
CASTLES IN CUMBRIA
THE CUMBRIA CYCLE WAY
WESTMORLAND HERITAGE WALK
IN SEARCH OF WESTMORLAND
CONISTON COPPER MINES Field Guide
SCRAMBLES IN THE LAKE DISTRICT
MORE SCRAMBLES IN THE LAKE DISTRICT
WINTER CLIMBS IN THE LAKE DISTRICT
WALKS IN SILVERDALE/ARNSIDE
BIRDS OF MORECAMBE BAY
THE EDEN WAY
WALKING ROUND THE LAKES

NORTHERN ENGLAND (outside the Lakes
BIRDWATCHING ON MERSEYSIDE
CANOEISTS GUIDE TO THE NORTH EAST
THE CLEVELAND WAY & MISSING LINK
THE DALES WAY
DOUGLAS VALLEY WAY
HADRIANS WALL Vol 1 The Wall Walk
HERITAGE TRAILS IN NW ENGLAND
THE ISLE OF MAN COASTAL PATH
THE LANCASTER CANAL
LAUGHS ALONG THE PENNINE WAY
A NORTHERN COAST-TO-COAST
NORTH YORK MOORS Walks
THE REIVERS WAY (Northumberland)
THE RIBBLE WAY
ROCK CLIMBS LANCASHIRE & NW
THE YORKSHIRE DALES A walker's guide
WALKING IN THE SOUTH PENNINES
WALKING IN THE NORTH PENNINES
WALKS IN THE YORKSHIRE DALES (3 VOL)
WALKS IN LANCASHIRE WITCH COUNTRY
WALKS TO YORKSHIRE WATERFALLS (2 vol)
WALKS ON THE WEST PENNINE MOORS
WALKING NORTHERN RAILWAYS EAST
WALKING NORTHERN RAILWAYS WEST

DERBYSHIRE & EAST MIDLANDS
WHITE PEAK WALKS - 2 Vols
HIGH PEAK WALKS
WHITE PEAK WAY
KINDER LOG

THE VIKING WAY
THE DEVIL'S MILL (Novel)
WHISTLING CLOUGH (Novel)

WALES & WEST MIDLANDS
THE RIDGES OF SNOWDONIA
HILLWALKING IN SNOWDONIA
HILL WALKING IN WALES (2 Vols)
ASCENT OF SNOWDON
WELSH WINTER CLIMBS
SNOWDONIA WHITE WATER SEA & SURF
SCRAMBLES IN SNOWDONIA
SARN HELEN Walking Roman Road
ROCK CLIMBS IN WEST MIDLANDS
THE SHROPSHIRE HILLS A Walker's Guide
HEREFORD & THE WYE VALLEY A Walker's Guide
THE WYE VALLEY WALK

SOUTH & SOUTH WEST ENGLAND
COTSWOLD WAY
EXMOOR & THE QUANTOCKS
THE KENNET & AVON WALK
THE SOUTHERN-COAST-TO-COAST
SOUTH DOWNS WAY & DOWNS LINK
SOUTH WEST WAY - 2 Vol
WALKING IN THE CHILTERNS
WALKING ON DARTMOOR
WALKERS GUIDE TO DARTMOOR PUBS
WALKS IN KENT
THE WEALDWAY & VANGUARD WAY

SCOTLAND
THE BORDER COUNTRY - WALKERS GUIDE
SCRAMBLES IN LOCHABER
SCRAMBLES IN SKYE
THE ISLAND OF RHUM
CAIRNGORMS WINTER CLIMBS
THE CAIRNGORM GLENS (Mountainbike Guide)
THE ATHOLL GLENS (Mountainbike Guide)
WINTER CLIMBS BEN NEVIS & GLENCOE
SCOTTISH RAILWAY WALKS
TORRIDON A Walker's Guide
SKI TOURING IN SCOTLAND

REGIONAL BOOKS UK & IRELAND
THE MOUNTAINS OF ENGLAND & WALES
VOL 1 WALES
VOL 2 ENGLAND
THE MOUNTAINS OF IRELAND
THE ALTERNATIVE PENNINE WAY
THE RELATIVE HILLS OF BRITAIN
LIMESTONE - 100 BEST CLIMBS

Also a full range of EUROPEAN and OVER-SEAS guidebooks - walking, long distance trails, scrambling, ice-climbing, rock climbing.

Other guides are constantly being added to the Cicerone List.
Available from bookshops, outdoor equipment shops or direct (send s.a.e. for price list) from
CICERONE, 2 POLICE SQUARE, MILNTHORPE, CUMBRIA, LA7 7PY

CICERONE GUIDES

Cicerone publish a wide range of reliable guides to walking and climbing abroad

FRANCE
TOUR OF MONT BLANC
CHAMONIX MONT BLANC - A Walking Guide
TOUR OF THE OISANS: GR54
WALKING THE FRENCH ALPS: GR5
THE CORSICAN HIGH LEVEL ROUTE: GR20
THE WAY OF ST JAMES: GR65
THE PYRENEAN TRAIL: GR10
THE RLS (Stevenson) TRAIL
TOUR OF THE QUEYRAS
ROCK CLIMBS IN THE VERDON
WALKS IN VOLCANO COUNTRY (Auvergne)
WALKING THE FRENCH GORGES (Provence)
FRENCH ROCK

FRANCE / SPAIN
WALKS AND CLIMBS IN THE PYRENEES
ROCK CLIMBS IN THE PYRENEES

SPAIN
WALKS & CLIMBS IN THE PICOS DE EUROPA
WALKING IN MALLORCA
BIRDWATCHING IN MALLORCA
COSTA BLANCA CLIMBS
ANDALUSIAN ROCK CLIMBS

FRANCE / SWITZERLAND
THE JURA - Walking the High Route and
Winter Ski Traverses
CHAMONIX TO ZERMATT The Walker's Haute
Route

SWITZERLAND
WALKING IN THE BERNESE ALPS
CENTRAL SWITZERLAND
WALKS IN THE ENGADINE
WALKING IN TICINO
THE VALAIS - A Walking Guide
THE ALPINE PASS ROUTE

GERMANY / AUSTRIA
THE KALKALPEN TRAVERSE
KLETTERSTEIG - Scrambles
WALKING IN THE BLACK FOREST
MOUNTAIN WALKING IN AUSTRIA
WALKING IN THE SALZKAMMERGUT
KING LUDWIG WAY
HUT-TO-HUT IN THE STUBAI ALPS

ITALY & SLOVENIA
ALTA VIA - High Level Walkis in the Dolomites
VIA FERRATA - Scrambles in the Dolomites
ITALIAN ROCK - Rock Climbs in Northern Italy
CLASSIC CLIMBS IN THE DOLOMITES
WALKING IN THE DOLOMITES
THE JULIAN ALPS

MEDITERRANEAN COUNTRIES
THE MOUNTAINS OF GREECE
CRETE: Off the beaten track
TREKS & CLIMBS JORDAN
THE ATLAS MOUNTAINS
WALKS & CLIMBS IN THE ALA DAG (Turkey)

OTHER COUNTRIES
ADVENTURE TREKS - W. N. AMERICA
ADVENTURE TREKS - NEPAL
ANNAPURNA TREKKERS GUIDE
CLASSIC TRAMPS IN NEW ZEALAND
TREKKING IN THE CAUCASUS

GENERAL OUTDOOR BOOKS
THE HILL WALKERS MANUAL
FIRST AID FOR HILLWALKERS
MOUNTAIN WEATHER
MOUNTAINEERING LITERATURE
THE ADVENTURE ALTERNATIVE
MODERN ALPINE CLIMBING
ROPE TECHNIQUES IN MOUNTAINEERING
MODERN SNOW & ICE TECHNIQUES
LIMESTONE -100 BEST CLIMBS IN BRITAIN

CANOEING
SNOWDONIA WILD WATER, SEA & SURF
WILDWATER CANOEING
CANOEIST'S GUIDE TO THE NORTH EAST

CARTOON BOOKS
ON FOOT & FINGER
ON MORE FEET & FINGERS
LAUGHS ALONG THE PENNINE WAY

*Also a full range of guidebooks
to walking, scrambling, ice-climbing,
rock climbing, and other adventurous
pursuits in Britain and abroad*

---

*Other guides are constantly being added to the Cicerone List.
Available from bookshops, outdoor equipment shops or direct (send for price list)
from CICERONE, 2 POLICE SQUARE, MILNTHORPE, CUMBRIA, LA7 7PY*